Race, Sex and Class under the Raj

Kenneth Ballhatchet

Race, Sex and Class under the Raj

Imperial Attitudes and Policies
and their Critics, 1793–1905

WEIDENFELD AND NICOLSON
LONDON

Weidenfeld and Nicolson
91 Clapham High St   London SW4

ISBN 0 297 77646 0

Printed in Great Britain at
The Camelot Press Ltd, Southampton

Preface

Many years ago an officer colleague of mine on an RAF station in England announced his intention of marrying a WAAF corporal. He was promptly posted overseas. On another occasion a colleague on a military station in India proposed to marry an Anglo-Indian, or Eurasian, girl. He was promptly posted to another station a thousand miles away. The former case threatened the social distance which was carefully maintained between commissioned officers and other ranks, both male and female: even drinking together in pubs off duty was forbidden. The latter case threatened the social distance between the ruling race and peoples of India. The preservation of social distance seemed essential to the maintenance of structures of power and authority. Marriages that threatened to bridge this social distance were sternly discouraged.

I was reminded of these incidents when I read Kate Millett's *Sexual Politics*, and in the present book I have tried to uncover the attitudes to women, to race and to class which underlay British attempts to control sexual behaviour in India in the interests of imperial power.

I have enjoyed the opportunity of speaking on various aspects of this subject at the Centre for South Asian Studies in Cambridge, at the European Conference on Modern South Asian Studies in Leiden and at the Royal Asiatic Society in London, and on each occasion I learnt much from the subsequent discussion.

I am very grateful for the help of librarians, archivists and others at the Archives Nationales (section outre-mer), the British Library, the Fawcett Library in the City of London Polytechnic, the Imperial War Museum (Department of Sound Records), the India Office Library and Records, the Institute of Historical Research, the London Library, the Library of the Society of Friends, the National Army Museum, the Library of the School of Oriental and African Studies and the Library of the Senate House, University of London.

Barbara Anderson read the whole of this book in typescript, and I am deeply indebted to her for advice and information, both on medical points and on various other matters. I am also indebted for information and advice to David Arnold, Christine Baxter, Lucy Carroll, Peter Hardy, John Harrison, Caroline Harte, Paula Iley and Ronald Hyam.

Anne Mackintosh and Marion Sweny have been most generous with secretarial help far beyond the call of duty, and I am very grateful to them.

Introduction

This is a study of attitudes to race, sex and class in nineteenth-century India, as revealed in official attempts to control sexual relations between English men and Indian women, in the criticisms which those attempts provoked and in difficulties experienced by individuals who transgressed or threatened the accepted conventions.

Ronald Hyam has suggested that sexual energy was a factor in imperial expansion, and he mentions a number of pugnacious proconsuls with tastes that could not readily be satisfied in England.[1] Some of them seem indeed to have been agreeably satiated overseas, and it is certainly possible that frustration urged many into imperial pursuits. On the other hand a considerable number of prominent empire builders were rigidly repressed, and many others seem to have confined themselves to matrimony. It seems probable that most of those who embarked upon an official career in nineteenth-century India were moved by very respectable motives. There may have been few inhibitions in frontier regions, but once British rule was firmly established the opportunities for irregularity were quickly reduced. It also seems probable that wherever they went the British were driven by similar impulses and troubled by similar tensions to those they felt at home, but in India at least they saw themselves as acting on a different and more public stage, where to perform in a proper manner seemed to be not only morally but politically imperative.

The hero of Tennyson's *Locksley Hall*, orphaned in the Maratha wars, was tempted by the delights he envisaged in union with a bride of a different race – in contrast, we may suppose, to the austerer pleasures to be expected with a Victorian lady – but he decided that such a union would hamper him in the progressive role in historical development which was appropriate to an educated English gentleman. Kipling later testified to the sexual as well as alcoholic possibilities of life east of Suez, but he was expressing sentiments suited to a member of the lower

1

classes. This, indeed, became a crucial distinction in the development of British attitudes to such questions.

Special provision seemed necessary for the sexual satisfaction of British soldiers because they came from the lower classes and so were thought to lack the intellectual and moral resources required for continence, while as ordinary soldiers they lacked the material resources required for marriage, except for the few who were allowed to marry 'on the strength' of a regiment and were accordingly allowed married quarters. The official elite, on the other hand, were supposed to shun Indian mistresses and content themselves with British wives, for rulers should be aloof from the people and so trusted as beyond corruption and feared as remote from the ways of common men. The prestige of the ruling race came to be a matter of serious concern.

For the greater part of the eighteenth century the East India Company's servants had seen themselves as merchants who had come to India in search of fortune. It was said that a favourite after-dinner toast was to turn the traditional lament 'Alas and alack-a-day' into 'A lass and a lakh a day !' – an aspiration natural to men who saw a *lakh*, or 100,000 rupees, as a proper object of ambition and a *bibi*, or Indian mistress, as a fitting companion. But as the Company came to concern itself more with government than with commerce, its officials were transformed from merchants into diplomats, administrators and judges. This change was completed by Lord Cornwallis in his capacity as Governor-General between 1786 and 1793. The Company's officials were assured of a good salary – significantly, 'a respectable competence' in the language of the time – and they had to abandon all thought of private profit. Indeed, the covenanted service was another name for what came to be known as the Indian Civil Service: on appointment each member entered into a covenant to the effect that he would not accept gifts or bribes or profit in any way from his duties. At the same time, these officials were coming to be seen as an aloof elite: this was justified on political grounds by the President of the Board of Control – the minister responsible for Indian affairs.

Anthony King has shown how the British ensured a physical separation between the life of the official elite and that of the Indian people by planning civil stations adjoining but apart from Indian towns.[2] There they lived in an ordered environment, in spacious houses enclosed by large gardens and joined by wide, straight roads. Indian towns, with their congested, winding streets, seemed a different world – mysterious and sometimes threatening. A similar seclusion was provided for the soldiers in cantonments, or permanent military camps. The authorities often revealed anxiety at the thought of British soldiers wandering beyond the controlled environment of the cantonment into mysterious places where they might be infected with dangerous diseases and tempted into Oriental vices. The typical cantonment contained regimental bazars as well as a central bazar, and the soldiers were expected to satisfy their needs there.

As there were relatively few British troops in India the preservation of their health and vigour seemed particularly important. By the middle of the nineteenth century there were some forty thousand, with six times as many Indian sepoys. After the Mutiny of 1857 there was an adjustment of these proportions so as to provide some sixty thousand British troops and only twice as many sepoys.[3] British soldiers now seemed less heavily outnumbered. But commanding officers of Indian regiments had previously expressed such faith in their sepoys' loyalty that the Mutiny seriously undermined British confidence. British rule now seemed all the more dependent on the British soldier. The authorities redoubled their efforts to enable him to satisfy his virility without endangering his health.

Although the Mutiny was followed by the abolition of the East India Company in 1858 and the proclamation of the Queen as ruler of India, there was little change in the structure of power. A Secretary of State replaced the President of the Board of Control. He had a council dominated by retired officials to advise him.[4] But retired officials had come to dominate the Court of Directors, the Company's governing body. The Secretary of State could override his council. But the President of the Board of Control had been able to alter the despatches of the Court of Directors as he thought fit. The main difference was that the Secretary of State had to face parliamentary criticism and pressure on his own, unlike the President of the Board of Control who was known to exercise merely a supervisory power over the Company. On the other hand, the charter under which the Company ruled was only renewed by Parliament for twenty years at a time: each renewal, in 1813, in 1833 and in 1853, was preceded by a detailed enquiry into Indian administration. Under Crown rule there was no such regular enquiry: reformers had to create their own opportunities for publicity.

The Company had come to India by sea, and in the nineteenth century British administration was still controlled from the great ports of Calcutta, Bombay and Madras, each the capital of a province or Presidency, governed by a President and Council. In Bombay and

Madras the President was called the Governor, in Calcutta the Governor-General – at first the Governor-General of Bengal, from 1833 the Governor-General of India. The Governor-General in Council, soon called the Government of India, exercised a general supervision over the other Presidencies. As British rule expanded, fresh provinces were added, under Chief Commissioners or under Lieutenant-Governors. British Burma was put under a Chief Commissioner in 1862 ; more Burmese territory was subsequently conquered, and Burma was put under a Lieutenant-Governor in 1897. When in 1858 the Queen was proclaimed sovereign of India the Governor-General acquired the prestigious title of Viceroy. But throughout this period he and the Governors of Bombay and Madras would act from time to time in a semi-regal manner, holding stiff and formal *darbars*, or receptions, like Indian rulers, and stiff and formal levees, like European monarchs.

Yet Calcutta, Bombay and Madras were bustling, modern cities, and it was sometimes difficult to maintain the prestige of the ruling race in such places. There was no room for spacious civil stations or cantonments. These great cities were also seen to contain many Europeans of the lower classes, and this circumstance sometimes led to problems that perplexed the authorities.

Eurasians also came to be regarded with uneasy disfavour, as threatening to bridge the social distance between the ruling race and the people. In the last decade of the eighteenth century, when covenanted civil servants were coming to be seen as an aloof elite, Eurasians were excluded from appointment, and they were also excluded from the commissioned ranks of the Army. To justify such discrimination, the officials were apt to appeal to Indian notions of birth, as they perceived them. Significantly, they would refer to Eurasians as 'half-castes'. Equally significantly, Eurasian spokesmen preferred the term 'Indo-Briton' ; later, in the twentieth century, they claimed, and were accorded, the name of 'Anglo-Indian', which had previously been applied to the British in India.

Missionaries also played an ambiguous part on the imperial stage. Although most of them followed a European lifestyle, they were professionally involved in close relationships with Indians. Many proved to be uncomfortable members of the ruling race, criticizing British as well as Indian immorality. In this role they were strengthened by close ties with religious and reforming groups in Britain. On the one hand, they were greatly stimulated by the evangelical revival during the first half of the nineteenth century and by the social purity movement subsequently. On the other hand, allies in Britain would often bring pressure to bear upon the Secretary of State: Liberal Governments, mindful of Nonconformist votes, were particularly sensitive in such matters. In general, however, the presence of missionaries of the ruling race encouraged the British to see themselves as more moral than Indians and to think that the preservation of social distance was morally justifiable.

Improved conditions encouraged more Englishwomen to live in India, and in various ways their presence seems to have widened the distance between the ruling race and the people. However, as we shall see, Englishmen were sometimes too ready to assume that the women necessarily approved of that distance. But some generalizations seem reasonable. As wives they hastened the disappearance of the Indian mistress. As hostesses they fostered the development of exclusive social groups in every civil station. As women they were thought by Englishmen to be in need of protection from lascivious Indians.

The British often suspected that Indians were by nature more lascivious than they were themselves. Child marriage and polygamy seemed to prove it. Such assumptions can be seen in British attempts to ensure that school textbooks were such as to inculcate loyalty and other estimable virtues. In the second half of the nineteenth century, when Western education seemed to be producing critics rather than collaborators, various officials examined the available literature for undesirable tendencies. Even the *Arabian Nights* aroused concern. The book was 'full of adventures of gallantry and intrigue, as well as of the marvellous', one nervous official commented. 'The latter is what the English boy's mind fastens on, but the Hindu, and especially the Muhammadan youth . . . gloats quite as much on the former, to his own moral harm.' One could not be too careful: 'Books that are innocuous to the comparatively pure and healthy morals of English boys may not be so to the more inflammable minds of Indian boys.'[5] Anxious attention was given to such matters by educational administrators.

Yet Indians, on the other hand, were often shocked by European manners, not only in eating, drinking and personal hygiene but in the indecorous behaviour of ladies baring their shoulders and even dancing on social occasions. Such things did not encourage Indians to loosen the restraints of caste or to abandon the traditional seclusion of respectable women. But it became a sore point with the British that when Indian gentlemen came to receptions they seldom brought their wives. This encouraged the feeling that white women were at risk. Indeed, the British in India were peculiarly prone to the jealousy felt by men of a dominant elite at the possibility of sexual relations between women of the elite and men of subordinate groups.

Racial feeling among the British became more explicit and more aggressive in the course of the nineteenth century and reached its peak during Lord Curzon's viceroyalty, between 1899 and 1905. The Mutiny of 1857 showed them the insecurity of their military power. The inauguration of regular census reports showed them how large the population of India was, and how small a minority they were. At first there was much imprecision, but in successive decades terminology was refined and methods of enumeration were improved. According to the 1901 census there were only 170,000 Europeans and members of 'allied races' in a total population of 294,000,000. There were also 89,000 Eurasians.[6]

A more insidious threat was perceived in the appearance of Indians among the official elite. Competitive examinations for the Indian Civil Service began in 1855, and an Indian candidate, Satyendranath Tagore, was successful in 1863. The Civil Service Commissioners reacted in characteristic fashion by manipulating the marking scheme so as to impede subsequent Indian candidates.[7] Even so, Indians occasionally passed into the ICS in ones and twos. In their early years they necessarily laboured in obscure posts, and the British could see little change in the structure of power and authority. Then in 1883 Courtenay Ilbert, as law member of the Governor-General's legislative council, introduced a Bill to enable Indian judges to try European British subjects on criminal charges. At that time there were only two Indians in the ICS with sufficient seniority to have such powers.[8] But there was consternation among the British. Vehement opposition was expressed in various ways – in bitter speeches in the Calcutta town hall, in letters and editorials in newspapers, and in official reports and memoranda. Even the high-minded Annette Beveridge, who had come to India with philanthropic purposes before marrying a member of the ICS, wrote an indignant letter to the *Englishman* about 'Mr Ilbert's proposal to subject civilized women to the jurisdiction of men who have done little or nothing to redeem the women of their own races, and whose social ideas are still on the outer verge of civilisation'.[9]

In the face of such opposition the Government retreated, and a hypocritical compromise was the result : a European British subject could claim to be tried before a jury of whom at least half were European British subjects or Americans. The race of the judge was not mentioned, but the implication was that an Indian judge could not be trusted alone with power over a British defendant. For us the episode has a dual significance. On the one hand, English womanhood is readily seen as at risk when the structure of British power and authority is threatened. The feelings expressed by Annette Beveridge were shared by many.[10] On the other hand, when the spread of Western education had enabled Indians to compete successfully for posts in the ics, the British could no longer assert their right to power on grounds of superior knowledge or intellect : instead they turned to arguments of racial superiority.

The Ilbert Bill episode demonstrated the Government's readiness to yield to pressure. Bearing this in mind, Western-educated Indians with nationalistic sentiments founded the Indian National Congress two years later, in 1885, and began to press for representative institutions. The British would often retort that such Indians were a minority of the population, like themselves, but they could not deny that they themselves were also a foreign minority. Again, to justify their power they tended increasingly to see themselves as members of a race with the right to rule because of their masterful qualities.[11]

In this context, Indian princes involved the British in fresh perplexities. Before the Mutiny their states seemed doomed to succumb to British expansion. After it the princes were guaranteed a place in the imperial structure as loyal but subordinate allies. They included rulers of large states such as the Nizam of Haidarabad, with 83,000 square miles, and lesser figures such as the Raja of Pudukkottai, with 1,000 square miles. Characteristically, British officials devoted careful attention to their social precedence. Salutes ranging from nine to twenty-one guns were assigned to different princes ; a prince with a salute of eleven guns or more was addressed as 'His Highness'. Such honours could be used to bring pressure to bear upon individual princes. In 1865 the Raja of Jabwa was deprived of his salute, and also fined ten thousand rupees, when the British learnt that he had allowed a thief to be punished in the traditional manner, by having a hand and a foot chopped off. But the social status of the princes often troubled British officials. They were not members of the ruling race, yet they ruled by right of birth. Indeed, their claims to aristocratic status were stronger than those of most if not all of the official elite, and such claims were recognized in Britain, especially at Buckingham Palace. It was rumoured from time to time that certain princes enjoyed the favours of white women. At the turn of the century, when concern for the prestige of the ruling race was at its height, Lord Curzon as Viceroy found such possibilities deeply disturbing.

Curzon and his colleagues assumed that the social hierarchy should correspond to the political hierarchy and that sexual behaviour should be subordinated to the need of both. Indeed, in the course of the nineteenth century the official elite had used the resources at their disposal to establish themselves at the summit of the European social hierarchy in India. Their precedence was ratified and reinforced in the social ceremonies held at every centre of government, great or small. On the other hand, when the typical ICS official went home on leave to England he was apt to find himself in a much less exalted position.[12] Yet aristocratic circles which were closed to him might well be open to any Indian prince.

Competitive examinations were repeatedly criticized for not attracting the best men. The 'competition-wallahs', who had passed into the ICS through such examinations, were often described as bookish, socially inept and physically inadequate.[13] In their turn they constructed similar stereotypes for their Indian rivals, the Western-educated *babus*. The officials were therefore the more anxious to see themselves as uniquely fitted to rule, living in an aristocratic lifestyle, respected by simple peasants and supported by 'martial races'.

Such stereotypes are of theoretical interest, for they fit the classical models of dominance and subordination. Members of the dominant group ascribe to themselves the qualities needed for the tasks which they wish to monopolize. They are unable to perceive such qualities in persons of subordinate groups, who are excluded from positions in which they can demonstrate such qualities. Persons of subordinate groups, on the other hand, are perceived as born with the qualities appropriate to activities involving obedience and subordination, and as they are confined to such activities they duly demonstrate that they do indeed possess these qualities. Such reasoning is vitiated by its circularity, but it is repeated in various forms by members of the dominant elite to justify their position. Within the dominant group women are perceived as a subordinate group but towards all other subordinate groups they are expected to display attitudes appropriate to the dominant group. In particular, they must show distaste for any relationship that might bridge the social distance between the dominant group and subordinate groups.[14]

There may seem at first sight to be a contradiction between the care with which the military authorities provided facilities for sexual relations between British soldiers and native women and the care with which other authorities tried to discourage sexual relations between British officials and native women. In both cases, as we shall see, the fundamental concern was for the preservation of the structure of power.

1
Lock Hospitals and Lal Bazars

Of all the areas of sexual behaviour which embarrassed the authorities, relations between British soldiers and Indian women proved the most troubling. The problem was concisely expressed by Dr W.J. Moore, Surgeon-General, Bombay, in 1886. He began with the premiss that 'physiological instincts must be satisfied in some way or other; or they must be repressed by force of will aided by severe physical exertion, abstemious habits, and the high moral capacity arising from culture'. But it was well known that the lower classes, from whom the rank and file of the army were recruited, would not repress their animal instincts in such ways. Perhaps, he hinted, they were fortunate, or at least healthy, in their lack of inhibitions: 'That such instincts can be repressed without ulterior serious consequences is a moot point on which it is not desirable to enter.' But the remedy seemed plain:

> For a young man who cannot marry and who cannot attain to the high moral standard required for the repression of physiological natural instincts, there are only two ways of satisfaction, viz., masturbation and mercenary love. The former, as is well known, leads to disorders of both body and mind; the latter, to the fearful dangers of venereal.[1]

This was the general view among army officers. An even more fearful alternative, referred to only in oblique terms, was homosexuality: it was despised as unmanly, and it was dreaded as a threat to military discipline.

British soldiers, then, seemed to need protection from the dangers of 'mercenary love'. The measures taken culminated in an elaborate system for registering prostitutes, inspecting them, and detaining them in hospital if they caught venereal disease. This closely resembled the system established by the Contagious Diseases Acts which prevailed in England between 1864 and 1886. After the successful campaign against these measures, a similar campaign was mounted against the Indian system. As in England, such measures were criticized as immoral, inhumane and ineffective. The Indian system was also criticized as sacrificing Indian women to British selfishness. This campaign and these arguments will be examined in due course. Our first concern is to analyse the process whereby a variety of measures taken at different times and in different places eventually became a coherent policy, and to identify the assumptions, the attitudes and the stereotypes involved in that process.

Similar steps were taken independently in the three Presidencies into which the British possessions in India were divided. There was, however, more discussion of first principles in Madras and Bombay than in Bengal, whose Governor-General in Council exercised a vague superintendence over the other two presidencies. In all three, alarm at the growth of venereal disease among soldiers prompted proposals for the establishment of Lock Hospitals. In the background, and without submitting formal proposals to Government, many regiments established *lal bazars*.

The term 'lock hospital' seems to have been first used of the London lock hospital, which was flourishing under that name in the early years of the eighteenth century. William Acton, the Victorian authority on such matters, thought that the name had always implied some form of restraint, as its site had formerly been that of an asylum where lepers were confined. In the nineteenth century it was accepted that VD patients would be locked up until they were cured, and it was invariably understood that these patients would be women prostitutes.[2] The *lal kurti*, or red jacket, was the recognized uniform of the British soldier, and this term was sometimes used as a synonym for the British cantonment, the barrack or camp area administered by the military authorities. But the term *lal bazar* came to have a special significance, as denoting the red light or brothel area of the regimental bazar, superintended by an elderly woman whose duty it was to ensure that the prostitutes were healthy, and that those infected were either expelled or sent to hospital.

Before the end of the eighteenth century, the Governor-General in Council had authorized the building of 'hospitals for the reception of diseased women' at Berhampur, Cawnpore (now spelt, more correctly, Kanpur), Dinapur and Fatehgarh. Their purpose was to check the spread of venereal disease among European soldiers, and although the term 'lock hospital' was not used, patients were forbidden to leave

11

until they had been certified as cured. *Lal bazars* were not mentioned either, but it was stipulated that the *kotwal*, the Indian official in charge of the regimental bazar, was to be responsible for the conduct of the women attached to it. Women found to be 'disordered' on 'the customary days of inspection' were to be sent at once to the hospital.[3] Similarly, on the recommendation of the Provincial Commander-in-Chief, hospitals for 'diseased Publick women' were established at Agra and Muttra in 1807.[4]

Meanwhile, more systematic consideration was being given to the matter in Madras in 1805, under a reforming Governor, Lord William Bentinck. Assistant Surgeon Price, of His Majesty's 12th Regiment of Foot, had written from Trichinopoly of 'the vast proportion of venereal cases' in his corps, and advocated appropriate measures. His letter was duly referred to the Medical Board, which was composed of senior medical officers. The Medical Board then produced a plan for 'the treatment of such unfortunate women as may be labouring under the venereal disease to the prejudice of the Troops at the different military stations'. This involved the establishment of lock hospitals, the appointment of special police to control the prostitutes and the holding of compulsory medical examinations. All this was to be done with the cooperation of the Civil Magistrate.[5]

At this point the Governor in Council felt the need for caution. 'Considerable inconvenience' might result from any connection with the Civil Magistrate. It would be more practical to leave it to commanding officers and medical officers to decide which women should be subjected to these restrictions. Magistrates, after all, might object to interfering with individual liberty. Another anxiety also troubled the Governor in Council: army officers must clearly understand that the system should be applied to 'those persons only who may be liable from their general habits to occasion the diffusion of the fatal complaint which it is important to counteract, as from the nature of the local usages of India much confusion might be produced by any measure tending to create an interference with the establishments attached to many of the principal places of Hindoo worship'.[6] With these prudent qualifications, the Madras Government sanctioned the scheme.

From London, the authorities eventually despatched their guarded approval: 'We consider the general idea of a measure of this nature to be poth politic and humane.' But they wanted more detail – and they wanted to know how much it was all going to cost.[7] The Madras

Government, thinking of economies, soon asked the Medical Board for an assessment of the effectiveness of lock hospitals, based on the available statistics.[8] The Medical Board were embarrassed to report, in 1809, that the number of European soldiers annually admitted into hospital with VD had more than doubled since the establishment of the lock hospital system. Did this mean that the system had failed ? Other explanations were readily produced. On the one hand, there had been the arrival of new regiments from Europe 'with many young men', and also of 'many young Recruits whose habits are ill calculated to guard against temptation'. On the other hand, the system had not been fully introduced. There were no efficient police to take 'all infected or suspicious women' to hospital ; instead, only the most wretched or the starving came. Also, 'all castes being huddled together in a miserable choultry', or shed, the more prosperous prostitutes preferred 'native medical assistance', for which they could afford to pay.[9]

The Government pressed for specific proposals. As an economy, the Medical Board suggested that nine lock hospitals should be closed. In charge of each of the remaining eight there should be 'a decent woman of caste and proper years'. The Board assumed, no doubt with reason, that the more prosperous patients, whom they wanted to attract, would be of higher caste. In the existing hospitals, however, there were over 1,300 patients, and many of them were 'wretched objects' who would suffer severely if hospitals were suddenly closed before they were cured : some provision should be made for them.[10] The Government duly sanctioned the closure of the nine hospitals, and Superintendent Surgeons were instructed that they should 'guard in the strictest manner against exposing the unhappy objects now under care in them to any unnecessary distress'. In other words, no new patients would be admitted, and hospitals would only be closed when they were empty.[11]

But the closing of lock hospitals soon aroused protests in military circles. Again, statistical evidence was produced. Lieutenant-Colonel Gibbs, commanding at Bangalore, wrote in 1810 that VD among the soldiers had greatly increased as a result : the proportion affected was now one man in seven.[12] The Commander-in-Chief urged that the lock hospital at Bangalore be reopened, and that as a matter of policy there should be one at every station where a European regiment was quartered.[13] The Government promptly agreed, and asked the Medical Board how the system could be improved.

Predictably, the Medical Board repeated their previous recom-

13

mendations for special police and 'appropriate buildings'. These buildings, they explained, should be 'erected at a considerable distance from the Barracks, so as to prevent any intercourse with the Troops, and with a few distinct apartments, for different descriptions of patients'. Less predictably, they also recommended a refinement of the *lal bazar* system – 'some internal regulations in Regiments, by which inducements might be held out to the men to attach themselves individually to individual Native women'. After all, 'It was well known, how much more efficient those Corps are, which have Native women attached to them, than those are which have not been so provided.' The Board perceived numerous advantages:

> The soldiers so attached, if they have been at all cautious in their choice, are not only kept free from the venereal infection, but have more attention paid to the providing and dressing of their victuals and to other comforts conducive to health than can be given in this climate by European women, who in general are not equal to the exertions necessary.[14]

In other words, what members of the Medical Board had seen in some regiments should be enforced by regulations in all. This was too much for the government to accept, but the proposal for special police was sanctioned.[15] After this, the lock hospital system continued to operate in the Madras Presidency until 1835.

The Bombay Government's attention was drawn to the problem in the 1820s, after its territories had been greatly enlarged, and its military responsibilities greatly increased, by the annexations that followed the British defeat of the Marathas in 1818. Its measures were, however, of a more temporary nature, and its purpose was sometimes to protect the health of Indian as well as of British troops.

In 1824, it was reported that VD was 'spreading to an alarming degree' in the Baroda Subsidiary Force – the contingent which the Gaekwad, the ruler of Baroda, was bound by the terms of his alliance with the British to admit within his territories. T. P. Weekes, surgeon to the 1st Bombay Light Cavalry, who was stationed there, was alarmed to find that two-thirds of his hospital cases were venereal. He thereupon established a lock hospital, and maintained it at his own expense for six months. As a result, he claimed, 'upwards of twenty unfortunate creatures were restored to perfect health who a few months before were labouring under a most loathsome disease'.[16] The Bombay Government therefore agreed to maintain the hospital: this was on behalf of an Indian regiment.[17] In the following year a lock hospital was established at Rajkot, because of the extent of vD among 'the soldiery and camp followers (both European and Native)'.[18] A lock hospital was also established at Poona, where there was much vD among British troops, and at Dapoli, where there was much vD among the 1st Grenadier Regiment of the Bombay Native Infantry.[19]

Lock hospitals were established at other military stations where vD was said to be rife. They were soon closed if vD was said to have abated. The lock hospital at Bhuj was closed in 1827 because it had only held two patients in the previous three months.[20] The lock hospital at Satara was similarly closed in 1830.[21] In short, in the Bombay Presidency there was no policy of establishing lock hospitals on a permanent basis merely for the benefit of British troops. They were opened wherever the need was reported, for the benefit either of British or of Indian troops, and they were closed when they no longer seemed to be needed.

Lock hospitals soon became accepted as in the nature of things at Bombay, so that when the question arose of providing for a Dr Kennedy who had lost his existing appointment, the proposal was made that he should be given charge of the lock hospital at Belgaum. Formal authorization was about to be given when William Newnham, who had worked his way up to the Governor's Council from the secretariat, pointed out that there was in fact no lock hospital at Belgaum.[22] It transpired that the idea had come from the bluff Sir John Malcolm a few days before he retired from the governorship. A characteristic letter was produced from Malcolm to the Commander-in-Chief, Sir Sidney Beckwith:

> My dear Sidney,
>   You agreed I believe that Doctor Kennedy should be staff surgeon at Belgaum, Deputy Store Keeper and have charge of the Lock Hospital. This is all in your patronage and you can propose it to take place from the 1st of December, the day on which Doctor Kennedy's appointment ceases.[23]

Newnham, with tongue in cheek, stated blandly that in these circumstances he accepted that Malcolm and Beckwith thought that there was a local need, although it was usual for that to be explained as the basis for such appointments.[24] The arrangement was duly sanctioned. But this was to tread on dangerous ground when there was a reforming Governor-General, Lord William Bentinck, at Calcutta, who was urging economies all round, and had been nicknamed the 'clipping Dutchman' for that reason.

More dangerous ground was soon revealed. Some lock hospitals had been supplemented by special police. In 1825 the Superintending Surgeon, Poona Division, argued that in view of the danger to British troops there two peons should be appointed to bring diseased women to the lock hospital ; he proposed a basic wage of five rupees a month, with a bonus of a quarter of a rupee for each woman brought in.[25] The Medical Board disliked the idea of such a bonus as liable to abuse, but it was strongly supported by the Commander-in-Chief, who suggested the appointment of 'two steady old police peons', or constables, on account of their knowledge of the regulations and of 'the haunts of prostitutes'.[26] This was sanctioned, and two years later the number was increased to four NCOs and twenty peons, while the bonus was increased to one rupee a head. Their duties were to arrest 'all strange women found in the lines of the European Regiments at Poona and to take them to the Regimental Hospitals to be examined'.[27] Soon enough it came to be accepted that similar police could elsewhere be appointed on the basis of one NCO and five peons for every European regiment, but in 1830, in response to Bentinck's call for economy, this was reduced to two peons without an NCO.[28]

Meanwhile in Bengal, Bentinck, as Governor-General, had begun to question the utility of lock hospitals, although as Governor of Madras he had once presided over the establishment of a lock hospital system. In 1830 the lock hospitals in Bengal were accordingly abolished, and the Governor-General in Council reported with satisfaction to the Court of Directors that this would save thirty thousand rupees a year.[29] The Bombay and Madras Governments were invited to do likewise. But the Bombay Government protested, and produced statistics in support of its argument that VD among the troops had decreased since the establishment of lock hospitals and *lal bazars*, although there had been some increase since the reduction in the number of peons.[30]

Bentinck was cautious about the Bombay statistics. There might be 'fluctuations', for example when a regiment moved from one station to another. More seriously, he thought it 'impossible' for peons to ascertain who were 'the idle and diseased women without intrusive, impertinent and disgusting research such as must be extremely offensive to the more decent prostitutes and from which research the more decent no doubt purchase exemption by submitting to any degree of extortion'.[31]

This humane argument was supplemented by Dr Burke, the Inspector-General of Hospitals for the King's forces in India. When a lock hospital was established, only the poorest and most wretched prostitutes could be induced to enter it : these were 'probably the most harmless', as they did not attract the soldiers. The others would go some distance away, and 'the soldiers consequently went in search of them, exposing themselves to all weathers, day and night, and thereby giving rise to Fevers, Dysenteries, Cholera, etc.'. With the abolition of the lock hospitals, 'the men became more healthy' ; also, 'a better class of prostitutes' came to attend to their needs. He agreed with Bentinck that these women found the lock hospitals 'horribly revolting to their habits and customs'. But he was unusual in suggesting that 'the native curative means' which they had known 'for years or ages' were 'held in estimation by them which would not be the case if they found them less efficacious than those employed by the Europeans'.[32]

Finally, Burke tried to deal with the figures. He presented statistics of the incidence of VD among British troops in Bengal :

	Total strength	*VD cases*	*Proportion of VD cases to total strength* (%)
1827	8760	2545	29
1828	8812	2746	31
1829	8315	2500	30
1830	8914	1891	21
1831	8898	2055	23
1832	7872	1584	20
1833	7431	1182	16

It seemed that VD began to decline in 1830, the very year in which the lock hospitals had been closed. Burke examined the statistics for Bombay, and argued that there was more VD in stations with lock hospitals than in stations without them. But this was to forget or ignore the Bombay Government's policy of opening lock hospitals where there was much VD and closing them where there was only a little. He also compared Poona with Kanpur and Mirat. At Poona, with its lock hospital and peons, VD cases in 1831 and 1832 were 36·5 per cent of strength. At Kanpur and Mirat, without lock hospitals, VD cases in the same years were only 12·9 per cent of strength. But such comparisons were unconvincing. They took no account of differences between the two areas, or indeed between different units in the same station : for example, in one troop of horse artillery at Poona VD cases were 41 per cent of strength and in another troop they were only 13·5 per cent.

Moreover, if we bear in mind the rough and ready methods of diagnosis and treatment, all such statistics must seem highly suspect – significant more for their effect on opinion and policy than for any relation to medical realities. Methods of treatment were hazardous, especially for syphilis : mercury and bichloride of mercury were of doubtful efficacy and had unpleasant side-effects; iodide of potassium, which was also in general use by the 1850s, was only a little more effective. The optimism with which the doctors claimed that they could cure patients, both men and women, seems to have been based more on self-confidence than on clinical evidence. Indeed, when the primary lesions disappeared, patients were discharged as cured. In the statistics no distinction was made between fresh cases and the readmission of former patients. However, when these reservations have been admitted, it may be granted that the confinement of patients in hospital during the most infectious stage of their illness did prevent them from infecting others when they were most likely to do so.

Dr Burke's explanation for the low level of VD at Kanpur and Mirat was the existence of *lal bazars*, which he inelegantly termed 'the Old Bawd system' : a procuress was paid five rupees a month from the regimental canteen fund to see that the girls were healthy. When Burke inspected the hospital of His Majesty's 11th Light Dragoons at Mirat he found only four VD patients, but when he came again three months later there were twenty-two. This, he thought, was because 'the Old Bawd had gone away as she had not been paid her salary'. He went to the commanding officer with his discovery. The good woman was persuaded to return, and VD thereupon decreased.[33]

Lal bazars functioned in the Bombay Presidency, as elsewhere. But at this time they came under ecclesiastical censure there. The Rev. Thomas Carr, Archdeacon of Bombay, found out what was happening and protested to the Commander-in-Chief in 1834. He described the system with accuracy and indignation : 'A number of females are kept in buildings in a Bazar called the "Lal Bazar" within the lines of the Regiment, and the men go there for the gratification of their passions.' He conceded that the system was defended on the ground that thereby the soldiers were 'saved from contracting disease and from getting into broils in the Bazars'. But this only made matters worse : 'My answer to these reasons is that it has pleased Providence to order that sin and misery should be connected, and the arrangement of which I complain is an attempt to make sinning safe.'[34]

This was an opportune moment for such a protest, as Bishop Wilson, the aggressively evangelical Bishop of Calcutta, was about to visit Bombay in the course of a lengthy journey through British India, during which he engaged in a number of lively controversies. Carr told him all about it, and renewed his complaints to the Commander-in-Chief: 'The iniquitous establishments which candidly viewed are nothing more nor less than licensed brothels, are still attached to every European Regiment under this Presidency, inviting the soldiers to licentiousness with the assurance that they may indulge their sinful passions, not merely with safety as far as disease is concerned, but with the sanction of their superiors.'[35] The Bishop of Calcutta in turn complained, in the same words, that *lal bazars* made 'sinning safe'. He also introduced a more utilitarian argument: they threw 'the rein on the neck of the very vice which most rapidly and certainly saps the principle, the courage, the animal power and the life of the soldier'.[36]

However, the Bombay Government went on its way, and calmly reported to the Court of Directors, in 1834, that it had sanctioned the erection of a lock hospital at Ahmadnagar at a cost of 1,161 rupees precisely.[37] The Court, always on the watch for unnecessary expenditure, promptly replied that lock hospitals had been discontinued elsewhere and must be abolished also in the Bombay Presidency.[38]

The Madras Government had apparently been convinced by Burke's arguments. It directed its Medical Board to draft an order abolishing all the lock hospitals in the Madras Presidency. The Board tactlessly began the draft with the words 'under instructions from the Supreme Government', but the Madras Government deleted this phrase before publishing the order.[39]

Some significant tendencies can be identified in this early stage of confused experimentation, when local initiatives culminated in a policy which was abruptly terminated. First, the health of the British soldier is the dominating criterion in policy discussion. Some attention was paid in Bombay to the health of Indian soldiers. But they were less affected by vD. Some officials expressed sympathy with diseased prostitutes, satisfaction at the thought that they might be cured and indignation at the possibility that police peons might oppress them. But the main argument against the lock hospital system was that it had not substantially checked the spread of VD among British soldiers. Secondly, certain stereotypes have emerged, which will continue to affect bureaucratic discussion throughout the century. The British soldier who satisfies his sexual desires by visiting a prostitute is assumed to be merely acting in a natural way, even if he catches VD, although Indians who behave in a similar manner are apt to be viewed in a different light. When General Sir Lionel Smith stressed the importance of a lock hospital at Ahmadnagar, in 1830, he argued that one reason for the prevalence of VD there was the presence of a large number of Muslims, 'the most debauched of any caste in this part of India'.[40]

On the other hand, official attitudes to the prostitutes visited by soldiers reveal great ambivalence. In satisfying the soldiers' masculine needs, prostitutes are seen as playing a positive role, helping their clients to remain manly. But they are also seen in a negative role, as threatening soldiers with diseases which might destroy their manhood. Medical officers arguing for lock hospitals would describe in unpleasant detail cases of soldiers with genital organs 'eaten away' by VD. The dilemma is often resolved by distinguishing between 'respectable' or 'decent' prostitutes, who live in the regimental bazars and submit to medical treatment when necessary, and 'idle' or 'disorderly' prostitutes, who live in 'haunts' beyond military control and tempt soldiers to wander dangerously far from camp. But there is no condemnation of prostitutes on moral grounds, nor is there any attempt to persuade them to change their occupation. It was generally recognized that religious attitudes were less rigid in India than in England, though social structures were more rigid : prostitutes were not denounced as sinners, but society permitted them no alternative occupation. Also, prostitutes were needed by British soldiers. Rehabilitation was precluded both by Indian realities and by British necessities. At least in the Indian lock hospitals there was nothing of the punitive regime so characteristic of their counterparts in England. But some degree of compulsion seemed essential to their advocates.

With the abolition of the lock hospital system, army officers lost their powers of control over prostitutes in cantonments. They feared that British soldiers were threatened by diseased Indian women, and they felt helpless. Brigadier Burton, commanding the important military cantonment of St Thomas's Mount, Madras, complained in 1839 that 'the disease in frightful form' had become 'lamentably prevalent'. He thought he could see 'diseased women abounding in this vicinity', while 'a considerable number of very healthy young men' had recently arrived from Europe. There had in fact been a draft of 150 recruits. Significantly, the Brigadier demanded the power to deal with these threatening women in a variety of drastic ways – 'their expulsion and punishment, confinement for cure, or removal to some distance under surveillance of civil authority'.[41] More simply, the Commander-in-Chief suggested that the officer commanding the police be empowered to expel from the cantonment any woman found on medical examination to be diseased and to punish her if she returned, under Madras Regulation VII of 1832, which subjected to military law Indians working in cantonments, such as officers' servants and camp followers.[42]

The matter was referred to the Company's chief law court, the *Sadr Faujdari Adalat*, which ruled that prostitutes did not come within the scope of this regulation : they remained subject to the ordinary courts, and army officers had no jurisdiction over them.[43] The Madras Government then consulted the Court of Directors.[44] The Court of Directors cautiously advised it to consult the Governor-General in Council.[45] With equal caution the Governor-General in Council contrived to sidestep such an embarrassing issue : 'the subject tho' difficult to be provided for by legislation may in the opinion of His Lordship in Council be well disposed of by judicious military and local arrangements.'[46] Finally, the Court of Directors solemnly advised the Madras Government to take special care when it devised these arrangements.[47]

Meanwhile many army officers had been deploring the abolition of the lock hospital system in the Madras Presidency. Dr Murray, Deputy Inspector-General of Hospitals for the Queen's troops, claimed in 1838 that there had since been a great increase in the number of VD cases. He produced a careful analysis, admitting that there seemed to be no general increase in 'virulence', only fluctuations in severity in different places and at different times in the same place : this he thought could be explained by 'some endemic or epidemic influence giving facility to the agency of the virus, and causing a predisposition in the body to its more severe action'. He conceded that lock hospitals had been offensive to 'the feelings and prejudices of the Natives'. Instead he suggested general civilian hospitals, each with a VD ward superintended by an Indian matron acquainted with 'the haunts and habits' of prostitutes.[48]

Murray's report put the Medical Board in a delicate position. They

21

had recently stated, in their report for 1837, that VD continued steadily to decline, whereas Murray now stated that it had greatly increased. They laboriously constructed several lines of defence. First they pointed out that they had considered only the last few years: in 1835, 1836 and 1837 the proportion of VD cases to the total strength of European troops was 29, 26 and 23 per cent respectively. This was a steady fall, though only over a few years. But Murray had begun with the year 1830, when VD cases were only 13 per cent of total strength. Even so the proportion had risen to 34 per cent in 1833 and 1834, although these unusually high figures could be explained as the result of famine years, with economic hardship driving more women into prostitution.[49]

This might have been thought an adequate explanation of the apparent disagreement. But the Medical Board went further than they need have done. They also commented that Murray had included as venereal what they called 'non-syphilitic' diseases of the genitals, such as '*bubo simplex* and *ulcus penis non-syphiliticum*'. This was unwise of them. Murray could – and promptly did – claim wide medical experience of the treatment of venereal disease, not only in India but in France, Spain and the Cape of Good Hope. Moreover, the Medical Board revealed themselves to be old-fashioned: they still thought that all venereal disease was syphilitic. The eighteenth-century physician Hunter had indeed argued that syphilis and gonorrhoea were the same, and for a time his theory had won considerable acceptance, but from early in the nineteenth century evidence had been accumulating of their essential difference even before Philippe Ricord established it definitively in 1837. In the 1830s most medical officers in India differentiated between syphilis and gonorrhoea. By *bubo simplex* the Medical Board presumably meant soft chancre: this is not syphilitic, but it is undoubtedly venereal, and Murray was correct in so regarding it.

The Medical Board also produced their own statistics of VD cases among European troops between 1802 and 1838.[50] Based upon uncertain diagnostic criteria and compiled in accordance with outmoded assumptions, these figures were unimpressive. Not surprisingly, the Board concluded that VD statistics seemed 'subject to extraordinary fluctuation'. Certainly they provided no support for the lock hospital system. Some of the statistics submitted by Murray seem a little more significant – at least when the figures over a period of years appear to have been compiled by the same medical officer, who presumably used the same criteria throughout. He produced, for example, one table giving, very unusually, the number of VD cases among Indian as well as European troops at Bangalore from 1833 to 1837. The annual proportion of VD cases to strength ranged from 32 to 45 per cent among European troops, but from only 2 to 4 per cent among Indian troops.[51] There is some reason to believe that such a low incidence of VD was characteristic of Indian regiments : no wonder the health of British soldiers dominated policy discussions about VD control. Not all the Queen's regiments reported an increase in VD since the abolition of lock hospitals. Of those which did, Murray found most alarming the figures for the 41st Foot, stationed at Belleri, which had fluctuated between 3 and 14 per cent of strength in the five years before 1835 but rose to 29 and 39 per cent in 1836 and 1837 respectively.[52]

In spite of their statistical disagreements with Murray, the Medical Board also thought that something should be done to check VD. They agreed that lock hospitals had been disliked by Indian women. Instead they suggested that each station with European troops should have a public dispensary to issue medicine to the sick, with a ward attached to it for 'female patients, whose cases might require particular attention', while each regiment should have an Indian matron to keep an eye on the prostitutes.[53] This was not very different from Murray's plan for general hospitals with special VD wards and matrons. The Madras Government cautiously submitted these ideas to its superiors in Calcutta : it would be 'useful' to have an infirmary, of course 'on a very limited scale', at every station with European troops, 'or perhaps a dispensary'. It was careful to explain that it disapproved of the idea of appointing matrons : it recalled that the matrons of lock hospitals had often 'made an improper use of the powers vested in them by levying contributions upon classes not of the description contemplated, under a threat of denouncing for examination'.[54]

But for all its caution it failed to conciliate the Government of India, who had no patience with such euphemisms as 'a ward for female patients whose cases required particular attention' and refused to sanction these proposals. There could be no return to a lock hospital system or anything like it. This prompted a fresh discussion of the subject in Madras. What other remedies could be devised ? The medical officers were again consulted. The Medical Board submitted another report. The only other conceivable measures were regular medical inspections in European regiments and 'the expulsion of suspected, or diseased, females from military cantonments'. In fact, weekly medical inspections were already held. But women could not be 'forcibly subjected to personal examination', nor did the military authorities have the power to expel them from cantonments. The Medical Board reverted to their proposal for public dispensaries with special wards and matrons. As it happened, public dispensaries had recently been established at two places where there were European troops – Bellari and Trichinopoly. Could the experiment be tried there ?[55]

Lord Elphinstone, the Governor of Madras, now intervened. Lock hospitals were 'doubtless liable to abuses like other institutions', but he thought that 'under proper management' they were 'very useful'. After all, in Paris the celebrated expert on public hygiene, Parent-Duchâtelet, had 'justified a much more vigorous system of surveillance than I believe was ever attempted in this country'. He was referring to Parent-Duchâtelet's monumental study of prostitution in Paris, which was then attracting some attention in England, where the *Quarterly Review* hailed its author as 'the Newton of harlotry', but deplored his detailed treatment of his subject.[56]

Elphinstone would have liked a reconsideration of the lock hospital system in India; but on reflection he and his colleagues had to recognize realities. The Government of India would never agree to it, or even to the appointment of matrons at public dispensaries. All that the Madras Government thought it prudent to do was to minute that 'His Lordship is of opinion that every encouragement should be given to induce diseased women to receive medical aid from these establishments'.[57] That was in June 1842. At this point the Court of Directors intervened, with unusual speed. In January 1843 they authorized the appointment of matrons at the public dispensaries at Bellari and Trichinopoly.[58]

It soon emerged that the new arrangements were as disagreeable to the patients as the old lock hospitals had been. The surgeon at Trichinopoly protested in 1844 that 'every pains has been taken to conciliate this class of unfortunate women by attention to their wants and comforts while in Hospital'. Many of them, who 'were almost in a state of nudity on admission', had been given clothing. In spite of this, he noted with surprise, some of his patients remained in hospital 'more under the threat of compulsion than of their own free will'. Indeed, 'an occasional desertion would occur, but those individuals who resided in the purlieus of the Regimental Bazars were soon recovered'. But the *kotwals*, or bazar officials, were 'inclined to support the prostitutes' rather than the matron.

The surgeon complained to the military authorities, and it was publicly announced that 'all those who would not be persuaded to come to the Hospital and there remain until they are cured should be Tom Tomed [*sic*] and expelled the Lines'. But in the first year he had only 12 patients with primary and 6 with secondary syphilis, and 86 with gonorrhoea, while in Her Majesty's 94th Regiment stationed at Trichinopoly there were 63 cases of primary and 4 of secondary syphilis and only 48 cases of gonorrhoea. Like most medical men, he had unbounded confidence in his methods of treatment, and these figures so puzzled him that he drew the curious conclusion that 'some of these cases entered as syphilis among Europeans may only have been simple ulcers, the result of excoriations and abrasions, consequent on impure coition, which so frequently is met with in this country'.[59] In fact, the regiment had a low level of vd – only 12 per cent of strength. There was indeed a discrepancy between the relative incidence of syphilis and gonorrhoea among women patients on the one hand and soldiers on the other, but there were many uncertain factors in the situation : for example, the surgeon himself realized that because the *kotwals* obstructed the matron, many infected women never went to hospital. At Bellari the incidence was even more with 31 women treated for primary and 11 for secondary syphilis, and 31 for gonorrhoea, while Her Majesty's 63rd Regiment stationed there had 112 cases of primary and 15 of secondary syphilis, and 125 of gonorrhoea.[60] The proportion of the regiment affected was however higher – 27 per cent of strength – and the number of women treated was smaller. The surgeon emphasized that no coercion was used at Bellari, and many women were therefore treated as outpatients : as such they were presumably free to infect more clients.[61]

There was a considerable increase in the number of women treated at Trichinopoly in the following year – 169, of whom 41 were outpatients. The surgeon again proclaimed his faith in 'the dread of being Tom Tomed' as an inducement to women to enter hospital. But his matron also seems to have behaved in a forceful manner. On one occasion an Indian police officer intervened when he saw her taking two 'notorious women' to hospital : he stopped her and sent the women away. The surgeon repeated his complaints against the police : if only they would cooperate, he said, he would have double the number of patients in his hospital. Demands from different officers for stronger police action and for more coercive powers soon came to dominate policy discussions.

When the Court of Directors reviewed these events they noted that 'some degree of compulsion' had been used 'in certain cases'. They thereupon enunciated a principle : 'As a general rule, nothing is more to be avoided than the employment of measures of coercion for bringing the natives to Hospitals or Dispensaries, such measures being calculated to create a prejudice against these Institutions.' But they inserted a guarded qualification : 'In cases where the result of persons not obtaining medical aid for themselves is to communicate diseases to others, some deviation from this strict rule is occasionally admissible, but the utmost discretion must be used in the application of anything partaking of the nature of constraint.' Then they urged the Madras Government to have a policy – 'not leaving a matter requiring such peculiar attention to the sole discretion of the surgeons at the several dispensaries'.[62]

What sort of initiative might be taken locally was seen in the cantonment of the Hyderabad Subsidiary Force at Secunderabad. In 1844 Captain Morgan, the Superintendent of Police, announced that every dancing girl and prostitute must pay a tax of two annas a month, as British and Indian soldiers were suffering severely from sickness and something had to be done. The money was to pay for a Hindu and a Muslim matron, who would give her medicine. If she received soldiers before she had been cured she would be 'most severely punished'. Captain Morgan concluded ominously that if a matron connived at any concealment of illness she would 'also suffer the punishments'.[63]

These arrangements came to light when there was a change of command in 1848. Brigadier J. P. James, the new officer commanding the force, promptly cancelled Morgan's order on the ground that it was liable to abuse. He learnt that it was 'no uncommon occurrence' for the matrons to 'threaten respectable women with a visit of examination, knowing they would receive a donation to keep away'.[64] The Governor in Council agreed, on the ground that 'compulsory measures cannot be authorized'.[65] In fact, what Brigadier James disliked was not so much the compulsory tax as the system which enabled matrons to abuse their powers.

When the 94th Regiment moved to Cannanore, Lieutenant-Colonel Milner, their commanding officer, complained that the cantonment was 'crowded with diseased prostitutes of the very lowest caste'. It transpired that he objected more to their medical than to their social condition : of ninety soldiers sick in the regimental hospital, fifty were VD cases.[66] Dr Young, the Superintending Surgeon, reported 'the astonishing fact that at this moment there are thirty eight prostitutes in these Bazars afflicted with the venereal disease in all its different forms'.[67] He thought that the commanding officer could expel them from the cantonment, but the commanding officer thought otherwise. In fact, the regiment now had appreciably more VD than they had at Trichinopoly in 1844, and at Trichinopoly the provision of treatment for infected prostitutes had presumably imparted a sense of security. The officers of the regiment got up a private subscription, and a temporary lock hospital was established with the proceeds. Young claimed that this had been medically successful. But there were difficulties. Lieutenant-Colonel Milner had put 'an intelligent though overzealous Non Commissioned Officer' at Young's disposal. Soon Young was 'obliged from prudential considerations to dispense with his services'. Instead he urged that the District Collector and the Superintendent of Police should provide special peons to force infected prostitutes into hospitals.[68] At this the Madras Government scented trouble : no compulsory measures could be authorized ; it cited the principle enunciated by the Court of Directors in 1847.[69]

Another principle then enunciated by the Court of Directors was that there ought to be a general policy, and this the Madras Government continued to evade. Instead it continued to respond to local demands. In 1855 a high level of VD was reported among Her Majesty's 43rd Light Infantry at Bangalore – 54 men in hospital, 'with the probability of an increase'.[70] In fact, the proportion of VD cases to the strength of the regiment at that point in time amounted to six per cent, and a lock hospital was proposed and sanctioned as a temporary measure.[71] The Court of Directors approved, on the understanding that there was thought to be an emergency and that patients came voluntarily.[72] According to the Superintending Surgeon, the hospital only accepted such women as 'seemed likely from age, general appearance and the nature of their complaints and other circumstances to belong to the class associated with the soldiery'. One patient told him that she had come with the 43rd from Madras to Bangalore and had since 'lived much among the men of that Corps'. To encourage such women to enter, 'every kindness' was shown to them : 'they have been as little restricted in diet as possible'. The surgeon noted with satisfaction that 'they appear contented'.[73]

Remarkable success was soon claimed. The hospital opened in June

1855; by November the proportion of VD cases to strength in the 43rd had fallen to between 2 and 3 per cent. A year after the hospital began, the proportion was still only 2·5 per cent. Presumably the emergency had ended, and the lock hospital was no longer necessary? Dr Cole, as Superintending Surgeon, asserted that on the contrary lock hospitals would always be necessary. Indeed, with a little help from the police, 'judiciously exercised', he could have even more patients in his hospital. He outlined the possibilities with unpleasing relish:

Where women are vagrants, prowling about the barracks of the European soldiers, without being able to show that they have any honest calling or occupation, they might be arrested, it seems to me, without unduly trenching on the liberty of the subject, and subjected to a little wholesome coercion for their own good and that of the community, by being sent to the Lock Hospital for examination, and detention there, if they are found to be labouring under disease.[74]

In the end the lock hospital remained in operation at Bangalore, but Cole's plea for coercion was rejected. Lieutenant-General Beresford, commanding Mysore Division, was adamant: 'It would give such an opening to the villainous extortion of Peons and other Native Subordinates who would have to be employed.' He had tried without success to use peons to control the situation. He stationed some 'in front of the barracks, to drive off the prostitutes, always the worst description, who collect there previously to Tattoo, and entice soldiers returning perhaps half tipsy to their quarters'. But they were ineffective: 'a Native Peon soon learnt the danger of interfering with the European Soldier when influenced by lust and drink.'[75] Beresford's suspicions were justified, not long afterwards, when police peons were brought to court at Bangalore and found guilty of demanding money from women by threatening to take them to the lock hospital.[76]

On the other hand, the services of the police were now welcomed at Secunderabad. Brigadier James had disallowed Captain Morgan's scheme in 1848, on the ground that the matrons abused their power, but a new commanding officer took over in 1855, and quickly instituted new policies. A ward was set aside in the civil hospital, and the police brought women there for examination and treatment. The surgeon explained unctuously: 'Thus these poor creatures are, by a salutary amount of coercion, for their own benefit, as well as to prevent extension of disease to others, compelled to subject themselves to care and treatment.'[77]

Prodded by Sir Patrick Grant, the Commander-in-Chief, who regretted the abolition of the lock hospital system, the Madras Government was edging slowly towards its restoration. In 1860 the Principal Inspector-General, Medical Department, drew up a series of rules providing for the periodical inspection of prostitutes by the hospital matron and for their detention in hospital if infected. Surgeons would ensure that 'women of respectability were on no account to be interfered with' and that 'no undue coercion was employed'. [78] The Madras Government did not think it advisable to enact these rules into legislation. That would have meant an application to the Government of India, which at this time had sole legislative powers. Instead it expressed approval of the rules and authorized their use at military stations where there were European troops. Prostitutes who disobeyed should be expelled from cantonments.[79] However, in 1863 the Principal Inspector-General reported with regret that comparatively few prostitutes had been induced to enter hospital at Bellari, Trichinopoly and Cannanore. 'These stations being in Regulation Provinces, there have been legal difficulties in the way of compelling persons to submit to examination'.[80] In settled territories under direct British rule, the administration was conducted in accordance with the Regulations, or written law, and the judges prided themselves on their independence of the executive.[81]

Meanwhile, the Bombay Government had encountered similar pressure for a restoration of the lock hospital system. In 1846, the Commander-in-Chief suggested recourse to euphemism: 'Should the term "Lock" usually attached to hospitals of this description be objectionable as bearing the inference of an encroachment on freedom, the appellation could be easily changed to "Hospitals for diseased Females".' The military authorities were doing all the right things: the troops were regularly inspected and VD was promptly treated. But these efforts, he claimed, were frustrated because there was no control over diseased women, who were at large in the neighbourhood of cantonments, where they had their 'usual haunts'.[82] The Medical Board could find no statistical evidence to justify a return to the lock hospital system but were disturbed to think of diseased women at large: they recommended that the civil and military authorities should combine to 'prevent the settling of vagrant women in the neighbourhood of European Cantonments'; they did not explain how the legal and practical obstacles to such executive action could be overcome.[83]

A year later Lieutenant-Colonel Twopenny, commanding the 78th Highlanders at Belgaum, urged the need for a lock hospital. The regimental surgeon reported that nearly half the sick in hospital were vD cases. In addition he referred vaguely to 'an immense number of Rheumatic diseases which arise from Venereal Taint'.[84] Various authorities added their recommendations that something should be done – the Brigadier Commanding, Southern Division, the Deputy Inspector-General of Hospitals for the Queen's Forces, the Commander-in-Chief himself.[85] The Medical Board elaborated upon the danger of 'vagrant women': to reduce vD was 'more a matter of police than of medicine'; the remedy lay more in 'lessening the opportunities of intercourse with women likely to be diseased than in the cure of those that are so'. In view of the state of medicine at that time, this argument might seem reasonable.

But there were difficulties which the Medical Board hardly took seriously. They recommended 'a rigid civil and military police' to exclude 'vagrant women' from cantonments and to control the prostitutes in the regimental bazars; there should be regular medical examination and compulsory treatment of infected women, on pain of expulsion; true the police had been guilty of 'extortion and bribery' in the past, but the authorities must exercise 'the utmost care and attention'.[86] From this the Bombay Government drew the conclusion that it was for commanding officers to deal with the matter. Perhaps aware that it might seem to be evading responsibility, it added some advice:

Taking Poona as an example, the Bazar Master might be called upon, under the orders of His Excellency the Commander-in-Chief, to state if he can establish such an effectual system of registration and licence among the Public Women resident in the cantonment as may bring them under the protection and supervision of the police.'[87]

Captain Morse, the Superintendent of Bazars, Poona, rashly asserted that there would be no difficulty about this. Vagrants should not be allowed within ten miles; matrons and peons should be appointed to the central and regimental bazars to supervise the prostitutes; a 'respectable pensioned apothecary' should be appointed to treat infected women in their homes.[88] The Commander-in-Chief was enthusiastic: these proposals seemed 'judicious and free from any objections of a legal nature'.[89] Lord Falkland, the Governor, agreed that the plan should be tried at Poona, with the cooperation of the local magistrate.[90] Yet difficulties soon emerged. Surgeon Lidingham, of Her Majesty's 83rd Regiment, reported that VD 'of rather an aggravated character' was on the increase among the men, and submitted an official complaint: 'There are several prostitutes of the lowest description located in the native village immediately behind the Hospital to whose society these men are in the habit of resorting.' He asked that they be removed.[91] But the removal of villagers was no part of Captain Morse's scheme. Dr Edwards, Superintending Surgeon, Poona, pointed out that as prostitutes had no other occupation it was impracticable for them to cease work when they were infected; they could be spreading infection even while they were under the Apothecary's treatment. Infected women should therefore be confined while they were being cured. He wanted 'a system of gentle control and coercion'.[92]

When Morse heard of Lidingham's complaints he commented mildly that the Apothecary inspected prostitutes three times a week, and sent medicines to their homes when they were ill; since the Government did not allow compulsion they could not be forced to see the Apothecary.[93] But Lidingham was all for 'more stringent measures': he thought that the existing rules were 'perfectly worthless'.[94] However, Morse soon produced some impressive statistics: from July to October 1848 there were 866 VD cases among the British troops; from July to October 1849 there were only 413, although the total strength was the same. But further statistical enquiries produced less encouraging evidence.[95] According to Lidingham's figures the total number of VD cases in his regiment during the last six months of 1849 amounted to 9 per cent of strength but rose to 11 per cent during the first six months of 1850.[96] In the 10th Royal Hussars the proportion rose from 9 per cent to 10 per cent over the same period.[97] Surgeon Arnott, of the 1st Bombay European Fusiliers, produced much more disturbing figures for the first six months of 1850: 193 cases, amounting to 22 per cent of a strength of 888. But from January to March there were only 42 cases; at the beginning of April the regiment arrived in Poona, and from then until the end of June there were 151 cases.

This was hardly a condemnation of the system at Poona, for in the three months before they arrived they had been on the march from

Peshawar. But Arnott demanded more effective measures, and praised the *lal bazar* system.[98] Lidingham was still complaining indignantly of the spectacle of 'numbers of prostitutes of the lowest description located about a hundred yards in rear of my hospital'; they were 'perfectly unmolested', although he envisaged them 'communicating this poison to numbers of the men'. The Medical Board renewed their recommendation that 'vagrants' be removed: such women left 'unrestrained and at liberty to pursue their calling as they please' were unlikely to seek medical assistance of their own free will, while 'the reckless soldiers' were unlikely to abstain from intercourse with them.[99] Edwards repeated his plea for coercion: Morse's voluntary system had proved to be 'more unsatisfactory than ever'; 'the spread of the venereal' was 'an evil of an enormous magnitude'; it would increase 'as long as the prostitutes and that class of females are left to themselves'.[100]

In the face of these attacks Captain Morse concluded sadly that his plan had 'altogether failed'. The women who accepted the Apothecary's services were only 'a very small proportion' of those visited by soldiers, and they were 'by no means regular in their attendance'. He had recommended that vagrants should be kept at a distance, but they were still at hand: 'These people are the most mischievous of all as they not only disease the men but entice them to their huts by selling them liquor . . . frequently robbing them when drunk.' He had given all who were not regimental followers notice to quit the huts behind Lidingham's hospital. With the cooperation of the civil authorities, vagrants and 'prostitutes of a drunken and disorderly character' should be banished from the neighbourhood of the cantonment. But complete security was impossible. The wives and mistresses of officers' servants and grooms often received soldiers: to control them would be impracticable.[101] Brigadier Wilson, station commander, added that although prostitutes and bad characters were often turned out of the cantonment for drunken and disorderly behaviour, they 'merely have to go a few yards beyond the limits, set up a hut and reside there unmolested'. The civil magistrate did nothing.[102]

Morse, however, found a powerful ally in Major-General Auchmuty, commanding Poona Division. He deplored all this fuss: 'in my opinion, the actual number of venereal cases amongst the Troops in Poona is not greater than what it would be in any large garrison town in England, though the climate of India may render the

disease more difficult and tedious to cure.' The increased VD among the
10th Hussars and 83rd Foot was trifling. It was indeed greater in the
Fusiliers but this was 'scarcely to be wondered at when it is borne in
mind that the Regiment had just returned to Cantonments after a
march from Peshawar to Poona'. After all, some women were being
cured. He agreed that people who had been banished ought not to be
allowed to settle themselves nearby. Apart from that, there were only
two alternatives – either 'a numerous and vigilant police with extensive
and almost arbitrary power' or 'a continuance of the present system of
holding out an inducement to diseased women to seek a cure by
offering it to them free from expense and publicity'. He preferred the
present system.[103] Auchmuty's robust advice convinced the Bombay
Government. Morse's system would be continued. With the advice of
the chief criminal court, the *Sadr Faujdari Adalat*, the magistrate was
informed that he could take appropriate action.[104] But judges and
magistrates were apt to sympathize with individuals whose liberty
seemed threatened by executive and especially by military officers.

The following year was more encouraging for Captain Morse. In the
10th Hussars the proportion of VD cases to strength fell from 10 per
cent in the first six months to 7 per cent in the second. Surgeon
Lidingham left Poona with the 83rd Foot, no doubt to Morse's relief.
Even in the 1st Bombay European Fusiliers the proportion of VD cases
to strength fell from 21 per cent in the first six months to 16 per cent in
the second.[105] But Edwards, Superintending Surgeon, once again
pressed for coercive measures. He asserted doggedly that the number
of men infected was 'still very considerable', that 'many of these men
become disabled by venereal rheumatism', and in general that 'the
evil' was 'of a gigantic character'.[106] The Medical Board also
disregarded the statistics now that they indicated that Morse's
voluntary system might be having some effect. In view of 'the
magnitude of the evil' they urged 'the institution of rigid Police
Regulations'. The prospect evidently roused unscientific emotions in
the Medical Board :

Were a little of the loathsome misery entailed on the thoughtless European
soldier by this vile scourge of his moral delinquencies inflicted on any class of
the community by an ordinary but less blameable breach of propriety, and
were its cause removeable by such blameless means as the compulsory cure of
the disease, the loudest disclaimers against the Lall Bazar system would not
hesitate to recommend the instant adoption of so simple and humane a
remedy.[107]

Brigadier Trydell, station commander, was quick to express his disapproval of *lal bazars*: 'They are objectionable in my opinion and should not under any circumstances be established.'[108] Major-General Auchmuty agreed: 'Their establishment under any circumstances whatever would evince a total disregard of all outward decency and morality.' Of course one had to be realistic: 'Where the number of unmarried men is as great as it is in a European cantonment, prostitutes of one class or other are sure to be found in the neighbourhood; their existence is unavoidable, but their actual presence and pursuits need not be so paraded as to shock all sense of public decorum.'[109]

It transpired that the 1st Bombay European Fusiliers did have a *lal bazar*. When the proportion of VD cases to strength fell from 16 to 14 per cent in the first half of 1851, Surgeon Arnott commented modestly that great attention had been paid to the regiment's *lal bazar*, although he was careful to add that a little government help would be advantageous.[110] But when the proportion of VD cases to strength rose to 17 per cent in the second half of the year he remarked more pointedly that he thought it 'a great pity' that the Government had not tried to help make the *lal bazar* more efficient.[111] But he had previously told Morse not to interfere as the regiment would be making their own arrangements. In the 10th Hussars VD remained at a relatively low level – 7 per cent in the first half of the year and 6 per cent in the second – but their surgeon criticized Morse's policy as ineffective.[112] In Her Majesty's 86th Regiment, newly arrived in Poona, the level was similar – 7 per cent in the first half of the year and 5 per cent in the second.[113] But Surgeon Edwards and the Medical Board continued to press for sterner measures.[114] It seemed clear that there would be no dramatic improvement. The Bombay Government concluded that as far as British troops were concerned the policy was 'plainly inefficacious', but could not think of any acceptable alternative. The extensive coercion proposed by Edwards and the Medical Board was out of the question. The Governor in Council resolved to continue 'the trifling expense' involved in the existing measures, since some women were being cured; the local authorities must see that this 'charity' was not abused.[115]

Thereafter there were no significant changes of policy on this matter in the Bombay Presidency until 1863, when Sir Bartle Frere as Governor asked whether lock hospitals were of any use. In England there had already been widespread discussion of the health of the

British Army, prompted by the Crimean War and the Indian Mutiny. In evidence presented to a Royal Commission on the Sanitary State of the Army in India, venereal disease was generally agreed to be a serious problem, and a number of witnesses urged that more soldiers should be allowed to marry. Frere now raised this question in Bombay, and professed his distrust of lock hospitals.[116] Sir William Mansfield, the Commander-in-Chief, agreed, on the ground that a lock hospital system could never be applied to all the available women. Instead he also turned to marriage as the best remedy. In Britain only 6 per cent of a regiment could marry, in India only 12 per cent. Why should this percentage not be raised to 20 or 25 per cent? Or should there be any limit? There would of course be some additional expense. But 'a man skilled in dealing with figures and uncertain quantities might not improbably be able to show that such additional cost would be more than compensated in actual money by the improved health and constitution of the soldiery taken as a body'. Meanwhile such elements of the lock hospital system as existed in Bombay should be abolished.[117] Frere agreed, and it was so resolved.[118] The Adjutant-General hastily pointed out that only a professional actuary with access to the records in London could perform such abstruse calculations.[119] The matter was thereupon referred to the Government of India.

Some support for such views came from the Madras Government, where the Principal Inspector-General examined his statistics for the previous 18 years and calculated that the annual average proportion of VD cases to strength amounted to 25·5 per cent among European troops but only 3·5 per cent among Indian troops : almost all Indian soldiers were married.[120] In Calcutta, on the other hand, it was noted that the proportion of married British soldiers had not in fact reached the permitted level of 12 per cent : in 1862 it was only 4·75 per cent in Bengal, 8·6 per cent in Madras and 6 per cent in Bombay.[121] But this was to overlook the fact that permission to marry lay with commanding officers : as Frere had observed, many officers thought that unmarried men made more effective soldiers. At this point the Government of India turned to a reconsideration of general policy, in connection with the report of the Royal Commission, to which the Secretary of State directed its attention.

Madras and Bombay had been moving in opposite directions, with Madras restoring the lock hospital system and Bombay abolishing such vestiges as remained. In the Bengal Presidency the Governor-General in Council had steadfastly opposed any return to the lock hospital system in the years after its abolition, but *lal bazars* were tolerated and indeed received the commendation of such authorities as Dr Burke. In 1852 the Government thought it prudent to proclaim that prostitutes could not be officially recognized as part of any regimental bazar, but commanding officers continued to make their own arrangements. As in the other Presidencies, judges and magistrates proved unwilling to help when medical officers urged that *lal bazars* were not enough and that control should be more widespread and severe.

Lucknow, however, was an exception. There a lock hospital was opened in 1859, a register of prostitutes was instituted under the auspices of the City Magistrate, and those registered were regularly inspected.[122] But Lucknow was the capital of Oudh, which had been annexed in 1856, had thrown off British control during the Mutiny, and had only been recaptured with the greatest difficulty. An efficient army was deemed essential there, and there were many army officers in the civil administration.

Similar measures were instituted at Mian Mir in 1859. This was the important military cantonment near Lahore, the capital of the Panjab, which had proved of great strategic value during the Mutiny. Again a healthy army seemed especially necessary there. A lock hospital was opened; prostitutes were registered; they were inspected weekly, and they were issued with tickets on which the dates of their inspections were recorded. Soon encouraging statistics were reported: VD admissions fell from 27 per cent of strength in the twelve months before the system began to 19 per cent in 1860.[123] But the city of Lahore itself was not touched, in spite of the protests of the military authorities.

Pleas for stronger measures came from various regiments, often coupled with complaints of a lack of cooperation on the part of the civil administration. Lieutenant-Colonel Priestley, commanding the 42nd Highlanders at Agra, reported indignantly: 'close to my Bazar are two establishments, one of about 12 and another of about 30 women, beyond the bounds of military jurisdiction.' His 'thoughtless young soldiers' were 'their victims', and VD was spreading in the regiment.[124] Assistant Surgeon Maclean claimed that 'the regimental prostitutes' were free from VD, but of 51 sick men in his hospital, 33 had VD. They must have caught it in the nearby villages.[125] Brigadier Troup, commanding Agra and Mutta District, asked the Commissioner of Agra, a civil officer, to have the diseased women 'turned out' of their villages, and the local *zamindars*, or landholders, heavily fined for harbouring them.[126] But the magistrate pointed out that the matter was not so simple. He might be able to 'exert a moral pressure' on the landholders but he could not coerce them; 'any recognizances would be cancelled by the Sessions Judge if the matter were brought to his notice'. Besides, he added, 'I am not myself aware what rules to observe; should the prohibition extend absolutely to "clean" and "foul" commodity indifferently, and if only to "foul" what is the allowance of "clean" permitted to the wants of the community? And how can the zamindars, or how can I ascertain the character of the same? It is a subject with which I do not feel competent to grapple.' He concluded coldly that it would be preferable for the military authorities, 'who seem accustomed to conduct such sanitary measures', to enforce their own rules. Perhaps the boundaries should be changed to enable them to do so.[127]

Similar difficulties were experienced in Allahabad. In Her Majesty's 77th Regiment the surgeon reported a 'steady increase' of VD. He proposed that women identified by soldiers as having infected them should be arrested, taken to hospital and detained there until they were cured.[128] The Brigade Major referred his proposal to the civil authorities, who proved unsympathetic. J. H. Morris, the magistrate, commented frostily: 'I cannot discover that prostitution is an offence punishable under the provisions of the Penal Code, nor am I aware that women subject to venereal disease have rendered themselves amenable to the Law. Under these circumstances, and in the absence of any distinct charge against these women, I must decline to arrest them, or carry out the Surgeon's suggestion.' He added a piece of advice which infuriated the Brigade Major: 'It is, I presume, within the power of the Brigadier to prevent prostitutes from coming into cantonments, or European soldiers from going into the City and Bazars, and if the evil is really as serious as represented to be, some such measures as the above can easily be adopted by the Military Authorities.'[129] Brigadier Rainier promptly complained to the Adjutant-General: 'Mr. Morris' remark, that it is within the power of the Military Authorities to prevent the men from going into the City or Bazars, is absurd: it would entail a well-conducted Regiment being confined to barracks during their stay at Allahabad, as their Lines are surrounded in every direction by Bazars that are in the civil jurisdiction.'[130] The Brigadier was duly informed of 'the impropriety of making use of the term "absurd" in an official communication', however 'impracticable' the magistrate's suggestion might have been, but the papers went forward to the Government of India as further evidence in support of the case for a lock hospital system.[131]

From Rawalpindi Dr O'Nial, surgeon to the 51st Light Infantry, explained simply that when the regiment arrived the *kotwal* 'was directed to provide women, who were placed in a house in the Bazar under the superintendence of a woman paid Rs. 5 per mensem from the Canteen Fund'. Similar measures were taken by other units there. Nevertheless, 6 Sergeants, 7 Corporals, 7 Buglers and 153 Privates caught VD during 1862.[132] One difficulty was that the Station Surgeon refused to admit prostitutes into the civil hospital or dispensary : 'were I to do so, no respectable woman in the district would come near the place'.[133] O'Nial urged the necessity of a lock hospital. The Deputy Commissioner objected on moral grounds, and recommended that more soldiers be allowed to marry. But the Brigade Major and the Commissioner both thought a lock hospital more practicable.[134]

From Multan Assistant Surgeon De Renzy, of the Royal Artillery, reported a steady increase in VD, which accounted for 60 per cent of those then in hospital. He put forward an idea which was to be heard with increasing force in the years to come : 'the blood of England is now being tainted with the venereal poison disseminated through the country from the Army as its great focus and factory'. He recommended that more soldiers be allowed to marry : married men he considered to be not only much less prone to VD but much healthier generally.[135] But Brigadier Errington, commanding Multan, wanted a lock hospital system like that established at Mian Mir. He had read reports of its success.[136]

In these and other documents accumulating at Calcutta reference was sometimes made to systems of vice control in Belgium, France and Germany. But Sir Hugh Rose, the Commander-in-Chief, urged that Mian Mir should be taken as a test case, and as reports of its success came in he repeatedly recommended that lock hospitals should be established wherever there were European troops.

Now Sir Charles Wood, the Secretary of State, nerved himself to make a positive recommendation on this delicate subject. In 1861, when he found Sir Patrick Grant, the Madras Commander-in-Chief, pressing for a lock hospital system, he reminded the Madras Government of Burke's conclusion that lock hospitals had been accompanied by rising VD statistics.[137] But when he forwarded to the Government of India, in 1863, the report of the Royal Commission on the Sanitary State of the Army, he recommended its suggestions.[138] These included a return to the lock hospital system. He also referred approvingly to the measures recently taken in Madras. Those measures had amounted to a restoration of lock hospitals, although the military authorities often complained that because of the attitude of the local judge or magistrate they had been unable to force women to submit to medical examination. It now seemed that a more coercive system could be divised.

2

The Contagious Diseases and Cantonments Acts in India

The Royal Commission on the Sanitary State of the Army in India prepared the way for legislation. Venereal disease was described in their report as the scourge of British troops there. Many witnesses had recommended that more soldiers should be allowed to marry, but in their report the Commission alluded vaguely to a possible disadvantage: when a regiment went on active service wives and children left behind might be exposed to temptation and distress. Instead, the Commission recommended improved facilities for 'occupation, instruction and recreation', and also a return to the lock hospital system, with such improvements as experience might suggest.[1] In the next two decades some ingenious improvements were indeed introduced, with disastrous results for the reputation of the military authorities.

Familiar arguments were presented to the Governor-General's legislative council in 1864 when a Bill was introduced to regularize the administration of civil and criminal justice in military cantonments. One clause provided that local governments could make rules 'for inspecting and controlling houses of ill-fame and for preventing the spread of venereal disease'.[2] A.A. Roberts, Judicial Commissioner, Panjab, opposed this on the ground that it was 'questionable whether the end would justify the means, and also whether immunity from this disease might not be purchased by a general loosening of moral principles and an increase of profligacy'.[3] Instead, he urged that more soldiers be allowed to marry, and pointed out that Sir Bartle Frere and Sir William Mansfield were agreed that this was the remedy. C. E. Trevelyan briskly disagreed: moral standards differed in different countries, and in India the prostitute was a respectable, professional person. Of course, marriage would be a better remedy, but 'where were wives to be found for successive relays of 70,000 men? Also, 'most young Englishmen preferred to retain their liberty, during the early active period of life'.[4] The Bill duly passed into law as Act XXII of 1864.

If most soldiers did not want to marry, the restrictions could presumably have been removed without much expense. In fact, there were many attempts to evade them, sometimes with the connivance of sympathetic commanding officers. Captain Christienson, of the *Flying Foam*, unwisely applied for compensation because two women had travelled to India in his ship without payment. He was carrying detachments of the 58th and 107th Regiments, and the women had boarded his ship secretly to be with their husbands. He only discovered their presence after the voyage had begun. Enquiries were duly instituted.

The officer commanding the 58th Regiment replied from Allahabad that Mrs Johnston, one of the women in question, had indeed married one of his men without permission. She could not be taken on the strength because of the regulations. He added blandly, 'She has however a room given to her in Barracks as she has no other place to go.'[5] The officer commanding the 107th Regiment replied from Hazaribagh that Mrs Burns, the other woman in question, had embarked without her husband's knowledge. He explained carefully that 'her reason for doing so was to accompany her husband to India and endeavour to be taken on the strength of the Regiment, Private Burns having been married without permission'. He added simply: 'Mrs. Burns has been taken on the strength of the Regiment.'[6] Colonel Atkinson, the Controller of Military Accounts, conceded that the cost of their passages would have to be settled, but he added with ill-concealed satisfaction that consideration must also be given to claims against the captain of the *Flying Foam* on account of 'short provisions to the troops and deficient messing of officers'.[7]

A special committee was appointed to draw up rules under the Cantonments Act. Characteristically, the committee proposed that prostitutes should be divided into two classes: the first class would consist of 'public prostitutes frequented by Europeans', the second of 'public prostitutes not so frequented'. Only first-class prostitutes would be subject to regulation. They would have to register with the cantonment authorities, and each would be given a 'printed ticket' in a prescribed form, together with a copy of the rules. She would be medically examined every month, and the result of each examination would be recorded on her ticket. If she caught VD she would be detained in the lock hospital until she was certified as cured.

Cantonment committees might make rules for the maintenance of prostitutes' houses in a state of cleanliness and for 'the provision of a sufficient supply of water and of proper means of ablution'. Soliciting in public must not be allowed in cantonments.[8]

In such ways the special committee made valiant attempts to regularize prostitution. They noted 'the tendency of well-meaning men to attempt to suppress prostitution, instead of looking upon it as an inevitable evil, which may be controlled, but which cannot be got rid of'. As on previous occasions, control seemed essential : to control prostitution was to legitimize it, almost to make it respectable, certainly to make it seem less dangerous. The committee professed an awareness of the danger of oppression : this had to be guarded against, for if prostitutes felt harassed they would not register with the authorities, and control would be lost. The committee therefore stressed the importance of appointing suitable women as *dhais*, or matrons, to supervise the prostitutes.[9] They also drew up detailed instructions for lock hospital doctors. The list of duties to be carried out by medical officers in charge of such institutions ended with these words :

It should be the special care of the Medical Officer that all arrangements for inspection should be delicately carried out ; that the comforts and interests of patients should be carefully looked after ; their residence in hospital rendered as little distasteful to them as possible ; that all complaints should be investigated and adjudged with kindness and consideration ; and that all duties connected with women performed by himself or his subordinates should be carried out with respect and feeling towards sex.[10]

When previous systems of control had failed to check the spread of VD, a frequent explanation had been that soldiers went to women living outside the cantonment and free from military supervision. In Act XXII of 1864 it was therefore provided that the new rules could be extended beyond cantonment boundaries.[11] This was done again and again. For example, the rules were introduced in Kanpur cantonment in 1867, and in 1869 Dr Jones, the medical officer in charge of the lock hospital, complained that the number of prostitutes on his register had dwindled from 119 to 67. The others had left for the city, where they were freer, and soldiers went to them there. According to the police there were more than three hundred prostitutes in Kanpur, and Dr Jones wanted to have all of them on his register.[12] A special conference was held on the subject when the Lieutenant-Governor visited

42

Kanpur. It was agreed that 'there were serious difficulties in bringing the whole of the prostitutes of so large a city under medical control, but it was suggested that the lower class, the only class that would be accessible to the soldiery, might be so treated'.[13] In other words, the first-class prostitutes visited only by Europeans, as envisaged by the Government of India's special committee, turned out in fact to be 'the lower class'.[14] It was eventually agreed that the cantonment rules should be applied to the whole of the municipal limits of Kanpur.[15]

But the Presidency capitals presented special problems. A great city like Calcutta could hardly be treated as an appendage of the military cantonment of Barrackpore. It was also a sea-port, and sailors as well as soldiers seemed to be at risk. In 1864 the Chairman of the Justices asked Fabre-Tonnerre, Calcutta's health officer, for his opinion. As might have been expected, the result was a memorandum to the effect that control was imperative : 'syphilitic disease' was spreading, not only among sailors but among all classes. The health officer seemed more troubled by moral than by medical anxieties :

Nowhere are the lower classes of Christians and Natives more debased, dissolute and unclean than in the metropolis of India. Everything about them bears the stamp of a total absence of every moral, religious and social feeling. Hence the great number of prostitutes, who not only swarm in the bye-lanes and back-slums of Calcutta, but who infest our principal thoroughfares, polluting the atmosphere of our neighbourhood, and who, by their indecent conduct, scandalize the morals of the population in the midst of which they are permitted to live.

There were so many in Chitpore Road, which he described as 'the great thoroughfare of the Native town', that he thought that 'no respectable Native' would 'allow his wife or daughter to pass through a street showing such degradation and debauchery'. He concluded : 'The moment for action has arrived.'[16]

Fabre-Tonnerre submitted another memorandum in 1867. There were upwards of thirty thousand prostitutes in Calcutta. Sobha Bazar and Dharmahatta Street were 'infested' with them ; Chitpore Road was 'swarming' with them, and so were Cornwallis and College Streets, 'the centres of educational establishments for the young Hindoo population'. He hoped that Calcutta would 'soon possess one of those institutions which are the pride of philanthropy, "a Lock Hospital".' He was perfectly serious. He also submitted a draft Act for the prevention of contagious diseases, and he added with unseemly eagerness : 'I beg to state that in addition to my usual duties, I am willing to undertake the organization of the new office, to superintend the registration of the prostitutes, as well as to take an active part in the sanitary inspection of the public women.'[17]

The Lieutenant-Governor agreed that Bengal's ports needed a Contagious Diseases Act on the lines of recent English legislation, which Fabre-Tonnerre's draft closely followed. The main difference was that in his draft it was compulsory for prostitutes to register, while in England action could only be taken after a police officer had laid information against a woman. The Lieutenant-Governor thought that Fabre-Tonnerre's alternative was better for Calcutta because there were so many prostitutes there.[18] This point was taken further in the Governor-General's Legislative Council. H.S. Maine, as Law Member, introduced a Bill based on Fabre-Tonnerre's draft. In India, he said, there might be 'grievous oppression' if it were left to police officers to take action. In other words, police officers could not be trusted. Even so, 'in certain cases', he conceded, there might be 'some degree of oppression'. But a law of this sort must be 'thorough'.[19] John Strachey, formerly Chief Commissioner of Oudh, claimed that the extension of the cantonment rules to Lucknow city had not resulted in any oppression there.[20]

The Bill was duly passed into law as Act XIV of 1868, known as the Indian Contagious Diseases Act. Its provisions could be introduced in places specified by a local government with the sanction of the Governor-General in Council. These provisions included the compulsory registration of brothels and prostitutes, periodical medical examinations and compulsory treatment of prostitutes found to be infected. Also, prostitutes could be forbidden to live in specified areas.

Such policies could hardly have been inaugurated without a certain unease. In 1870 the *Friend of India* provided unctuous reassurance. Those in charge of lock hospitals were 'medical men, enthusiastic, sternly and gravely enthusiastic, in their profession'. At the Calcutta lock hospital there could not be seen 'anything to call forth an improper thought, or anything to degrade the women subject to the Act. There is cleanliness, fresh air, proper treatment, sometimes character raised, and very frequently life saved.'[21]

In Bombay, however, there was vigorous opposition. The Government of India ruled that half the cost should be met from municipal and half from Government funds. The Bench of Justices at first objected but eventually sanctioned Rs 40,000 for 1870, and the

Bombay Government approved a grant of the same amount. But in 1871 the Bench of Justices reduced this to Rs 30,000 and the Bombay Government similarly reduced their grant to the same amount. The Justices later rescinded their decision and refused to pay anything, leaving the Government to pay the full sum. This was at a time of bitter conflict between the Bench of Justices and the Municipal Commissioner, Arthur Crawford, who at a time of economic difficulty persisted in collecting taxes harshly to pay for lavish improvement schemes. In 1872 the Bench of Justices, part-British and part-Indian, unanimously refused to contribute any longer to the expenses of the Contagious Diseases Act. Dr Dallas, who moved that they refuse to pay, argued that as the Act was intended to protect seamen the cost should fall on imperial and not on local revenues.[22] The Justices also declined responsibility for the lease of a building for the lock hospital which had been executed by Crawford without their knowledge. The Government thereupon terminated the working of the Contagious Diseases Act in Bombay.[23]

Public opinion in England was now preoccupied with the working of the English CD Acts. A Royal Commission pondered the matter in 1871, and in the course of their deliberations heard some evidence about the system in India. What was said provoked a protest from the Baptist Missionary Society. They particularly objected to statements by Dr Ross, Surgeon of the 92nd Highlanders, to the effect that an establishment of camp followers, including prostitutes, would be 'told off' for a regiment when it arrived in India, that these prostitutes were housed in the bazars, looked after by 'the matron appointed for the purpose', and 'superintended and examined by the surgeon of the regiment'.[24] They concluded that 'no considerations of health, economy or expediency can justify or excuse legalized prostitution', and urged that 'the present obnoxious system of limitation of marriage in the Army should be repealed'. They must have realized that they could not expect much support for reform in India while the CD Acts were in force in England. But they pointed out that in India, unlike England, there was no attempt to persuade prostitutes to change their occupation.[25]

Some members of Gladstone's Cabinet were naturally perturbed by the prospect of Nonconformist pressure. Cardwell, at the War Office, proposed to send them to the India Office, and wrote a note to Argyll, the Secretary of State for India, to warn him.[26] Argyll, also a true politician, replied the following day that he had already seen the deputation and informed them that their proposal for a change in the marriage regulations was a matter for the War Office. Undeterred, Cardwell tried to divert them to the India Office again. But the Rev. E.B. Underhill, Secretary of the Baptist Missionary Society, would not be fobbed off. Cardwell thereupon expressed the unrealistic hope that the short-service system had 'materially diminished the evils of celibacy', and added that it would be very expensive to send 'a large number of women' to India.[27]

Argyll did in fact send the Baptist memorial to India, and there the bureaucracy reacted in a characteristic manner. The Commander-in-Chief referred the memorial to five selected regiments, including the 92nd Highlanders. In due course, Major-General Johnson, the Quartermaster-General, drew up a cautious reply, based upon the comments he had received from these regiments. Prostitutes were never 'told off' for a regiment. They did indeed live in the bazars, but in this they were 'like other people who ply a trade'. They were subject to Contagious Diseases legislation, and therefore were periodically examined by the medical officer in charge of the lock hospital. Also, 'for the purposes of discipline', they were placed under the supervision of a matron paid by the Government. He concluded in reassuring language : 'Unceasing and not unsuccessful efforts are made to control prostitution and to mitigate, so far as may be, its attendant evils : but neither the Government, nor its officers, either directly or indirectly, encourage it. It is not the practice of prostitution that is "legalized", but the attempts to avert its consequent and accompanying disease.'[28] There the matter lapsed, but only for a time.

Cardwell claimed that the evils of celibacy would be mitigated when soldiers enlisted for a shorter period. Until 1847 they had enlisted for life, or until discharge on medical grounds, and in that year the period of enlistment had been reduced to 21 years in the infantry and 24 in other corps, with an initial engagement for 10 and 12 years respectively. In 1870 Cardwell reduced the initial period of enlistment to 6 years with the colours and 6 in the reserve. Although re-engagement for a total of 21 years with the colours was still allowed, most men left after their initial period of service. The short-service system was much criticized for filling the army with inexperienced young men, and in 1881 the initial period with the colours was increased to 7 years, with 5 in the reserve.[29] But the VD statistics, which had fallen for several years after the introduction of the cantonment rules, rose again steadily in the 1870s, and the short-service system was frequently blamed. It involved an increase in the arrival of new men every year, an increase in the youthfulness of the troops generally, and an increase in the proportion of unmarried men. These factors were seen as favouring the spread of VD.

Meanwhile, the military authorities redoubled their efforts to make the cantonment rules more effective. The Quartermaster-General sent a series of circular memoranda on the subject to General Officers Commanding Divisions and Districts. In 1870, for example, 'Officers commanding troops on the line of march are directed to ensure the effective inspection of prostitutes attached to their regimental bazars'.[30] In 1876, the spread of VD revived the old suspicion that soldiers were not confining themselves to women who had been registered and inspected. Commanding officers were told to take care of three matters. First, there should be enough women : 'In most cases the number of women on the register is not in proportion to the number of men who visit them.' Secondly, the environment should be suitable : one must consider 'the improvement of the conditions under which the women ply their trade, such as greater privacy, facilities for ablution, etc., etc.' Thirdly, prostitutes should not be alienated by the system : one must ensure 'the kind treatment of the women, and every reasonable inducement being held out to them to attend the lock hospital when suffering from disease'.[31]

But no spectacular improvements followed. The VD statistics continued their steady ascent. Then two vigorous proconsuls took a fresh look at the situation, and came to different conclusions. As Governor of Bombay, Sir Richard Temple, an experienced official, tried to force the Bombay municipality to pay half the cost of the CD Act. At the same time, Lord Ripon, a devout Roman Catholic who became Governor-General with no previous experience of India, began to ask whether the CD Act could not be repealed. He could claim some previous knowledge of the subject : as Secretary for War he had helped to frame the first CD Act in England, and he was not opposed to such legislation on principle.[32] But he was soon confronted by problems both in Bombay and in Bengal.

In Bombay, Temple was displaying energy rather than subtlety. First he tried to flatter the municipality into compliance. Calcutta and Madras, he said, were operating the CD Act : 'Considering that in no other respect is Bombay surpassed by any city in India, His Excellency in Council cannot believe that in this important matter it will remain behind the other two presidency towns.'[33]

This encouragement was despatched to the Bombay municipality in January 1880. Two months later Commander Charles Woodruffe, of HMS *Beacon*, was pressing for a system of medical police in Bombay. When forty of his sailors went on shore leave, eight caught VD, and his surgeon thought that some of them would be 'permanently affected'. Rear-Admiral Gore Jones, Naval Commander-in-Chief, supported this plea: 'As Bombay is the headquarters of Her Majesty's ships stationed in the East Indies, the remedying of this evil is a matter of most vital importance in maintaining the ships and crews under the Admiral's command in a state efficient for service.'[34] The Bombay Government promptly resolved to reinstitute the CD Act in April. With a curious ignorance of local opinion they recorded their confidence that the municipality would contribute.[35]

Opposition was quickly organized. A memorial was signed by such personages as the Bishop of Bombay, the senior chaplain of the Church of Scotland and Vishvanath Narayan Mandlik, Chairman of the Municipal Corporation. They had followed the controversy surrounding the English CD Acts. Thus they claimed that the efficacy of such a measure was doubtful, and cited Professor Huxley. They denounced it on moral grounds and cited the Rev. F.D. Maurice and John Stuart Mill. They had also made a fruitful study of the incautious statements of officials. In particular they drew attention to the 'painful avowal' of Bombay's health officer to the effect that the CD Act had even proved beneficial in an unexpected way: 'To the women themselves the Act was of the greatest benefit, not only physically but professionally. The registration ticket was equivalent to a clean bill of health and a certificate of competency.' They also elaborated upon an argument which had in the past been amply justified by experience: such policies exposed respectable women to oppression.[36]

The Bombay Government thereupon told the Police Commissioner 'to be careful not to interfere with or attempt to register women in the position of mistresses of wealthy persons or kept women'.[37] But to their astonishment and indignation the municipality held firm, and merely offered to contribute Rs 15,000 when finances permitted, to be used for 'the mitigation of diseases'. In October the Government returned to the attack: the municipality's finances seemed adequate, and so Rs 15,000 would be deducted from the grant of Rs 90,000 which the Government made for Bombay's police.[38]

Mandlik appealed to Ripon. The CD Act had been suspended in 1872 because it had failed, he asserted. In fact, it had been suspended for financial reasons. On surer ground, he then proceeded to explain that the Corporation thought it 'not to be adapted to the mixed population of Bombay'.[39] But the Governor-General in Council declined to interfere, as the future of the Contagious Diseases Act itself was under consideration.[40]

From the first Ripon had misgivings. The arrangements in India seemed harsher than those in England. There was no fixed limit to the time a woman could be detained in hospital, and there was no way for her to appeal against her detention. Also, in Calcutta the Chief Presidency Magistrate had detected vagueness in the wording of the Act and 'expressed his intention to issue process for illegal confinement in any case in which a prostitute complains of arrest'.[41] This gave Ripon the opportunity for a reconsideration of the policy behind the Act. A committee was appointed, consisting of B.W. Colvin, a civil servant, as Chairman, and four medical officers as members. They heard evidence on a variety of matters.

Lambert, the Deputy Commissioner of Police, testified that 'the Act is very unpopular with all classes of Natives. They have no sympathy with it, because they consider it was introduced to benefit Europeans.'[42] Surgeon-General Cunningham asserted that the results of the Act were 'altogether insufficient to justify the expenditure of money and the interference with the people in their most intimate social relations'. It cost five thousand rupees a month. Yet the evil effects of vp were 'a mere nothing' compared with the ravages of fever, dysentery and other Indian Diseases : the money ought to be spent on curing them. Also, it was impossible to work the Act effectively without extending it to include the suburban area of Howrah. But this would double the number of prostitutes under supervision to a total of eighteen thousand – a much smaller number than Fabre-Tonnerre had envisaged, but much too large to cope with.[43] The Colvin Committee also looked at the figures. The average annual incidence of vp among the European troops in the garrison of Fort William had fallen from 328·2 per 1,000 in the decade before the Act to 192·7 per 1,000 in the decade after it. They concluded that the Act had had 'a measure of success'. But did this justify it ? Three of them thought that it did, two that it did not.[44]

Meanwhile the Bengal Government abandoned the attempt to work the Act throughout Calcutta and decided to limit it to prostitutes frequented by Europeans.[45] They also raised the question of fairness. Should the cost be met from the general revenues of Bengal, or could not the prostitutes be taxed to pay for the Act? Ripon and his Council quickly thought of 'the objections which could fairly be taken to Government raising a revenue from prostitution'. By now they had decided that the Act ought to be repealed, although the Commander-in-Chief and Whitley Stokes, another member of Council, disagreed. When they told the Secretary of State, they repeated some of the arguments put to the Colvin Committee: the Act was unpopular, it involved an interference in intimate social relations, it was expensive, and the money could be better spent on improving the drains and water supplies.[46]

But Hartington, the Liberal Secretary of State, replied that it would be 'at least premature' to repeal the CD Act. Yet another select committee of the House of Commons had been considering the operation of the system in England, and concluded that it should continue. Indeed, they thought that it would be beneficial to extend it, but public opinion made that impracticable. Also, some people thought that the Act had been reasonably successful in India. In these circumstances, he could not allow it to be repealed. But it could be suspended as an experiment.[47]

The Act was promptly suspended in Calcutta. Meanwhile, the position in Bombay was arousing some perturbation. The Government of India eventually pronounced against the Bombay Government's deduction of fifteen thousand rupees from the police grant to pay for the working of the CD Act. H.S. Maine, who had steered the Bill through the Governor-General's legislative council, was now a member of the Secretary of State's Council. His sympathies were with the Bombay Government. He dismissed the agitation against the Act as the work of 'a few English clergymen and a small number of native gentlemen who join English ideas to Indian dislike of taxation'. He added, 'Bombay is infamous for the virulent forms of these diseases which it produces and which it diffuses through the world through the crews of the ships entering the Port.'[48] But Hartington was unimpressed. He told the Bombay Government that the Government of India had rightly disapproved of its deduction of fifteen thousand rupees as 'impolitic' and 'unfair', and he ordered it to refund it. The Bombay Government at once protested. If the Government of India disapproved so strongly, why had it declined to interfere in 1881, and so allowed the Bombay Government to do it again?[49] Thus challenged, the Government of India conceded that it was 'perhaps to be regretted' that it had not expressed 'a more decided opinion' in 1881. But this, it explained, 'left us free to take such future action as we might think fit'.[50]

The Bombay Government seemed to have the better of the argument. Kimberley, who had succeeded Hartington as Secretary of State, was confronted with an office minute in favour of Bombay. The order to refund the money was 'naturally felt to be very galling and humiliating'. The Government of India had said nothing for two years, and 'now at length they come down upon the Local Govt. with this terribly severe decree of reimbursement'. Its letter was 'an extremely weak one, and rather supports than otherwise the position of the Govt. of Bombay'.[51] Kimberley noted awkwardly, 'I am disposed to disagree from this minute and to support the previous decision that the Govt. of Bombay should refund.'[52]

He turned for support to the Statistics and Commerce Committee, but they declined to help him out: 'As the Govt. of Bombay acted to the best of their judgement and in perfect good faith in the allotment of these funds, it is expedient that the order previously given for the refund of the amount deducted from the Police Grant should be withdrawn.'[53] They submitted a draft despatch to that effect, which he duly signed. Although the Bombay Government's proceedings were 'open to objection', it had acted in accordance with its view of the public interest, and should not be made to refund the amounts it had deducted, but it must not deduct any more.[54]

When he heard of the suspension of the CD Act in Calcutta, Sir James Fergusson, Temple's successor, wrote privately to Kimberley of its advantages in Bombay. Only recently the Commander of HMS *Dragon* had given him an encouraging report. His men had been for a long time without shore leave. When they arrived he granted it freely, and they drew out as much as six hundred pounds from the savings bank to spend in Bombay. Even so, only two mild cases of gonorrhoea had resulted! Surely this was evidence of the beneficial nature of the CD Act?[55] Kimberley protested that he himself had always believed in such legislation, 'but how long it may be possible to maintain the acts anywhere against the powerful Parliamentary pressure for their abolition, I cannot say'.[56] For the time being, that pressure was directed against the English CD Acts.

The Government of India soon advised the Bombay and Madras Governments to suspend the CD Act. Bombay did so, with some protesting. But delaying tactics were attempted in Madras. Surgeon-General Cornish admitted that the Act was 'one of our legislative failures. It was a weak-kneed production from the start.' It only applied to seven or eight hundred women, of whom about 50 on average were detained in the lock hospital : such as it was, this was to achieve something. Surely the Commander-in-Chief's opinion should be ascertained ?[57] The Madras Government appointed a Committee, which recommended that instead of suspending the Act it should be extended, 'not *upwards*, among classes whose privacy may be unduly invaded, but *downwards*, in order to reach the unfortunate casuals infesting the neighbourhood of the barracks and plying their trade in an open and shameless manner'. Most of the VD caught by soldiers was caught from 'non-registered women, especially those who haunt the vicinity of barracks after dark and waylay the soldier going to and from his quarters in the fort'.[58] Here was the familiar picture of the soldier threatened by unauthorized women 'haunting' the barracks and 'infesting' the neighbourhood after dark.

Sir Frederick Roberts, the Commander-in-Chief, promptly responded to the Surgeon-General's call. He expressed his agreement with the Madras Committee and added : 'I find it impossible to persuade myself that the same penalties lie in wait for the descendents of a man who has suffered from dysentery or fever, as those which are so often bequeathed by constitutional syphilis.'[59] But the Government of India quickly identified the weak point in the Madras argument. There were only five or six hundred soldiers in the garrison at Fort St George : 'It cannot be argued that it is justifiable or necessary to exercise surveillance over 700 or 800 women of the town merely for the protection of these few European soldiers.'[60]

Soon Kimberley was confronted by another office minute. Surely the Bombay and Madras Governments should be allowed to decide for themselves ? This was also the view of the Statistics and Commerce Committee.[61] But Kimberley had the last word. He noted simply : 'I think it is better we should not send out any despatch.'[62]

Ripon now turned to the cantonment rules. The Surgeon-General, Bengal, obligingly denounced them. With a VD rate of 259.1 per 1,000 British troops in 1881 he pronounced the system a failure. It was 'impracticable' to rely on 'the registration and the segregation of a few women called prostitutes, out of a multitude of unchaste women'. Also, there was the 'hopelessness' of detecting VD in women. Instead he suggested that the system be discontinued at a few stations so that the figures there could be compared with those at stations where the system was in full force.[63] The Government of India accepted this suggestion with alacrity. Ten lock hospitals were closed in Bengal, three in Bombay and two in Madras, and the Government of India settled down to await results.

When the results arrived there was a new Governor-General, Lord Dufferin, who had none of Ripon's moral objections to such policies. There was also a new Surgeon-General, who readily produced fresh statistics. He compared the average annual VD admissions per thousand troops in the decade preceding the closure of the lock hospitals with those for 1885 and 1886. For the ten stations in Bengal where the hospitals had been closed the figures were:

1875–84	*1885*	*1886*
210·3	351	450·4

For twenty other stations in Bengal where the hospitals remained open the figures were:

1875–84	*1885*	*1886*
270·13	329·06	364·31

In short, although VD was increasing in places with lock hospitals, it was increasing much more quickly in places without them.[64]

The figures for Bombay pointed in the same direction. The lock hospitals were closed at three stations, although at one of these, Ahmadabad, the increase in VD in 1885 so alarmed the authorities that the hospital was opened again in 1886. With the exception of Ahmadabad in 1886, the figures were:

1875–84	*1885*	*1886*
234·4	436·2	631·6

For the seven stations in Bombay where the hospitals remained open the figures were:

1875–84	*1885*	*1886*
203·8	231·3	282·9

In Madras the results were less conclusive. The lock hospitals were closed at two stations – Bellari and Cannanore. The statistical results at Cannanore were of little significance, although the hospital there was closed for two years. However, it seemed that there were some local difficulties at Bellari. The hospital was closed on 1 April 1885, but in February 1886 the Station Commander asked for permission to reopen it. He reported that a member of the local municipal council had 'begged' him to do so because of the increase in vp, because prostitutes were 'flocking' into Bellari from neighbouring villages, because of the 'shameful' way in which they solicited custom and because 'very soon after dark prostitutes frequent every available place, even the compound of the Masonic Hall'.[65] Such shocking behaviour had to be checked, and the lock hospital was reopened shortly afterwards. Although it was official policy that the rules should not be so operated as to drive prostitutes away, here the system was clearly valued as keeping their numbers down, and as a means of control.

The statistical evidence was accepted by the Governor-General in Council as sufficient to justify the reopening of the lock hospitals that had been closed.[66] But the increase in venereal disease seemed inexorable, with or without lock hospitals and the rules associated with them.

The military authorities continued to submit familiar explanations, which they reinforced with fresh examples. Captain Chatterton, secretary to the Cantonment Committee, Rurki, suggested in 1878 that the reason why vp affected British infantrymen more than the Royal Engineers or students of the Engineering College was that 'the men of small means prefer the cheap or unregistered women – coolies and grass and milk sellers – to be met with on the canal banks, to the more expensive bazar residents'.[67] The authorities at Lucknow also suspected unregistered women : one in particular who was found to be 'resident in a rum-barrel' was considered a 'source of much mischief'.[68] Dr Scott Reid, surgeon in charge of the lock hospital at Agra, thought that cheapness was not the only reason why a soldier might go with an unregistered woman : 'There is a greater amount of privacy and, if I may be allowed to use the term, "romance", in meeting a woman whom he does not look upon in the light of a regular prostitute than in going to the bazar with deliberate intent and consorting with women who he knows are visited by numbers of his comrades.'[69] But it was more usual to regard the soldier as similar to an unreflecting animal, although this did present problems. Colonel Emerson, Cantonment Magistrate at Dinapur, therefore thought it 'a most remarkable circumstance' that there was so little vp among Indian troops. Although they were mostly married, they did not have their wives with them: 'I presume that a native soldier has as great a desire for gratifying himself as a European.' How could it be that 'he would seem to escape unscathed, while his white-skinned comrade gets diseased' ? It was 'indeed wonderful'. That married soldiers might remain faithful to their wives did not occur to him. Instead, he put forward a cultural explanation : 'Can it be that the native does use water and that he washes himself clean while the European remains unwashed ?'[70] Meanwhile, the authorities at Lucknow were finding fresh evidence of the uncontrollable urges of the British rank and file : a soldier patient was detected in sexual intercourse in a hospital ward ; another soldier 'effected such intercourse in the dining hall of his barrack'.[71]

Impelled by such notions, the military authorities strove manfully to make the lock hospital system as comprehensive as possible. In 1883 the Quartermaster-General issued another circular memorandum to General Officers Commanding Divisions and Districts. When cantonment funds permitted, reliable matrons should be appointed to supervise 'the registered women'. These matrons should ensure that 'the women under their charge consort with none but Europeans'. They should inspect the women daily, between the periodical inspections made by the medical officer. They should ensure that the women only entertained men in their own houses, which should be numbered : it was known that men were reluctant to point out a woman who had infected them, but they would probably be more willing to mention the number of her house.[72] In the following year the Quartermaster-General turned his attention to the provision of suitable quarters for registered women, and quoted with approval from a report on lock hospitals in the North-Western Provinces and Oudh. Quarters should not be 'too pretentious, prostitutes delighting in dark little dens'. There were merits in simplicity : 'quite inexpensive places of mud-built walls and tiled roofs, of village character, best suit the occasion.' The advantage of having special quarters was that 'the women can be well-managed and easily found for examination, and that the soldiers know where to go as soon as they arrive at the station'. Also, it was 'customary for certain women to attach themselves to a regiment, moving with it as it marches – a desirable arrangement from a lock hospital point of view – and it is very suitable for these women to find a recognized resting place on arrival at a station with the regiment'.[73]

Systematization could hardly have gone further. Stated in such terms, the arrangements seemed wholesome and almost respectable. But in the quest for efficiency the military authorities did go further. On 17 June 1886 Major-General E.F. Chapman, the Quartermaster-

General, issued yet another circular memorandum, which he was bitterly to regret. In it he explained that the Commander-in-Chief was anxious to do everything possible to check the spread of VD. In particular, he wanted Indian practitioners to specialize in methods of treating it, and he hoped that sufferers would be inspected and treated wherever the need arose, not merely in lock hospitals. Then the Quartermaster-General went into enthusiastic but indiscreet detail. In the regimental bazars, he went on, it was 'necessary to have a sufficient number of women, to take care that they are sufficiently attractive, to provide them with proper houses, and above all to insist upon means of ablution being always available'. If 'young soldiers' were 'carefully advised' about such matters they might be 'expected to avoid the risks involved in association with women who are not recognized by the regimental authorities'.[74]

Yet in 1886, the same year in which Chapman issued this circular, the campaign against the English CD legislation had come to a climax with its repeal. The reformers were now free to campaign on other fronts, and they soon turned to India.

Characteristically, the military authorities in India continued on their way without regard for the outside world. In January 1887, Dr William Collis, Deputy Surgeon-General, Peshawar District, reported that he and his colleagues had done their best to comply with the Quartermaster-General's circular memorandum of June 1886: 'efforts have been made and with some success to provide a more attractive lot of women'. But this made the system of control all the more important, for if 'an attractive woman and a favourite' caught VD and left the regimental bazar, the men would follow her all the same.[75] Two months later, Sir Frederick Roberts, the Commander-in-Chief, wrote privately to Lord Dufferin from Rawalpindi that there were 101 VD cases out of 177 British troops in hospital, and this was not unusual. The reopening of the Lock Hospital, which had been experimentally closed, should do 'much good'. But more should be done. Local governments should be persuaded to treat VD as they did cholera or smallpox, 'or any other loathsome disease'. One had to be resolute: 'the subject is an unsavoury one, but we cannot well shirk it'.[76]

But to their astonishment and indignation the military authorities found that their own activities came to be regarded in England as unsavoury, once the reformers had set to work. The campaign began in London in May 1887, with a meeting at Exeter Hall under the auspices of the 'Gospel Purity Association', which had been active in the agitation against the state regulation of prostitution in England. The chairman of the meeting was George Gillett, a Quaker who had worked energetically with Alfred Dyer, another Quaker, in uncovering the traffic in women from England to Belgium.

Dyer, a partner in the religious publishers Dyer Brothers, was a seasoned publicist. He was the author of such works as the twopenny pamphlet *Facts for Men*, which boasted a print run of fifty thousand copies in 1884, and in which he warned against the evil effects of all sexual activity outside marriage, but also advocated early marriage and criticized parents who opposed it for materialistic reasons. His weekly journal, the *Sentinel*, also criticized drinking, smoking, vivisection, armaments and imperialism. He turned with zest towards India. Others present at the Exeter Hall meeting were the Rev. Hugh Price Hughes, the militant Methodist preacher, and James Stuart, Fellow of Trinity College, Cambridge, a loyal supporter of Josephine Butler in the campaign against the English CD Acts and a specialist in the asking of awkward questions in the House of Commons.

Hugh Price Hughes took his cue from an article by a 'Public Servant' which had appeared in the *Pall Mall Gazette* the previous day. The author had asked 'Is Empire Consistent with Morality?' and answered 'No!' England sent out Englishmen to the East but could not afford to pay them enough to marry on. He challenged Hugh Price Hughes and his colleagues to tackle such problems : 'At every turn they will find the necessity, the universality, and the eternity of sexual vice assumed as the basis of action and legislation.'[77] Hugh Price Hughes had his answer ready. The old empire-builders were heathen at heart. But it would be different with 'the new democracy'. As evidence of the immorality of Indian administration he produced a prostitute's official ticket.[78] Other speakers also criticized the Government of India. The meeting was well reported in the Nonconformist press, but there was now a Conservative Government at Westminster, and the campaigners were carefully ignored.

Then the Bishop of Lichfield asked in the House of Lords about the existence of official regulations for the provision of prostitutes in regimental bazars in India. This prompted Cross, the Secretary of State, to send enquiring telegrams, despatches and private letters to the Governor-General. 'With a democratic Parliament', he confided to Dufferin, 'these sensational questions are very disagreeable.'[79] The matter was duly referred to the Quartermaster-General. Chapman promptly quoted his predecessor's reply to the Baptist memorial in

57

1873, to the effect that it was not the practice of prostitution that was legalized, but the attempts to avert the consequent disease. The Bishop of Lichfield was surely mistaken, he added suavely: 'the military authorities anxiously strive to mitigate the evils of prostitution', and 'no act of theirs' could 'justly be interpreted as encouraging vice'.[80]

Trying to discern the signs of the times, the British Indian Association, a society of substantial Bengali landholders, submitted a protest against the possible reintroduction of the CD Act into Calcutta. Their Secretary, Babu Peary Mohan Mookerjee, asserted that the Act was 'wholly repugnant to the feelings of the entire native community' and facilitated police oppression.[81] The Bombay Government, on the other hand, argued that such measures were entirely proper according to Indian ideas: 'Prostitution is a profession recognised in the Hindu law books, and the regulation of courtezans in the public interest offends no native susceptibility, although in their general eagerness to find fault with the measures of Government a certain class have shown themselves ready to borrow a cry on this subject, as they would on any other, from European agitators.'[82]

In fact the reformers had adroitly chosen a different field for their campaign. They were not concerned with Indian ideas, whatever they might be. The Quartermaster-General had asserted, with the approval of the Government of India, that prostitution was neither legalized nor encouraged. Alfred Dyer now went to India to see for himself. What he saw he indignantly described in successive issues of the *Sentinel*. He also quoted damaging passages from official documents.

At Lucknow in December 1887 he found the 4th Rifle Brigade in camp; adjoining their encampment were thirteen tents for the registered prostitutes who had accompanied them from Chakrata. He went on to quote from the annual report on lock hospitals in the North-Western Provinces and Oudh for 1886: 'It is proposed to endeavour to induce a greater number of prostitutes to reside in cantonments by making their residence there more attractive.' Help would be provided from cantonment funds to enable them to buy furniture so as to make their houses more convenient for themselves and their visitors. He also quoted a request from the medical officer at Faizabad for the prostitutes there to be replaced by 'others who are younger and better looking'.[83]

He went to Bareli, where he described the camp of the 2nd Battalion, the East Kent Regiment: 'While the Temperance tent is in a comparatively obscure corner, the tents of the Government harlots confront the troops from morning to night, separated from their own tents only by a public thoroughfare, without any buildings or trees intervening.' He went to Delhi : there 'the principal quarters of the women licensed to sin are in Esplanade Row, a leading thoroughfare facing the fort and barracks, and within eighty paces of the entrance to the Baptist Chapel'.[84] He went to Ambala : there he described one brothel where the women were 'licensed to sin with natives only', and others where the women were 'licensed for Europeans only'. He also reported that prostitutes had been injured by soldiers, and argued that the system encouraged English soldiers to despise Indians.[85]

Week after week in Parliament James Stuart and his supporters asked questions based on Dyer's revelations, and Sir John Gorst, the Under-Secretary of State, could only reply that information was awaited. The bureaucracy had in fact been stirred into hectic activity, and there was much correspondence between the military authorities and the Government of India.

Meanwhile the Anglican bishops of India and Ceylon had passed some resolutions on the subject of 'Purity'. In particular, they declared it to be a 'fundamental principle' that 'the discouragement and repression of vice are of far higher importance than the diminution of suffering or of other evils resulting from vice, and that consequently in all efforts to mitigate the physical effects of impurity no sanitary or material gain can justify measures which in their operation afford facilities or encouragement for vicious indulgence'.[86] Like their predecessors in the 1830s, they disapproved of attempts to make sinning safe. But it was becoming clear that the Government would have to make some concessions to this increasing pressure.

Dufferin wrote privately to Cross that he and his colleagues were prepared to suspend the CD Act in Bombay and Madras, as it had already been suspended in Calcutta, but he added hopefully that they were very anxious to retain the cantonment rules. To demonstrate that this was a respectable hope he even drew attention to the presence on his Council of Sir Charles Aitchison, an industrious and upright administrator : 'We are all unanimous on this point, and the fact that Aitchison, who is a very religious man, a low churchman and a Scotchman, takes this view, and takes it very strenuously, ought to have some weight with those who would be willing, apparently, if they had their way, to allow disease and death to be propagated wholesale throughout the British Army.'[87] Cross agreed, but in his official despatch, which was published, he pointed out that Dyer had indicated in the *Sentinel* that the regimental bazar system was still in force. Such practices should be stopped.[88]

When it came, the Quartermaster-General's reply to Dyer's allegations was unconvincing. *Lal bazars* had been in force since the Company's days, but had only been brought under supervision in the 1860s. The system was authorized 'with the idea of controlling the evils which are complained of by the writer in the *Sentinel*'. In Dyer's use of the report on lock hospitals 'the facts' had been 'greatly contorted'. How was not specified. But the Commander-in-Chief had now prohibited the residence of prostitutes in regimental bazars, and they were also forbidden to accompany troops on the march.[89] In forwarding this document to the Secretary of State, the Governor-General in Council declared loftily that they did not 'propose to reply in detail' to Dyer's allegations. His statements were 'not all in accordance with facts'. However, they admitted that 'the blots upon the present system' were 'so serious' as to require 'earnest consideration'. The regulations would be revised. Also, 'much has been done of late years to raise the tone of the British soldier'. There was more 'temperance and sobriety'. However, 'the young soldier' would always be subjected to special temptations in India, 'in the midst of a population, certain classes of which are unaccustomed to regard prostitution as other than an ordinary condition of life'. In other words, there was a need for special measures in India, if not in England.[90]

Meanwhile, Dyer, in an impassioned article entitled 'The Infidel Government of India', had published Chapman's circular memorandum of June 1886, advocating the supply of a sufficient number of attractive women, together with a document emanating from the officer commanding the 2nd Cheshire Regiment, headed 'Requisition for extra attractive women for Regimental Bazar (Soldiers)'. This was dated 9 July 1886. It was addressed to the Cantonment Magistrate, Ambala, who was informed that the regimental strength was four hundred, that they had six women and needed six more. The message concluded with the words, 'Please send young and attractive women', and cited the Quartermaster-General's circular memorandum of June 1886 in support of this simple request.[91]

The uproar that followed these disclosures was enough to enable the reformers to carry a resolution through the House of Commons in June 1888 to the effect that 'any mere suspension of measures for the compulsory examination of women, and for licensing and regulating prostitution in India, is insufficient, and the legislation which enjoins, authorises or permits such measures ought to be repealed'.[92] Cross duly transmitted this to India with an enigmatic comment: 'It will, of course, receive at your hands that careful consideration which a Resolution of the House of Commons deserves. . . .'[93] The Government of India now took prompt and public action to do what had already been agreed. In July Aitchison introduced a Bill into the legislative council to repeal the Contagious Diseases Act. In doing so he made a short speech in which he claimed that this was what the Government of India had wanted to do in 1882 but had been prevented from doing because a select committee of the House of Commons had at that time recommended that the system should be continued.[94] Upright Scots Presbyterian as he was, Aitchison was somewhat disingenuous here, for the Government's attitude to such matters had changed since Ripon's time.

The cantonment rules were now the vital issue, and Dyer's revelations had put the Government in a weak position. Cross had acted quickly after the publication of Dyer's article. More than a fortnight before the House of Commons resolution he had sent a despatch to India in which he enjoined the Government to revise the rules so as to avoid anything like the legalization of prostitution, and expressed his 'deep regret' that Chapman's circular memorandum had been issued. He added that he could not reconcile it with Chapman's reply to the Bishop of Lichfield's allegations.[95] To send this despatch he had overridden the majority of his Council: he went to the Cabinet for support in doing so.[96]

Dufferin wrote privately to Cross to express his mortification: 'Our military friends have undoubtedly brought down the catastrophe upon their own heads by their silly and wanton misrepresentations.' The Government's credit had been damaged, 'we were asked a question, and we told a falsehood in reply'. Was the Cantonments Act threatened? The difficulty was that official statements might not be believed in future: 'Any despatch or statement which we may hereafter send home in defence of any policy which may run counter to the prejudices of what I may call the "hysterical" interests, will be disbelieved and denounced as misleading and untrustworthy.' Even their statistics might be distrusted because they did not agree with 'the wishes of "the shrieking sisterhood"'. Dufferin tried hard to dissociate the civil Government from the military authorities: 'Of course none of us civilians knew anything about the exhortations issued to the Commanding Officers of various British Regiments to obtain pretty women for their men, or of the various other objectionable notifications which seem to have been sown broadcast over all our military stations.' It was 'certainly most unfortunate'.[97]

There was no alternative but to cancel the circulars and suspend the cantonment rules. Great care was devoted to drafting a new Cantonments Bill and new rules in suitably circumspect terms. There was to be no mention of prostitutes, or venereal disease, or lock hospitals. But there would be hospitals for the treatment of persons with infectious or contagious diseases. If a medical officer supposed that someone had such a disease, that person (sex unspecified) would be required to report to the hospital, and could be expelled from the cantonment for refusing to go to the hospital or for leaving it before being pronounced free from disease. Cross sent a reassuring telegram to Dufferin about this: 'If woman refuses to go to hospital, she is ejected from cantonments for refusal; or if she goes to hospital, medical officer cannot compel examination, but cannot leave until pronounced free from disease. She must either submit or stay in hospital for indefinite period. If she leaves hospital, she is ejected from cantonments for leaving.'[98] In other words, the new system might not be compulsory, but it was not exactly voluntary.

When the Bill was introduced in the legislative council, General Chesney stated that since the rules governing 'the supervision of a certain class of persons liable in a special degree to contagious disease' had been suspended, there had been 'an alarming increase of disease' among British and Indian soldiers. The new rules provided for the same precautions to be taken for this disease as for smallpox or measles; they were 'the least coercive that could be imposed, short of according special favour and protection to the propagation of the disease in question over all other contagious diseases'.[99]

With less circumlocution the Commander-in-Chief asserted that VD had increased in numbers and virulence among the troops since the abolition of the lock hospital rules in 1888. The rules to be promulgated under the new Act were therefore essential. There would be some interference with personal liberty: 'those who voluntarily adopt prostitution as their trade cannot reasonably complain if they are placed under greater restrictions and disabilities than persons engaged in reputable occupations'.[100] This hardly accorded with another argument dear to the military authorities – that prostitution was hereditary and therefore not immoral by Indian standards. But it revealed some understanding of one argument in the reformers' campaign – that such regulations infringed individual rights. Finally, Lord Lansdowne, who had succeeded Dufferin as Governor-General, claimed that the new arrangements would not infringe the two principles upon which the House of Commons had insisted – that there should be no compulsory examination of women and no licensing or regulation of prostitution.

'The C.D. Act is gone, and there is not the faintest chance of its being revived.' This was the optimistic view expressed in the *Indian Spectator*, a Bombay weekly edited by B.M. Malabari, a Parsi journalist with an enthusiasm for social reform. There would be no more of those 'shameless' demands for pretty girls. However, he would have preferred to see a more repressive policy as well: 'The women should be hauled up to the hospital or turned out of the station, if diseased; and the soldier, who injures his health in this way, ought to be fined by way of warning.'[101]

But Walter McLaren, an ardent campaigner on behalf of such causes in England, warned him that if women were forced into hospital the old system could return.[102] W.S. Caine, a Nonconformist who specialized in temperance agitation, told Malabari that he thought that in England at least the proper remedy lay in 'harrying' the women. With unpleasant enthusiasm he explained: 'When the authorities really drive the women hard – as hard as they can under the law – the trade becomes so unpopular that every woman who can get out of it does get out of it.'[103]

Malabari forwarded this malignant advice to the Commander-in-Chief, but also warned him that the reformers in England would be watching carefully to see if the Indian authorities really did work the hospitals on a voluntary basis: 'The element of *compulsion* will prove fatal to your plan, I am afraid.'[104] Roberts consulted Lansdowne before replying to Malabari. They agreed that he should be assured that there would be no more compulsion.[105]

But it was soon suggested that the new arrangements did not differ greatly from the old. In January 1890 the Social Purity Committee of the Wesleyan Conference protested to Cross that the new Cantonments Act was compatible with the old lock hospital system.[106] The Calcutta Missionary Conference similarly protested to the Government of India that the new rules could be so operated as to force women to agree to a medical examination under the threat of expulsion from the cantonment.[107] The Governor-General in Council merely commented that this was not compulsion : anyone supposed to be suffering from an infectious or contagious disease who objected to a medical examination 'would be at liberty to quit the cantonment and by so doing to escape the necessity of submitting to medical examination or treatment'.[108] But to ignore the force of the opposition was unwise.

In the *Sentinel* Dyer was quick to denounce the Cantonments Act of 1889 as 'an impudent defiance' of the resolution of the House of Commons.[109] In the *Banner of Asia* Maurice Gregory, an associate of Dyer's, denounced the new rules under a suitably provocative headline : 'Anarchy! The Governor-General of India in Council flatly disobeys the commands of the House of Commons.' Just as the campaigners against the English CD Acts had denounced the corruption of working-class girls by the decadent upper classes, he now contrived to appeal to his Nonconformist readers by arguing that 'respectable Native shop-keepers and residents' had to 'pay for the Government education (by example) of their sons in the doctrine of the necessity of vice, and the very possible debauchery of their daughters by English officers'. He went on to argue that it was 'principally for the *officers*' that the system was maintained in India : when 'a wicked officer' lusted after the daughter of a respectable Indian tradesman, he would persuade his friend the medical officer to have her summoned for an examination, after which she would be too disgraced to return to her family and would therefore be available.[110] This was fantasy, but the military authorities had so damaged their own credibility that such things could be said with impunity.

In fact, the new rules had indeed created alarm among Indian shopkeepers and others living in cantonments. Three public meetings were held in Kasauli cantonment and a memorial was drawn up in protest against the 'general and too indefinite' language of these rules. The signatories asked the Governor-General in Council to tighten the rules so as to 'restrict their operation to women of known immoral character'. Since the new rules merely specified 'infectious or contagious disease' they feared that people of 'the respectable class' might be forced into hospital where they would be 'huddled together with men or women of inferior creeds, castes and denominations'. Also, 'it would be repugnant to their feelings to be waited upon by men or women of the *chamar* or sweeper class, who alone hire themselves for service in hospitals'.[111] Similar protests were received from many other

64

cantonments. This was the sort of anxiety that English officials understood, and the Lieutenant-Governor of the Panjab commented that he thought such objections were 'well founded'.[112] In their turn the Governor-General in Council assured the Secretary of State that they would take care not to offend 'respectable persons'.[113]

There was also some adverse comment in the Indian press. The *Sanjivani*, a Bengali weekly, accused the Government of hypocrisy in employing Christian priests and building churches while secretly continuing the system of prostitution which had been officially abandoned.[114] Another Bengali weekly suggested that a more effective solution for the problem of VD in British regiments would be to employ Indian soldiers, who did not suffer from it.[115] But the Government of India was undeterred by Indian protests on such matters.

In London the new rules were also attacked by James Stansfeld and James Stuart, the two Liberal MPs who had led the parliamentary campaign against the English CD Acts. They wrote a joint letter to Cross in which they argued that the threat of expulsion from the cantonment could be used to persuade a woman to enter hospital, and that 'being once within its walls she may be kept prisoner there for an indefinite time and submitted to a personal examination under the same compulsion'.[116] Cross, however, replied that he preferred to trust the Government of India unless there were 'some solid ground' for suspecting it intended to evade his instructions.[117]

Fresh statistics were soon produced to strengthen the resolution of the military authorities. Surgeon-General Thomson, Principal Medical Officer to Her Majesty's Forces in India, produced corrected figures for Bengal to show that VD admissions among British troops in Bengal had increased from 281 per 1,000 in 1866, when the lock hospital system had begun, to 291 per 1,000 in 1884, when it was in full force, and to 491 per 1,000 in 1889, when it had been abandoned. To explain the increase in 1884 he blamed the short-service system. But in 1889, 'the disease unchecked was allowed to run riot among young and foolish soldiers, recklessly ready to expose themselves to it'. In 1884 'the young and foolish' had been 'partially saved' by the lock hospital system. In 1866, soldiers were 'older and more knowing and cautious, and more of them were married'. VD admissions among Indian troops were slight, but he thought them significant: VD admissions had fallen from 54.4 per 1,000 in 1866 to 34 per 1,000 in 1884, but rose to 42.1 per 1,000 in 1889. Surely this showed the efficacy of lock hospitals? Of course, the generally low rate of admissions among Indian troops was because they were older and married.[118] But the age factor was only significant for the period of the short-service system among British troops, and VD admissions were also much lower among Indian troops before that system had been introduced. The constant factor was the higher marriage rate, which entered into all such comparisons.

Maurice Gregory, in the *Sentinel*, described a visit to a camp of Indian soldiers in Poona cantonment – 'street after street of neat homes provided by the Indian Government for the Native soldiers. Each man lives with his wife in a bright little home of his own, with his children growing up around him.' He compared this with 'the hideous scenes of licentiousness' which he had observed among British soldiers camped at Lucknow. He even found an example in recent history : 'everyone knows how the German army of respectable fathers marched with a steady tramp on Paris in 1870, after the complete overthrow of the harlot-accompanied French army.'[119]

That more soldiers should be allowed to marry was also a point made by the *Indian Spectator*. On these issues there was a significant coincidence of views. On one such occasion the *Indian Spectator* mentioned with somewhat patronizing approval 'our vigilant little contemporary', the *Sentinel*.[120]

But in some Indian journals there was more scepticism about Dyer's campaigns. The *Almora Akhbar*, a Hindi weekly, criticized him in 1888 for a lack of realism : 'Not to provide women for European soldiers who are drunk and mad with lust would be like letting loose beasts of prey.'[121] Clearly, the stereotype of the uncontrollable British soldier could be deployed as an indirect criticism of foreign rule. So the *Hindustani*, an Urdu weekly of Lucknow, extended the argument a few years later : 'A European soldier who is pampered at the expense of the taxpayer and is elated with the pride of race, cannot be expected to exercise any restraint on his carnal desires.' If military brothels were abolished, Englishwomen should be imported for the soldiers. Otherwise respectable Indian ladies would be at risk.[122] And although Dyer and his colleagues did argue that soldiers should be allowed to marry, such arguments were either ignored or dismissed as impracticable.

Yet there was a cultural explanation for the scenes which shocked Nonconformist observers. The soldier had little to do after finishing his early morning drill. He was confined to barracks for most of the day. And because the authorities feared the power of the sun he was forbidden to expose himself to it during the hot season and was supposed to keep in the shade from noon until evening. Because the authorities feared that contact with Indian life had mysteriously demoralizing effects, the soldier was discouraged from 'wandering' in the 'native city'. The canteen and the *lal bazar* were his only means of recreation – hence the drunkenness and dissipation depicted by Dyer and Gregory. Sir Frederick Roberts, a Commander-in-Chief revered for his sympathy with the needs of the ordinary soldier, encouraged the formation of regimental institutes with reading rooms, and the provision of sporting facilities. A special room was sometimes provided where teetotallers could drink such beverages as tea and ginger beer. But for most soldiers, kept from contact with the life of the country, their situation must have been irritating and frustrating. This was implicitly recognized in the arrangements made by the military authorities. Dyer had noticed at Bareli that 'the Temperance tent' was much less prominent than 'the tents of the Government harlots'.

3

New Cantonments Acts and Rules

There was a deliberate vagueness in the wording of the new Cantonments Act and in the rules issued under its authority. Precautions could be taken against infectious and contagious disease in general, but venereal disease was not specifically mentioned. This vagueness had aroused alarm among 'respectable' Indians in cantonments, who protested that the authorities might operate the rules against them instead of concentrating upon prostitutes, but it had aroused suspicion among reformers, who protested that the authorities would so operate the rules as to concentrate upon prostitutes. After all, when Sir Frederick Roberts supported the new Cantonments Bill in the legislative council he had harped upon the danger of venereal disease among the troops. Would the military authorities use the threat of expulsion from cantonments to compel women to submit to periodical examinations? The Governor-General proclaimed his intention of respecting the wishes of the House of Commons. The Secretary of State proclaimed his confidence in the Governor-General and the Indian authorities.

That confidence was shared by many missionaries. The matter was raised at the decennial conference of Protestant missionaries in India, which met at Bombay in the last week of 1892 and the first week of 1893. In the final session one missionary proposed a resolution expressing abhorrence of 'regulated vice' and the hope that British officials would obey the 1888 resolution of the House of Commons. But this was opposed by the Rev. Dr Miller, the Principal of Madras Christian College, on the ground that the issue had not been debated, and also because 'no good would come of the matter, as Government would see that they were divided on the subject'.[1] Another missionary, who supported Miller, said that medical missionaries were not in agreement on this issue. In the *Sentinel* Dyer was bitterly critical of Miller. He described him as Principal of 'Madras "Christian"

College'. He mentioned that Miller had been made a CIE, or Companion of the Indian Empire – a recognition of meritorious service which was accorded to distinguished officials. He pointed out that Miller kept 'in the closest touch with high officials'. Miller was even a member of the reception committee when Prince Albert Victor visited Madras. Indeed, on that occasion he attended a nautch party, with an entertainment by dancing girls, in honour of the Prince. He attended another nautch party in honour of Lansdowne, the Governor-General. One could not imagine, Dyer concluded triumphantly, 'one of these great missionary *burra-sahibs* dining in a native Christian hut'.[2]

These arguments were part of a long-standing controversy among Protestant missionaries. Miller was a prominent example of the missionaries who devoted themselves to education, especially higher education. But they were opposed by radicals among the Nonconformists, and by some in the evangelical wing of the Church of England, who argued that missionaries should concentrate on 'gospel preaching' and on work among the poor. Higher education would only benefit the higher castes, who were unlikely to be converted. This reasoning appealed to radical Nonconformists in England, such as Hugh Price Hughes, who was afraid that Methodism was too middle-class. Henry Lunn, a Methodist medical missionary, resigned for such reasons and returned to England. From this vantage point he criticized missionaries who lived 'in a style which cut them off from the natives', who mingled with the official elite and were influenced by them not to criticize government policies such as the regulation of vice. He too attacked Miller for his role at the Bombay missionary conference.[3]

These divisions among the Nonconformists blunted the force of Dyer's accusations. His revelations had made an effective impact on public opinion in England in 1888. But when he asserted in the *Sentinel* that the old system was continuing, little notice seemed to be taken. New tactics were required, which would have a fresh impact. The reformers invited two American women to investigate – Mrs Elizabeth Wheeler Andrew and Dr Kate Bushnell, both members of the World's Women's Christian Temperance Union. This was an astute move. Mrs Andrew was the widow of a Methodist minister and Dr Bushnell had medical qualifications: it would be difficult to challenge their evidence. Moreover, the thought that two respectable ladies had seen indelicate things sanctioned by the military authorities was bound to excite Victorian public opinion.

The two women had already completed their enquiries, and their evidence was being sifted by Stansfeld and Stuart, when the Bombay Conference gave publicity to the disagreements among missionaries. They arrived in India towards the end of December 1891, and visited ten military stations during the next three months. They visited hospitals and inspected registers of prostitutes, they visited brothels and interviewed prostitutes, and they brought back careful notes. Later in the year they were followed by John Hyslop-Bell, a retired North-Country journalist and newspaper proprietor, who made similar enquiries and confirmed their findings. It seemed that the old system was in force with the new Cantonments Act and rules.

By now there was a Liberal ministry under Gladstone, and Stansfeld wrote with some satisfaction to George Russell, the Under-Secretary of State : he recalled that Cross had asked for solid ground for suspecting the good faith of the Indian authorities and he claimed that the evidence was now available. He demanded a committee of the House of Commons.[4] In the India Office Arthur Godley, an experienced official, advised Lord Kimberley, once again Secretary of State, that Stansfeld should first be asked to produce his evidence. Then they could think about a committee.[5]

Stansfeld and Stuart promptly drew up a 'statement of facts' about the working of the Cantonments Act and rules : systematic provision was made at military stations for prostitutes for the exclusive use of British soldiers ; periodical examinations were compulsory and so was detention in hospital if necessary ; there was even a fixed tariff payable by soldiers, graded in accordance with their rank.[6] Kimberley attempted delaying tactics : he offered to lay the case before his Council, with a view to asking the Government of India to reply. But Stansfeld was too shrewd to accept this offer. 'We must obtain this committee or bring the matter before the House.'[7] But Kimberley realized that a parliamentary committee in these circumstances might be unmanageable. Instead he quickly appointed a departmental committee to ascertain how far the Indian authorities were complying with the 1888 Resolution of the House of Commons. George Russell was to be the Chairman, with two old India hands from the Secretary of State's Council – Sir Donald Stewart and Sir James Peile – and two MPs – Stansfeld himself and another Nonconformist, H.J. Wilson, a man of rigid principles who had once envisaged legislation to prohibit fornication.[8]

Kimberley also sent the 'statement of facts' to the Governor-

General in Council, who thereupon appointed their own commission of enquiry with Denzil Ibbetson, an experienced civil servant, as Chairman and two other members – Surgeon-General Cleghorn, Inspector-General of Civil Hospitals, and Maulvi Sami-ullah Khan, a former District Judge. They worked fast: they visited four cantonments and completed their report in three weeks. Ibbetson and Cleghorn were then despatched to London to give evidence before the Russell Committee.

Mrs Andrew and Dr Bushnell testified that in the great cantonments such as Ambala, Lucknow, Mian Mir and Mirat the old system was still flourishing. Ibbetson and his colleagues conceded that it had not been completely abolished. Their enquiries were not as extensive as those of the American ladies. But they found that not all the military authorities had obeyed orders with their accustomed precision.

There seemed to have been some curious misunderstandings. For example, the Government of India had issued orders in 1888 that registered prostitutes should no longer be allowed to live in regimental bazars. Soon afterwards they issued orders abolishing the registration of prostitutes. At Ambala and Mirat the prostitutes were duly turned out of the regimental bazars, but they were later allowed to return on the ground that the former orders had merely prohibited the residence of registered prostitutes in regimental bazars, and registration had subsequently been cancelled: the military authorities reasoned, somewhat speciously, that there could be no objection to the residence of prostitutes who were not registered.[9]

Mrs Andrew and Dr Bushnell also said that at Ambala prostitutes had pitched their tents near the encampments of two Highland regiments – the Gordons and the Argyll and Sutherlands. Lieutenant-Colonel Gildea, commanding the 1st Battalion of the Gordons, explained that he had only arrived in India in January 1892 and nobody told him that this was forbidden.[10] Captain Trotter, commanding the 2nd Battalion of the Argyll and Sutherland Highlanders, stated that he told the women that he would not interfere with them provided '(a) [that] they kept outside the limits over which I had jurisdiction, (b) that I did not find the men contracting venereal from them, (c) that decency and order were observed, (d) that they availed themselves of any medical aid attainable'. A public road separated them from his regiment. He claimed that this was not licensed prostitution. Considerations of health and decency always led him to encourage his men to 'devote their attentions to women who

71

can, if they wish, obtain medical aid, instead of having promiscuous intercourse with diseased villagers and city prostitutes'.[11] Brigadier-General Pretyman, commanding Sirhind District, explained that it was merely through 'an oversight' in his office and also in the office of the Cantonment Magistrate, Ambala, that the orders had not been conveyed to Gildea and Trotter. As the orders were marked 'strictly confidential', they had been locked in a confidential box, and so had escaped notice.[12]

A similar disarray was revealed at Mian Mir. The Station Commander admitted that prostitutes lived in the regimental bazars and accompanied troops on the march. This was then denied by the commanding officers of the regiments concerned. Major-General Viscount Frankfort, commanding Lahore District, telegraphed for an explanation of these 'contradictions'.[13] The Station Commander thereupon withdrew his statement on the ground that it was 'based on former customs, and not on actual facts at the time of reference'.[14] It was becoming strangely difficult to establish precisely what was happening at any particular place and time.

When the old rules were suspended in 1888 the lock hospitals were renamed 'voluntary venereal hospitals'. According to the new Cantonments Act and rules VD was to be treated like any other contagious disease, and there were to be hospitals in each cantonment for the treatment of infectious and contagious diseases in general. Mrs Andrew and Dr Bushnell claimed that the old lock hospitals were still operated as such by the authorities, whatever the change of name. Surgeon-Major O'Connor, in charge of the 'cantonment general hospital' at Mirat, told the Ibbetson Commission in June 1893 that until three weeks ago all sixty of the cantonment prostitutes came to hospital once a week for examination. But there was no register of prostitutes. Of course there was a list of those who came. Indeed, he added vaguely, 'new women turn up almost every week, without my having sent for them, or even having heard of their existence before'. But if a woman then failed to attend on several occasions, he would send for her, and if she disobeyed he would report to the Cantonment Magistrate that he supposed her to be diseased. The Magistrate would then give her the choice of going to hospital or leaving the cantonment. In 1892 he had received an order from the Quartermaster-General to the effect that there were to be no special examinations for VD. 'On receipt of this order I asked the Cantonment Magistrate whether this meant that I was to stop my weekly inspections; and I was told to continue them as before.' But just three weeks back Colonel Reid, station commander, 'said he thought they had better be stopped'.[15]

Major Campbell, Cantonment Magistrate at Lucknow, told the Ibbetson Commission that periodical examinations had indeed been stopped there, though only in 1892. But a few months later he had had such reports of increased vd that he asked soldiers to point out the women who had infected them. He then told these women to leave the cantonment or go to hospital.[16] Surgeon-Major Hamilton, in charge of the cantonment general hospital, confirmed that he had thereupon recommenced the periodical examinations.[17] Lieutenant-Colonel Macpherson, Cantonment Magistrate at Mian Mir, coolly asserted that 'there was no intention whatever of overlooking or disobeying any orders that had been passed: they were simply not thought of'. A hospital had been built: his assumption was that 'it would of course be worked on former lines'.[18] Major-General Viscount Frankfort, commanding Lahore District, merely commented that Macpherson's reasoning was 'inexplicable'.[19]

Were the new cantonment general hospitals used merely for prostitutes suffering from venereal disease? Mrs Andrew and Dr Bushnell found that they were still known as lock hospitals, and Hyslop-Bell stated that at Mirat, for example, there seemed only to be women patients. Major-General Nairne, commanding Mirat District, contradicted this. The cantonment hospital was open to all who came, regardless of sex or disease. On the other hand, he added, there was also 'the literal fact' that 'hardly any but prostitutes do come, owing to the fact that the money required for the cantonment buildings as sanctioned has never yet been allotted, and the present buildings are only those of the original lock hospital; it is unlikely therefore that many other than those of the prostitute class would yet avail themselves of treatment'.[20] General White, who had succeeded Roberts as Commander-in-Chief, produced a more convincing refutation in the statistics for seventeen cantonment hospitals in 1892. Of a total of 62,051 cases, only 3,475 were venereal. Even at Mirat there were only 176 venereal cases out of a total of 447.[21]

Mrs Andrew asserted that the same tariff prevailed in various cantonments – one rupee for Sergeants, eight annas for Corporals, six annas for Bombardiers and four annas for Privates.[22] This was stated to be a matter of immemorial custom, and the military authorities generally claimed that it was nothing to do with them. But Sergeant George, 2nd Derbyshire Regiment, explained that as an NCO in the military police at Ambala he would visit the brothels every night to take drunken soldiers into custody and turn out anyone trying to stay after hours – ten p.m. for those without a pass, midnight for those with one. If a woman complained that a soldier had failed to pay, he said simply, 'I make the man pay.'[23] He argued that this was essentially the same procedure that he followed if a shopkeeper complained that a soldier had failed to pay. He regarded this as the right thing for the police to do, and in the circumstances of cantonment life it seemed reasonable enough : no doubt it was the usual procedure.

Were prostitutes still reserved for British soldiers ? The authorities claimed that this was no longer so. Major-General Graham, commanding Rohilkhand District, admitted that there might still be discrimination in practice : 'no doubt the bawdy house-keeper tried to reserve her prostitutes for British soldiers, but she had no official assistance in so doing.'[24] But the military police seem at least sometimes to have acted under different assumptions. Private Macnally, Garrison Provost Sergeant at Lucknow from 1891 to 1893, told the Ibbetson Commission that the military police invariably turned Indians out of brothels used by British soldiers : 'there is no order to that effect ; but it is not right for natives to go where British soldiers go for their women.'[25] Sergeant George acted similarly at Ambala, at first with authority. The Cantonment Magistrate told the military police to ensure that Indian males did not enter. Later he told the police that they had no power to do so. Now, Sergeant George explained in June 1893, his orders were not to turn Indians out except in order to avoid a disturbance. But he seems to have interpreted this in his own way : 'If soldiers come down here and find native men here without business there would very likely be a disturbance.'[26] The Ibbetson Commission accepted this reasoning : 'If English soldiers and natives were openly to consort with the same sort of women, jealousies would certainly arise, and quarrels, which are specially to be deprecated as inter-racial, would frequently occur.' They hastened to explain that this did not affect 'the better class of natives', who would not want to be associated with women frequented by British soldiers. 'The same objection is felt in England by the better class of Englishmen.'[27] This was hardly a tactful line of argument to pursue in meeting Nonconformist criticism, and it revealed a significant

ignorance of the class hostility invoked during the agitation against the
CD Acts in England.

It was generally admitted that prostitutes travelled with regiments.
But was this with official help or approval? The regimental
Quartermaster of the Gordon Highlanders saw prostitutes following
the regiment on the march to Subathu. He asked the *kotwal*, the Indian
official in charge of bazar arrangements, who had ordered it, and the
kotwal replied that 'they used to follow the regiment in former years,
and had done so now'.[28] Major-General Nairne, commanding Mirat
District, asserted that prostitutes who accompanied a regiment did so
'on their own private account'. Nobody could stop them. 'The mere
fact of removing all authority from Commanding Officers prevents
them from interfering with their movements; and the well known
axiom that when there is a demand supply is sure to follow, is as true of
sexual intercourse between men and women as of every thing else in a
free country.'[29]

General White, as Commander-in-Chief, pushed this line of
argument to a broader conclusion in a valiant attempt to defend the
record of the military authorities. Ambala cantonment had as many
inhabitants as York, Bath or Paisley. Such cities contained 'prostitutes
plying their trade with the cognizance of the municipal authorities. Yet
the Mayor of York is probably not accused of making official and
systematic provision of prostitutes; nor is it conceivable that the
municipal authorities in these three towns could exclude all
prostitutes.'[30] But the military authorities had been revealed as playing
a much more active role than any municipality. When the Ibbetson
Commission submitted their report even the Governor-General in
Council admitted to the Secretary of State that 'in certain cases' officers
had gone beyond their powers or misinterpreted orders. But they
assured him that strict orders were now in force prohibiting the
residence of prostitutes in regimental bazars, and they urged that it
would be most unwise to try to exclude them from cantonments. This
would involve a great interference in private life, and it would drive
soldiers to look for women outside cantonments, where sanitary
precautions could not be enforced and where the soldiers themselves
would be 'less within the reach of military discipline'.[31] Here was that
recurrent fear of the mysterious dangers that lay beyond the ordered
world of the military cantonment, and the enduring wish to keep the
soldier under control.

But more damage had already been done to the reputation of the military authorities. Sir Frederick, now Lord Roberts, who had retired as Commander-in-Chief, unwisely allowed himself to be interviewed when he landed in England. The reporter approached the great man with fitting reverence as the hero of the Mutiny and of the march from Kabul to Kandahar. He described Roberts as 'a rather slightly-built man, of medium height, with a sun-tanned skin, and keen grey eyes'. He then went through the allegations made by Mrs Andrew and Dr Bushnell, and to each Roberts replied with soldierlike brevity.

Systematic provision was made for prostitutes in cantonments ? 'I deny it.' There were compulsory medical examinations ? 'It is not true.' Infected women were compulsorily detained in hospital ? Here Roberts was less definite : this would be 'quite possible – and desirable – though I have no knowledge of it'. The reporter helpfully suggested that 'officers wink at some things that are contrary to orders – when it suits them ?' The answer was categorical : 'Impossible ! They dare not do so.' The reporter tried again : 'Might not some things as are described exist without coming to your lordship's cognisance ?' Again the answer was categorical. 'No sir. An occasional breach of the regulations might occur, but a wholescale organised system, under official sanction, is impossible !' Then how could these allegations have been made ? This prompted an indignant outburst : 'Why didn't these ladies, when they were in India, make their complaint to *me* ? Surely I was the proper person to be approached. If they had come to me with a specific charge I would at once have gone at all costs and investigated it.' He added incautiously : 'That the old system is abolished is pretty plainly proved by the fact that disease is fast spreading in our Indian Army.' The reporter seized his chance : 'Am I to understand that your Lordship thinks the "old system" better than the new ?' Robert hastily replied, 'I do not say that. I merely mention a fact.'[32]

The reformers were delighted. Roberts had played into their hands. The interview was published in the *Christian Commonwealth*, and a week later the same journal carried a reply from James Stuart : 'either Lord Roberts knows or he does not know that this horrible system has never been swept away. If he knows it, he has been a party to wilful disobedience of the House of Commons. If he does not know it, he has neglected his duty.'[33] W. T. Stead also made the most of it in the *Review of Reviews* : 'But a Commander-in-Chief who does not know what is going on in half-a-dozen of the most important military stations in

India, is not by any means the kind of Commander-in-Chief that Lord Roberts is believed to be. To be found not guilty of disloyalty by proving that you have been hoodwinked by your subordinates is not a pleasant position for one of the most capable of our military chiefs; but it is difficult to see what other way of escape there is – always assuming that the facts are as stated before the Departmental Committee.'[34]

Roberts gave his unfortunate interview in May – after Mrs Andrew and Dr Bushnell had testified before the Russell Committee and before the Ibbetson Commission had drawn up their report. After he had seen the Ibbetson Report he confronted the Russell Committee and admitted that the 1888 resolution had not been fully observed. There were 'slight shortcomings' at first. 'Natives of India live guided by habit and custom, and this makes it very difficult to carry out any change.'[35] He was asked about the circular of 1886, and tried to evade responsibility. The Commander-in-Chief, he said, was not aware of all the orders issued in his name. He had indeed told Major-General Chapman, then Quartermaster-General, how important it was to have doctors with experience in treating VD, and that part of the circular accorded with his views. But he would not have approved of the part which advocated the supply of pretty women for soldiers. Stansfeld pressed him on this. Such ideas were 'repugnant to the ideas of an officer and a gentleman'. Roberts conceded that they were 'very improper'. Stansfeld pressed harder: 'Am I going too far in saying repugnant to the ideas of an officer and a gentleman?' Roberts would not be pushed any further: 'They are not at all proper ideas to have.'[36] He knew that officers and gentlemen often had very improper ideas on such matters. However, Major-General Chapman, now Director of Military Intelligence at the War Office, crisply declined to accept responsibility for the circular. Had Roberts seen and read the 1886 circular? Chapman was adamant. He did not know, he said drily, whether Lord Roberts approved of such ideas now, but then 'he certainly did approve of them'.[37]

Shortly after these unmilitary attempts to escape responsibility, Roberts publicly apologized to Mrs Andrew and Dr Bushnell. He had now studied all the documents, and he considered that the ladies' statements were 'in the main correct'. But he still asserted that 'it would have been better if the missionary ladies had been commended to the care of the authorities in India'. Any 'omissions and shortcomings' on the part of the authorities could have been remedied on the spot, and 'a great deal of unpleasantness would have been avoided'.[38] Such protestations only did more damage to the credit of the military authorities. 'Unpleasantness' might well have been avoided by cooperating with them, but at the cost of concealing realities. The *Tribune* of Lahore sombrely predicted that Roberts himself would suffer in his future career, and hinted, probably correctly, that the affair had put the viceroyalty beyond his reach : this verdict was quoted triumphantly by the *Sentinel*.[39]

The Russell Committee finally submitted a majority report to the effect that the 1888 resolution of the House of Commons had been disregarded in the ten cantonments visited by Mrs Andrew and Dr Bushnell. The new rules had been so operated as to make periodical examinations virtually compulsory. The orders issued by the Government of India had not ended the old system of 'regulated and licensed prostitution'. Legislation was therefore necessary.[40] Sir Donald Stewart and Sir James Peile tried to defend their old colleagues in a dissenting minute which did not carry much conviction. They argued that there had been a genuine attempt to enforce the new policy, but it was bound to take a little time to overturn a system which had lasted so long. After all this publicity the new rules would certainly be enforced everywhere. Legislation was therefore unnecessary.[41] However, the general impression conveyed by these proceedings was that such changes as had been made were in response to the reformers' pressure, and that without their campaign nobody would have realized how little change there had previously been. James Stuart, ready with a memorable turn of speech, had said, in the course of the newspaper interview in which he criticized Roberts : 'Passing a resolution in the House of Commons is like pulling at a bell-handle with no bell at the other end.'[42] There seemed to be no alternative to legislation.

The Governor-General in Council hastily submitted drafts of possible rules to give effect to the views of the majority of the Russell Committee. Not that they agreed with those views. Indeed, they claimed that any such legislation would either be 'vague' or it would accord 'to prostitutes an immunity from that supervision and control to which all other residents in cantonments are liable, and to venereal disease an exemption from the sanitary precautions taken to guard against the spread of all other contagious maladies'. Their underlying fear was that reformers would go on to press for the exclusion of prostitutes from cantonments. So they told the Secretary of State that to go beyond the 1889 Cantonments Act would fail to diminish prostitution but 'would certainly lead to the spread of disease and not improbably to the prevalence of far graver forms of immorality'.[43] This was their trump card, and they were correct in their assessment of the direction that future reforming activities might take.

In December 1893 the Madras Missionary Conference forwarded the report of a committee of missionaries who had enquired into seven cantonments in the Madras Presidency. They found that 'immorality' prevailed among British soldiers 'to an appalling extent', and that officers did not try very hard to suppress 'impurity'. This was no doubt an accurate observation, although most officers would not have thought it either possible or wise to attempt such a task. Instead, the missionaries urged that all prostitutes be expelled from cantonments. But they also argued forcibly that more soldiers be allowed to marry. These recommendations travelled along the usual bureaucratic channels, and attracted characteristic responses. The official view was that prostitutes fulfilled a socially necessary function. The Government of India commented: 'The absence of prostitutes in cantonments where large numbers of young unmarried soldiers are living would probably lead to offences such as criminal assault, rape and unnatural crime.' In a departmental minute at the India Office it was recognized that an increase in the marriage ratio 'might have a good effect on the morality and health of the troops'. But it would be expensive, and a reduction in the number of married soldiers was 'one of the advantages claimed for the short service system'. Economy must be the first consideration.[44]

At the same time the Army Sanitary Commission were carefully pondering the low incidence of vd among Indian troops. They admitted that most of them were married, but firmly rejected this as a possible explanation on the ground that usually their wives were not with them, thus ignoring the obvious possibility that married men might remain faithful to their wives. Instead, they suggested more esoteric explanations: 'It may be that in the case of Native soldiers religion, habits, diet, especially as regards the use of meat, alcohol and opium have some influence, and it is desirable that these points should be investigated.' They also envisaged simpler ways of reducing the surplus energies of the British soldier: 'Commanding Officers should be urged to encourage in every way all forms of athletic amusement, as physical fatigue acts as a deterrent to sexual indulgence.' They agreed with the Indian authorities that commanding officers should still be empowered to reduce temptation by preventing women from coming into the lines after dusk and by putting out of bounds places where soldiers were thought to have caught vD.[45] This was to come perilously near the recommendations of the Madras Missionary Conference.

Kimberley, however, was in no danger of going as far as this. He insisted that the Cantonments Act be amended to preclude such practices as compulsory examination and to provide penalties such as 'a moderate fine' or a short term of imprisonment for any official who disobeyed.[46] To send this despatch he had to override his whole Council. Peile put on record a dissenting minute in which he repeated the arguments he had used when he dissented from the Russell Committee Report. There had no doubt been some disobedience of orders, but no more than one might expect in such a vast area and with regard to practices which had existed for so long. But the result of this despatch would be that the diseased prostitute would 'possess an altogether exceptional exemption from control'.[47]

At the same meeting Kimberley also had to override his whole Council to approve the levy of an import tariff that excluded cotton goods in deference to English manufacturing interests and Liberal voters. Arthur Godley, Permanent Under-Secretary at the India Office, who made a habit of writing indiscreet letters to Viceroys behind the backs of his political superiors, quickly wrote to Elgin that this was a 'record'.[48] Kimberley's Council, however, saw their Secretary of State as recklessly sacrificing the moral and material interests of the British raj to hypocritical Liberal and Nonconformist pressure. The Government of India had produced, as evidence of the need for some regulation of prostitution, the difference between vD admissions for British troops of 166·7 per 1,000 in 1873 and 409·9 per 1,000 in 1892. This was, he conceded, 'a remarkable increase'. But if the figures were broken down into two periods the increase for the decade beginning in 1873 was 62 per cent whereas for the subsequent decade it was only 51 per cent. In other words, it was greater in the period when the lock hospital system was operating in full vigour.[49] But he had already accepted the Russell Committee's conclusion that the system was continuing in defiance of orders until 1892.

Kimberley wrote privately to Elgin that he personally had 'no sympathy with Stansfeld's views'. But politically Stansfeld had the majority of the Commons behind him. To Kimberley, an experienced politician, this was a clear justification for subordinating his own views. In parliamentary terms, it made sense. 'The late Conservative Govt found it impossible to resist Stansfeld and his followers in the

House of Commons, and if they could not with their great majority resist, you may suppose how perfectly hopeless it would be for us to attempt it.'[50] Elgin took the point. But he was aware of Indian criticisms of the sacrifice of Indian to English manufacturing interests on the tariff question. He warned Lieutenant-General Brackenbury, Military Member of his Council, to be careful when the Cantonments Act came up for amendment : 'This is another case in which the House of Commons is too strong to be resisted, and I think that we had better not have to say that again just at this moment.'[51]

Meanwhile there was anxious discussion of the wording of the new Bill and rules. When the affable Kimberley was succeeded by H.H. Fowler, a Nonconformist with strong views, Elgin was soon playing the Government of India's trump card in private correspondence. The ultimate course might well be to forbid 'disorderly houses' in cantonments and expel all prostitutes. But General Brackenbury had only just been talking to him about this, and it seemed that this might lead to 'even more deplorable evils'. Elgin forced himself to be more specific : 'I regret to say his allegation is that there is already an increase in unnatural crimes.'[52]

When Sir Alexander Miller, as Law Member, introduced the new Bill into the legislative council in July 1894 he explained merely that it was done to comply with the wish of the home Government to give effect to the views of the majority of the Russell Committee. He did not fail to mention that that majority had been three to two, and he added that he did not wish to express any opinion on the Bill's provisions.[53] Sir Griffith Evans, a non-official member, subsequently pointed out that Miller had not introduced the Bill 'as having any merits but simply as having been ordered by the Secretary of State'.[54] When Fowler saw the report of the debate in *The Times*, he reacted strongly. He wrote privately to Elgin, 'Sir A. Miller appears to have adopted the course of openly dissociating himself from the policy of the measures which it is his duty to introduce!' He explained the principle of Cabinet solidarity – that ministers must loyally support Cabinet decisions or resign – and asserted that it should apply equally to the Viceroy's council. 'I must therefore ask you to convey to him that I regard this matter as a most serious one, affecting as it does the relations between Her Majesty's Government and the Government of India, and that I hope that in the future I may rely upon his loyal co-operation with your Government.'

But Miller was unrepentant. In the Government of India, he told

Elgin, 'no one is bound by the class of ties which so often vitiate the action of members of the House of Commons'. Also, Fowler did not realize that it was no part of his duty as Law Member to introduce a Cantonments Bill: 'I only did so to oblige Brackenbury, and because the feeling in Council was so strong that no Member was willing to father the measure, and I believed that I could do so with less repugnance than any of the others.'[55]

The Bill provided that there should be no rules permitting the compulsory or periodical examination of women for VD, or the registration of prostitutes, or sanctioning the practice of prostitution in cantonments. Any official disobeying this would be liable to a fine of a hundred rupees or imprisonment in lieu. The Government of India then invited official comment.

Officials generally disapproved of the idea that an official might be punished for disobeying orders. The Chief Commissioner of Assam protested that it would 'lower the credit and injure the *morale* of the public service', if officials were not trusted.[56] The Chief Commissioner of Burma feared that it might 'open the door to vexatious claims against public servants'.[57] The rest of the Bill aroused similar indignation. Some confined themselves to indignation. Colonel Fendall Currie, the Commissioner of Faizabad, for example: 'The less said about the present Bill, fathered by morbid married faddists and sexless unprofessional sisters, the better.' It involved 'thousands' of men in hospital, and 'thousands and thousands cast on the world to propagate disease to unborn generations'.[58]

The Deputy Commissioner, Naini Tal, forecast trouble with villagers: 'As long as prostitution is regulated the soldier has little temptation to make advances to women outside cantonments, but in the case of the large cantonment of Ranikhet the abolition of regulations was followed by complaints from villagers that their women were solicited.'[59] The Commissioner in Sind was prompted to witticism: 'Mr James cannot but believe that, as a question of practical politics, the great pox can and should be repressed as vigorously as the small pox.'[60]

The Acting District Magistrate of Ahmadabad expressed the general view among officials and army officers:

Private soldiers are young men taken from the classes least habituated to exercise self-contol – classes who in their natural state marry very early in life. You take such men, you do not allow them to marry, you feed them well –

better in most cases than they have been accustomed to be fed, and you give them a sufficient amount of physical work to put them into good condition and no more. It is asking too much to expect that a large majority of such men will exhibit the continence of the cloister.[61]

Other officials were laconic. For example, the Commissioner of Pegu : 'I think the Bill to amend the Cantonments Act is well adapted to effect the object stated – an object the expediency of which is, I think, very doubtful.'[62] Or the Commissioner of Tenasserim, who replied simply that 'in my opinion the Bill is a bad Bill, as if it becomes law it can only do harm, and that unless it is imperatively necessary to pass such a law it ought not to be passed'.[63]

One voice questioned the necessity, and an original argument emerged from outside the bureaucracy. The European and Anglo-Indian Defence Association had been founded to oppose the Ilbert Bill, which was introduced in 1883 to enable Indian judges to exercise criminal jurisdiction over Europeans. The ensuing agitation had alarmed the Government of India sufficiently to concede to Europeans the right to trial by jury. After this the Association had continued to watch sullenly and suspiciously over European interests. Now, however, its President was roused to argue that undue deference was being paid to a resolution of the House of Commons, although Parliament consisted of the Queen and the Lords, as well as the Commons.[64] But this was to deal in constitutional niceties rather than practical politics.

A more serious constitutional point was raised by Fowler's insistence that members of the Viceroy's executive council should support government measures. At first it only seemed that Sir Charles Pritchard, a senior official from Bombay, would vote against the Bill, and Elgin urged Fowler to be tactful : 'If I might advise, I should not send any order to Sir Charles to vote. He is rather anxious to have it, as it would give him firmer ground for a grievance, and, if it is merely a question of his one vote, I am told there is no fear of the Bill, and I should let him take the responsibility of abstaining if he chose.'[65] Elgin reassured Fowler that the other members of the executive council would support the Bill.

But it then emerged that Sir Alexander Miller was thinking of voting against it on its second reading. Elgin soon had to warn Fowler that there was 'a practical difficulty' in view of the 'considerable non-official element' in the legislative council since the reforms of 1892. A

Liberal such as Fowler could hardly object. He also explained that there was 'more than one opinion of the proper attitude of a member of the Government in face of an order of the Secretary of State from which he disagrees. General Brackenbury avows that he must obey it, or resign. Sir A. Miller, on the contrary, says if he does not obey he can be dismissed, but cannot be compelled to resign, and he would not do so.'[66] Fowler's response was indignant expostulation. If Miller did not resign in such circumstances, he would be dismissed. But he ought to resign.[67] Three weeks later, such was his irritation, he reverted to the matter in a postscript to a letter on a different subject altogether : 'I think that the Lord Chancellor, the Cabinet and myself are quite as competent to form an opinion as to the "constitutional" position of the Executive Council as Sir A. Miller.'[68] He was now facing similar opposition to his insistence on imposing a countervailing excise duty on Indian cotton goods to ensure that they enjoyed no advantage in competing with British goods subject to import duty. James Westland, Finance Member of the Viceroy's executive council, had minuted that an excise duty on Indian cotton manufactures was 'an expedient worthy of the middle ages' : Fowler indignantly resolved to cut this out of any published version of the documents.[69]

There was also much disagreement about the rules to be issued under the new Bill once it became law. The Government of India wanted to give commanding officers power to expel infected women from cantonments. Fowler refused on the ground that it would be impossible to tell if a women had VD without examining her : 'this would undoubtedly lead to a recurrence of the practices which have given rise to the agitation.' Alternatively, they wanted to give them power to expel anyone from cantonments without giving a reason. Again Fowler refused : the same objection would apply if it were intended to expel individual women, and it would be impracticable to exclude prostitutes as a class.[70] The Government of India asked if commanding officers could be empowered to expel women with VD who refused treatment. Again Fowler refused, and he insisted that the Government of India comply with his instructions.[71] He made a point of telling Elgin in a private letter that he had overridden his whole council on the matter.[72]

It seemed that the new policy could not be evaded. General White, the new Commander-in-Chief, wrote home to the Duke of Connaught, recently Commander-in-Chief at Bombay, that there had already been 'a terrible increase' in VD. 'The addition to human suffering that this represents ought to influence right-minded men to oppose the grievous wrong worked by Stansfeld & Co to our boy soldiers.'[73] But Stansfeld and his collegues had made such an impact on public opinion that no strings could be pulled against them with any effect. Lord Reay, former Governor of Bombay, assured Elgin that his own sympathies were with the military authorities, but 'democracies, like autocrats, have their hobbies'.[74]

Shortly before the Bill was due to come back to the legislative council, there was a meeting of the Indian Medical Congress, composed of doctors in private practice and also in Government service. Surgeon-Colonel Harvey, their President, told Sir Antony MacDonnell, of the Viceroy's executive council, that his colleagues were 'absolutely unanimous' that the clause imposing penalties for disobedience was 'an undeserved affront'. These colleagues included 'a number of medical missionaries and medical women strongly opposed to the C.D. Acts'.[75] MacDonnell quickly forwarded this information to the Viceroy's Private Secretary with the comment, 'One cannot blame the doctors.'[76] After hasty enquiries and calculations he reported that the non-official members of the legislative council would oppose the Bill, and that it would be defeated.[77]

The Viceroy and the Secretary of State exhanged anxious telegrams. Elgin warned Fowler that two members of his executive council – Pritchard and Westland – would oppose the Bill, or at least abstain : 'No desire to shirk responsibility, but feel, If I am required to insist on hopeless division known to entail compulsory withdrawal of Colleagues who have unanimous sympathy here, my position would be seriously weakened and might be rendered untenable.'[78] Faced with this threat, Fowler prepared for a speedy retreat. He telegraphed to Elgin that he would take the matter to the Cabinet and asked him to postpone further discussion for a week.[79]

But discussions were continuing, and on the following day Elgin telegraphed news of a possible compromise. Sir Griffith Evans offered, on behalf of the non-official members, to let the Bill go through if the clause imposing penalties were dropped.[80] This was already under discussion at the India Office, and the fact that Gladstone had been succeeded by Rosebery made it feasible, as Godley explained defensively to Elgin :

You will say why was this not done before ? Of course it is easy to see now that it is a great pity the penal clause was ever introduced ; but at that time we had a Prime Minister who was very much in sympathy with Stansfeld and Co ; and I doubt whether even now the Cabinet would have agreed to face a row in Parliament on the subject, if they had not before them your telegrams showing how disastrous would be the results of proceeding with the clause.[81]

Fowler duly agreed to drop the penalties clause on the ground that the Government of India considered that the existing law provided adequate penalties for disobedience.[82] To facilitate the stretching of Fowler's Nonconformist conscience Elgin got Sir Alexander Miller to record a legal opinion to the same effect.[83]

The Bill therefore had a peaceful passage through the legislative council. Evans excelled himself. He criticized dictation from London. He cited St Paul to the effect that all men had not the gift of continence, and condemned the War Office for merely ensuring the physical fitness of recruits and not 'their fitness for celibate orders'. He did not oppose the Bill, but he uttered grave warnings against 'sacrifices to the Moloch of syphilis'. In his enthusiasm he apparently forgot that he was speaking in the Indian legislature as he concluded, 'The subject is one of national importance. The disease strikes at the vitality of the race – sooner or later the English nation must deal with it.'[84]

In the previous enquiries conducted by the Government of India the only authoritative voice raised in support of the Bill had been that of an Indian – Justice Muttuswami Aiyar of the Madras High Court, who declared himself to be opposed to the registration and compulsory examination of prostitutes as 'a measure incompatible with the requirements of sound legislative policy'.[85] But the moderate Indian politicians on the legislative council had different views. Babu Mohiny Mohun Roy described Muttuswami Aiyar's opinion as 'faint praise' and said that the Bill should be dropped, while Gangadhar Rao Madhav Chitnavis said that the British army should not be weakened by disease.[86] Various official members now dutifully produced various reasons why the Bill should be passed.

But Sir Charles Elliott, Lieutenant-Governor of Bengal, criticized the Bill for vagueness of expression. The Bill was then going to a carefully chosen select committee, and to Elgin's alarm Sir Alexander Miller proposed that Elliott be added to the committee. Scanning newspaper reports of the debate, Godley at the India Office commented mildly, 'Sir Charles Elliott seems to have sailed rather near the wind.' Godley held unquestioningly to the Whitehall view that civil servants, 'whether they be very great or very small men', must be prepared to cooperate in measures of which they disapproved.[87] Elgin wrote quickly to assure Fowler that his wishes would be obeyed : 'as soon as we met in Executive Council, I took Miller to task, and Brackenbury backed me up. It was then that I impressed on my colleagues that we were bound to insist on the rest of the Bill, and none of them, not even Pritchard, made any real objection.'[88]

The changes made by the select committee were innocuous enough. Instead of the provision that there should be no rule sanctioning prostitution, it was stated that there should be no rule giving legal sanction to prostitution. Instead of the provision that there should be no registration of prostitutes, it was stated that there should be no special registration of prostitutes – for all the inhabitants of a cantonment might be registered, whatever their occupation. Elgin telegraphed his obsequious regret at asking Fowler for 'further concessions', and emphasized that these modifications did not affect the substance of the Bill.[89] Fowler graciously assented.

If the penalties clause were indeed superfluous, as Miller claimed, it was remarkable that its deletion enabled the Bill to pass. The explanation seems to be that it had a symbolic importance : it was seen as a slur on the prestige of the official elite, and by implication on the prestige of the ruling race. Evans, a prominent Calcutta barrister, who negotiated the compromise on behalf of the non-official members, had negotiated the Ilbert Bill compromise a decade ago. But there were many expressions of anxiety about the effects of the new policy on the health of young soldiers, and warnings that this must be watched. If the military authorities had lost this battle, the ground for the next was already in sight.

In the new rules, VD was not mentioned. Instead, the medical officer in charge of a cantonment hospital was empowered to require the attendance of anyone he supposed on credible testimony to be suffering from cholera, smallpox, diphtheria or typhoid. This prompted a protest from some of the inhabitants of Mirat cantonment. There ought to be provision, they said, for 'respectable and well-to-do persons' to be treated in their homes. 'Even hopeful cases may end fatally through mental depression and physical exhaustion from removal from his home comforts.'[90]

This sad prospect aroused no sympathy among the military authorities, who embarked upon a rudimentary sociological analysis. Captain Sutherland, station Staff Officer, classified the signatories. He reported that 38 were 'Bengali babus being Government servants', 5

'Bengali babus not being Government servants', 6 'Government servants other than Bengali babus', 23 'well-known respectable persons', and no less than 124 'persons of small repute (not known, no fixed profession, owning no property, paying no taxes)'.[91] Major-General Sanford, commanding Mirat District, was impressed by Sutherland's findings. They illustrated the role that Bengali *babus* were apt to play, he explained. In other words, 'persons of this class in Government service are as prone to make complaints and foster agitation as they are when in independent employ'. He concluded that the petition was unworthy of consideration, but as it was addressed to the Governor-General in Council he was unable to stop it.[92] Lieutenant-General Sir W. K. Ellis, commanding Her Majesty's Forces in the Bengal Presidency, agreed that the petition was unworthy of consideration.[93] But the Government of India issued instructions that the rule should not be operated with regard to 'well-to-do and respectable persons', and a polite reply was returned to the petitioners.[94] The military authorities could no longer go about their business without regard to public opinion, English or Indian.

In this difficult period, when they saw British soldiers deprived of protection from VD, the military authorities again tried to formulate explanations for the relative immunity of sepoys. The Principal Medical Officer to the Forces in India and the Commander-in-Chief identified a number of reasons apart from marriage. As Indians, sepoys were seen as having certain advantages: 'being Natives of the Country they have better information and a wider field for illicit sexual intercourse'. So far as Hindus were concerned, 'the obligations of caste' saved them from the dangers of 'promiscuous cohabitation'. On the other hand, 'a religious operation and a religious injunction as to hygiene are believed to give Mahomedans some protection'. In general, the sepoy was 'less prone to drink' and therefore 'more discriminating in his choice of a temporary companion'. Also, his staple food was not as 'stimulating' as that of a British soldier. An economic explanation was also possible: the sepoy sent much of his pay home to his family; when he had fed and clothed himself he had 'little margin out of his pay to spend on pleasure'.[95] In all these respects the British soldier seemed the more vulnerable.

The statistics soon confirmed this. The Government of India reported in November 1896 that the annual VD admissions among British troops in India had risen to 522·3 per 1,000.[96] The idea that over half the British army in India had VD had an explosive effect on

English opinion. In an editorial headed 'The Great Military Problem', the *Pioneer Mail* of Allahabad urged the authorities to follow the example of the French and German armies, in which the regulation of prostitution had reduced the incidence of VD to insignificance.[97] In London *The Times* treated the matter with appropriate solemnity. The *Lancet* referred with approval to the *Pioneer Mail*. England must certainly learn from Europe. 'We must look the facts in the face. Nature has implanted in every man, in common with the lower animals, an appetite so strong that it is hopeless to suppose we can successfully war against it.' Nor should young soldiers be allowed to marry : for a young man to marry regardless of his ability to maintain a wife and family meant 'misery, suffering and an early death'.[98] This gloomy, if dramatic, line of reasoning led to the conclusion there was no alternative to regulated prostitution.

The urbane Lord George Hamilton was now Secretary of State in a Conservative ministry. He appointed a departmental committee under the Earl of Onslow to consider the problem, but before the committee reported he had already decided what should be done. He wrote privately to Elgin in February 1897 : 'We must do something at once to revive the old precautions in force in India. We shall have a bitter controversy here, but it must be faced.'[99] He noted with satisfaction that there had been 'a great change of opinion here amongst educated persons'.[100]

It was soon apparent that a number of educated persons were energetically applying the means of pressure open to them. The Royal United Service Institution was a convenient forum. Major-General Dashwood lectured there on the high rate of VD among British troops in India as compared with the low rates in European armies. The Government of India, he said, should be given a free hand. *The Times* promptly called for a change of policy.[101] The Army Sanitary Commission produced a recantation: they had previously pronounced the old system of regulated prostitution to be 'a failure' ; now they realized that although it had failed to lower the level of VD it had at least checked its increase. Some 'control of prostitution', they concluded, seemed 'a reasonable method' of checking the further spread of VD.[102] The Royal College of Surgeons and the Royal College of Physicians both expressed concern at the figures and urged a change of policy.[103]

The Onslow Committee made effective use of statistics. They found, taking the mean of the three years from 1890 to 1892, that the VD admissions of British troops in India were much higher, 438·1 per

1,000, than those of British troops at home – 203·7 – and that European armies had much lower figures – for example, 27·3 per 1,000 in the German army and 43·8 in the French. They also described in harrowing detail the effects of tertiary syphilis on young soldiers disfigured and slowly dying in Netley hospital.[104]

Much publicity was given to this. The *Daily Telegraph* called it 'a simply appalling document'. The Liberal Government had sacrificed young soldiers to 'the prejudices of a few score of masculine women and womanish men'.[105] Three days later the *Daily Telegraph* returned to the attack : the Secretary of State should now call upon the House of Commons to 'rescind the monstrous resolution by which the Indian authorities were compelled to establish free trade in contagious disease'. It was only because of 'the abject cowardice which preferred to sacrifice an Army rather than to defy a canting clique' that this resolution had not met with the 'contemptuous neglect' with which the authorities had treated the more recent Commons resolution in favour of holding simultaneous ICS examinations in India as well as England to benefit Indian candidates.[106] In his agitation Earl Fortescue wrote a letter to *The Times* to demonstrate the threat to the English people : deaths from VD had risen from 499 in 1893 to 2,011 in 1894.[107] It was several days before another correspondent pointed out that the troubled earl had compared the figures for London in 1893 with those for England in 1894.[108]

It might have been expected that the recognition, in the Onslow Report, that the Indian figures included readmissions, would have blunted their effect. If readmissions were excluded, the figure for 1895 would be reduced to 391 per 1,000. This was only mentioned in a footnote in the Onslow Report, and it was duly noted in *The Times* and the *Lancet*, but such a detail was overshadowed by the graphic description of sufferers from syphilis in Netley hospital.[109] But even those who concerned themselves with accuracy may well have reflected that a ratio as large as 391 per 1,000 justified some change of policy.

Elgin wrote privately to Hamilton that he was afraid of going too far. Some of his colleagues were 'disposed to ride the turn of feeling very hard', but he feared that the result might be 'only too probably another swing of the pendulum and all that we gain now will be swept away'. The doctors wanted compulsory examinations. He accepted that the problem was that a soldier would not betray the woman who had infected him, and that doctors therefore had difficulty in detecting which women had VD. He suggested that voluntary examinations be allowed again, together with the power of expulsion from cantonments, which could be used as a means of persuasion. But he did not want officers to be again in the position of disregarding the Commons resolution. Could it be rescinded ? Also, men who caught VD should be penalized by stoppage of pay while in hospital. This would have two advantages : first, 'it takes away the reproach that we only punish and harry the women' ; secondly, 'these young fellows go astray a great deal from simple thoughtlessness, and anything that would make them reflect for a moment would have a restraining influence'.[110]

At the same time, Onslow privately warned Elgin not to go too far. Any more circulars about the need for young and good-looking women would put the ministry in a difficult position in Parliament. Anything which had 'even the appearance of facilitating, sanctioning or making vice more attractive' would alienate potential supporters.[111] This was a fair assessment of the climate of opinion in England.

Towards the end of March 1897, Hamilton decided that the time was ripe to announce a change of policy. The Onslow Report, he told Elgin with satisfaction, was 'still making a great stir', and he felt confident of the support of a large majority in Parliament.[112] A lengthy despatch was constructed, with extensive quotations from the Onslow Report. Although it was addressed to the Governor-General in Council, its arguments were clearly devised for the benefit of opinion in England. Hamilton knew that he had no need to convince the authorities in India. Some solemn warnings were therefore included to the effect that there should be 'no provision of women for the use of soldiers', and no registration of prostitutes except for that which applied to all inhabitants of cantonments. Nor were prostitutes to be allowed to live in regimental bazars. But nothing was said about their presence in the *sadr*, or main, bazar of each cantonment, where they now in fact lived. After these protestations of respectability, the new policy was explained as a decision to treat VD like other contagious diseases. This meant compulsion, and there followed an elaborate justification :

It may be argued that the examination of women which may, but need not necessarily, be held under these rules, is in effect compulsory. Her Majesty's Government do not share this view. But if there be any compulsion it is precisely of the same kind as that which has been accepted as necessary and enforced without any objection in the case of diphtheria or scarlet fever. There will be no obligation on women to attend hospital, but as an alternative to doing so they will be required to leave the cantonment, and rightly so, as an almost certain cause of disease to others.

The old suspicion that solders were infected by a 'low class of women' who haunted the barrack areas after dark and tempted them was expressed in a general admonition to reduce as far as possible the number of women employed there, and there was also an exhortation to improve the facilities available to the troops for 'instruction, occupation and recreation'.[113]

Hamilton was delighted with the reaction to his despatch in England. It had had 'an extraordinary success', he told Elgin. Stuart and his colleagues were powerless. Elgin could treat the new policy as a reversal of the previous one. The 1895 Act could be repealed forthwith and new rules should be drafted, which could be published in a parliamentary paper. 'In this way we could again challenge the Social Purity party, but so long as feeling remains as it now is, the anti-restriction party will not be able to do much.'[114]

The reaction was even more satisfactory than Hamilton had expected. A memorial was drawn up in favour of effective protection for the British soldier and signed by a number of society ladies headed by a Princess and including a variety of Duchesses, Viscountesses and others, not to speak of Mrs Humphrey Ward and Florence Nightingale, although the last two only signed subject to the establishment of further local enquiries.[115] The British Committee of the Federation for the Abolition of the State Regulation of Vice submitted a memorial to the effect that the new policy amounted to a restoration of the old.[116] But Lady Henry Somerset, President of the World's Women's Christian Temperance Union, wrote to Hamilton to urge even stronger measures : prostitutes should be confined to a specific part of the cantonment, and men who went there should be registered and medically inspected. She justified this on the ground that it would be 'a system as stringent for men as for women'.[117] At this point, the reformers seemed to be disagreeing among themselves. A few months later Mrs Josephine Butler, a veteran of many such campaigns, resigned from this organization in protest against Lady Henry Somerset's propositions.[118] Lady Henry Somerset subsequently retracted.[119] But such disagreements were comforting to the authorities.

Hamilton's confidence was unbounded. The Commons resolution

need not be rescinded. To rescind it would be inconvenient, for it might imply that a Commons resolution ought to be obeyed – and there was no intention of obeying the resolution in favour of simultaneous examinations for ics candidates.[120] Some tact might, however, be prudent when the papers were presented to Parliament. Onslow pointed out that it would be 'quite clear' that 'a system of periodical examinations' would be set up under the new rules. 'If any disease exists amongst soldiers in a cantonment there will be prima facie evidence that disease exists among the women there and a threat of expulsion will at once bring them all to submit to voluntary examination.' The important thing was to ensure that the new policy was efficacious. 'If we try to disarm the opposition of Messrs Stuart and Wilson by concessions to their opinions we shall only weaken the hands of the Executive in India.' If the vd figures then increased, the reformers could begin another campaign. On the other hand, something could be done to conciliate those who wanted to raise moral standards. Onslow confessed that he had not 'much hope in that direction'. But there would be advantages in bringing to Parliament the orders to be issued by the Commander-in-Chief at the same time as the new rules were presented.[121] When they considered the new rules, members were therefore edified to read, in an accompanying paper, a General Order in which the Commander-in-Chief urged officers to encourage their men in 'healthy exercise and physical recreation', not forgetting 'social recreation, interesting mental occupation and reading'. Also, suitable officers should give 'lectures to the men on the moral and physical degradation which is the almost certain result of consorting with loose women in India'.[122]

Hamilton meanwhile reassured Elgin in a private letter that 'we may safely risk associating periodical examination with some form of indirect pressure'. He understood that the women had no real objection to these examinations, although he did not explain how he had learnt this. However, 'the mere knowledge that the Government tendency inclines towards examination will, I believe, be quite sufficient to ensure their coming in'.[123] He welcomed the proposal to impose penal stoppages from the pay of men admitted to hospital for vd because it would show a determination to punish men as well as women for contracting such a disease, and the reformers were apt to argue that such policies of control discriminated against women.[124] However, the War Office refused to allow this on the ground that it would encourage men to conceal their infection. Also, it would be unfair that the more serious a man's illness and the longer his stay in hospital, the greater would be his penalty.[125]

A few local difficulties attended the introduction of the new policy. The grass cutters of Fort William protested against the exclusion of their wives from the area. Presumably they felt strongly enough to employ a professional petition-writer. They began in traditional style: 'Sir, we are your Honour's poor servants and earn our honest bread by cutting grass in the fort.' The substance of their complaint seemed reasonable enough. Hitherto they had done their work 'comfortably' with their wives, 'without which [sic] we cannot possibly earn enough to keep a married couple in a station like Calcutta where living is so dear'. There was no danger to the soldiers: 'As for our women, they are of good character and all married. We come to work daily at about 11 a.m. accompanied by our wives; in up-country those people most likely have accommodation close to the lines of British troops where there are [sic] every chance of such occurrence.'[126] The Garrison Quartermaster strongly recommended that this be treated 'as a special case on condition that the women confine their work to the outer ditches of the fort'.[127] This was duly allowed, 'provided they are confined to the ditch and leave the fort before dusk'.[128]

In general the new system was soon operating smoothly, or at least to the satisfaction of the military authorities, and gratifying statistics were quickly produced. Admissions for VD seemed to be declining almost at once: 485·7 per 1,000 in 1897, 362·9 per 1,000 in 1898. The *Shield*, a reformist journal, suggested that medical officers might well apply stricter standards when there were no rules than when they felt that health was safeguarded by rules. The *British Medical Journal* also suggested that methods of treatment were improving: there was a growing tendency to treat patients until they were cured, rather than until the symptoms disappeared. In other words, readmissions might be diminishing.[129]

The figures fell again to 313·4 per 1,000 in 1899 and to 298·1 in 1900. By then, Surgeon-General Taylor, Principal Medical Officer to the Forces in India, felt that some explanations were necessary. The decrease, he admitted, was 'partly unreal, and due to the treating of venereal cases as out patients'. But he claimed that it was also partly real, and as contributory factors he mentioned the new Cantonments Act and rules, the more prolonged treatment of cases, 'improved discipline and moral tone', lectures on moral dangers, 'games and athletics', and 'the provision of lotions and towels for the men in barracks'.[130] In 1901 he conceded that there was a 'personal element' in diagnosis, and he explained the low ratio in the Royal Engineers by reference to the large number of married men in that Corps.[131]

Perhaps Dyer was right after all ? But the spirit had gone out of the agitation. Mrs Andrew and Dr Bushnell returned to India on another visit of inspection in 1899. On their return in 1900 they painted a discouraging picture. The *Shield* commented that the 1888 resolution of the House of Commons had in effect been nullified.[132] The military authorities had won the last battle in a long campaign.

4
On the Margins of Social Distance

When Lord Cornwallis left India in 1793 the East India Company's servants had been transformed into a bureaucracy with exclusive rights to responsible posts, with security of tenure and with high salaries. That it was proper for them to function as a small, aloof elite was an assumption increasingly held from the end of the eighteenth century. It was bluntly explained to the House of Commons in 1793 by Henry Dundas, who as president of the Board of Control had a general oversight of the affairs of the East India Company. He strongly opposed the idea that Europeans should be allowed to settle freely in the Company's territories. The result, he argued, would be to 'annihilate the respect paid to the British character, and ruin our Indian empire'. If the British came to India in any number, this would 'eradicate that feeling, which is so general among the natives, of the superiority of the European character'.[1]

Eurasians had already begun to suffer from this transformation. It soon became obvious that their social and economic position was inferior to that of their counterparts in territories under the rule of other colonial powers. Even in nearby Ceylon the Burgher community enjoyed a much better position. But British rule only began there in 1796, after almost three centuries of Portuguese and Dutch rule, and the Dutch were particularly tolerant of intermarriage.[2]

At first, however, the English in India accepted Eurasians as colleagues and friends. In the seventeenth century the East India Company encouraged the growth of a Eurasian community as a support for English activities. In 1687 the Court of Directors wrote to their officials at Madras that 'the marriage of our soldiers to the Native women' was 'a matter of such consequence to posterity that we shall be content to encourage it with some expense and have been thinking for the future to appoint a Pagoda to be paid to the Mother of any child that shall hereafter be born, of any such future marriage, upon the day the child be christened, if you think this small encouragement will increase the number of such marriages'. They added prudently 'but, if you think it will not have any considerable effect that way, we had better keep our money, which we leave to your consideration . . . '.[3] The payments were duly instituted.

Army officers and civil servants also had children by Indian wives and mistresses, and for the greater part of the eighteenth century Eurasian youths with influential fathers became civil servants or officers in the Company's armies. But as British rule prospered these posts became more desirable, and the Cornwallis reforms were increasing their desirability : the Court of Directors became the more eager to exert their rights to this patronage, unimpeded by such claims. In 1791 they resolved that Eurasians could no longer be appointed to the Company's civil, military or marine services. This meant their exclusion from the covenanted or higher grade of the civil service, from commission in the army and from officer posts in the marine.[4] This exclusion did not apply generally to those already appointed, although one marine officer not long in the service asked to be allowed to remain and was refused.[5] The local recruitment of Eurasians to clerical posts continued, although they were also excluded from all but non-combatant posts in the rank and file of the army. There were some exceptions.[6] But however many exceptions there might be, there was discrimination, and Eurasians resented it.

When Parliament enquired into the East India Company's affairs, before renewing its charter in 1833, John Ricketts, a leading Calcutta Eurasian, came to London with a petition on behalf of his community. He was himself a locally appointed official, as Deputy Registrar of the Board of Customs in Calcutta. He appeared before select committees of both Houses of Parliament, and answered their questions with an impressive command of detailed argument.

The main objection which officials put forward against the advancement of Eurasians was that Indians despised them. This idea appeared in different forms. Officials liked to think that besides being few and strange they were respected because they were gentlemen. William Chaplin, who had served in responsible office in western India, told a parliamentary select committee in 1830 that 'the respect and reverence the natives now have for the English' would be diminished by the presence of 'Europeans of the middling or lower classes'.[7] In fact, few of the covenanted service were of aristocratic birth, but all lived in an aristocratic style in India. Restrictions on the entry of Europeans were abolished in 1833, and some more came, as planters, lawyers and businessmen, but the official elite kept their distance.

It was also suggested that Indians objected to Eurasians because of their mixed birth. Chaplin argued that it would detract from the prestige of the official elite 'to admit persons of half-blood to higher situations, for the native gentry of the country would look upon them with no respect; they look down upon them very much'. Foreign birth was not the point at issue. Muslims of high status would claim that their forefathers came from central Asia, or from Iran, or from Arabia. High-caste or 'twice-born' Hindus would claim descent from the Aryan-speaking invaders who came into India in the second millennium BC. But the Hindus at least objected to intermarriage between castes. It might have been expected that they would therefore despise Eurasians. But to the pious Hindu all Europeans were unclean, whether they associated with Eurasians or not. Also the fact was that many Eurasian officers had commanded Indian troops with great success, and some were employed as officers in the armies of Indian rulers.

But Major-General Sir Jasper Nicolls testified in 1832 that Eurasians should not be given commissions in the army because there was 'so strong a prejudice against them on the part of the natives'.[8] More crudely, Ricketts was asked by a member of the House of Commons select committee whether the exclusion of Eurasians from higher posts was not based on 'the belief of your appearance and your colour being likely to affect you in the estimation of the natives of India ?'[9] He denied that Indians did in fact despise Eurasians.

Ricketts also told the parliamentary committees about several outstanding Eurasian officers, including Colonel Stevenson, Quartermaster-General, Bengal, who had been commissioned before 1791. The celebrated Colonel Skinner was another example. R.D. Mangles, an experienced civil servant, told the House of Lords select committee that Skinner was a man with much property. Moreover, he was 'a man of great influence among the native population; he could raise, I should think, 10,000 men at any time'.[10] But the British were unlikely to see this as an argument in favour of improving the prospects for Eurasians. Such men might be dangerous. At the turn of the century there had been fears that a strong Eurasian community might be a political threat: there was talk of Eurasian leadership in the revolt in Haiti.

In fact few Eurasians were rich or influential. Many, especially those of Portuguese origin, were poor Roman Catholics whom the British tended to distrust for their religion and despise for their poverty. Although many possibilities of prosperous employment had been closed to them by government policy, their lack of prosperity was often cited as evidence of fecklessness and lack of enterprise, and the fact that few Eurasians attained positions of eminence was often cited as evidence of a lack of ability and energy. Similar stereotypes were applied to Western-educated Bengalis, or *babus*, later in the century. Both Eurasians and babus might be expected to know more of India than Englishmen, and so to have strong claims to be appointed to responsible posts. Their claims could be undermined by stereotypes which implied a deficiency in character and morals.

However, in the Act that renewed the Company's charter in 1833 it was provided that neither religion, birthplace, descent or colour should be a bar to official employment. Eurasians now hoped for better things. But these were slow to appear. Even the christening payments at Madras were formally abolished in 1835:[11] James Metcalfe, the Eurasian son of Sir Charles Metcalfe, a distinguished Company official, was appointed to a military cadetship in 1836, and Lord Dalhousie, who became Governor-General in 1848, chose this same Lieutenant Metcalfe as one of his aides-de-camp. Less highly connected Eurasians still had to content themselves with subordinate employment in government offices, in the police and as officials in newly conquered territories.

When Parliament next enquired into the Company's affairs, before renewing its charter in 1853, Eurasians complained that little had changed in twenty years. Some Eurasians of Bengal protested in a memorial that 'A gulph divides the subordinate from the dominant class, which the former is not allowed to pass. In many cases experience and efficiency must submit to be ruled by a covenanted superior possessing no knowledge or previous experience.' Official witnesses again asserted that Eurasians were not respected. But the Eurasians retorted that 'The members of the covenanted service, indeed, evince small consideration or respect for either East Indians or natives, or even for Europeans, out of the pale of those services.'[12]

There was one exception – Charles Trevelyan, Macaulay's brother-in-law, a brilliant civil servant with a reforming reputation. Before an unsympathetic parliamentary committee he protested that the language used by several witnesses about Eurasians had been 'very ungenerous'. They had to struggle against the disadvantages of a marginal position : 'their situation is unfortunately very equivocal, midway between the Natives and the Europeans – not owned by either – and whatever faults they have, are mainly due owing to the sensitiveness caused by that unhappy situation.' A common saying among the British was that Eurasians shared the vices of both races, but Trevelyan asserted that they united 'many of the good qualities of the English and of the Natives of India. With the amiability and quickness and tact of the Natives of India, they unite a great deal of the energy and high moral qualities of Europeans.' They would be valuable in all government departments. He cited examples. A committee member asked whether these were a fair sample. 'The only reason why we have not more like them is because they have not had fair play given them.' Also Eurasian women were 'among the best of wives and mothers'. Lord Ellenborough interjected : 'Are not the ladies of that class physically much better than the gentlemen ?' Trevelyan denied it. 'Are not the generality of Indo-Britons a class of poor weakly-looking persons, very sallow and unhealthy in their appearance, and very small in stature ?' Similar questions followed. 'Are they not inferior to the Natives in physical qualities ?' 'You would not say that the persons called Crannies were a fair sample of the human race, should you ?' The word 'Cranny' was a contemptuous nickname for a Eurasian clerk. To these questions Trevelyan replied that Eurasians varied in stature and appearance just as Englishmen did. If Eurasians were not as strong as Indian peasants, neither were many Englishmen.[13]

When Trevelyan became Governor of Madras in 1859, these statements were recalled in the local press, and it was noted that Eurasians as well as Europeans and Indians were invited to his levees. Perhaps the fortunes of the Eurasian community were about to improve ? After all, the Mutiny of 1857 had enabled them to show their support for British rule. Charles Forjett, Bombay's intrepid Superintendent of Police, was a Eurasian, and during the Mutiny he had displayed his courage and resourcefulness in many heroic exploits, often in disguise. Publicity was also given to Eurasians who had served with credit in various medical capacities with the Bengal and Madras armies.[14] But the case of Assistant Surgeon Gillies, a Eurasian who had encountered difficulties, was then attracting attention. He was one of six former students of Madras Medical College who had passed their professional examinations in England

and had thereafter been appointed to commissions with Indian regiments. Another had been given a commission in the Queen's army.[15] These developments were denounced in the editorial columns of the *Madras Daily Times* : such men had been 'elevated out of the sphere in which they were bred and born', and did not know how to behave among gentlemen ; they were crammed with book knowledge, but they could not read the page of nature and make good use of their knowledge.[16] A Eurasian spokesman retorted that English doctors appeared 'too much like *burra sahibs* in the eyes of the natives to win their confidence'. The Government should at least appoint Eurasians as civil surgeons and give 'the people of India, at a less cost, practitioners whom they can fully appreciate'.[17]

Here in a new form was the Eurasian challenge to the British monopoly of responsible posts : by virtue of their birth they were more suited to certain posts than the 'burra sahibs', or great men of the English elite. Officially, there was now no racial bar to office. Also the technical competence of these Eurasians was admitted. But were they gentlemen? Physicians and surgeons in England had earnestly struggled towards this desirable status, and had only recently achieved it.[18] Their colleagues in India were sensitive about such matters. There was also much dissatisfaction at promotion prospects in the Indian army. Assistant Surgeons in the Queen's regiments, complained an anonymous correspondent in the Madras *Athenaeum*, were promoted to the rank of Surgeon in about five years. Yet the senior Assistant Surgeon in the Madras army had served for over eighteen years and was still waiting for promotion.[19] But within official circles there was also concern about standards. There had been a very unfortunate case a few years ago.

A succession of adverse reports had been received about the incompetence of a certain Surgeon Supple. It was said that his patients had been 'reduced to a state of extreme debility' as a result of his practice of dosing them with harsh laxatives. When the acting Superintending Surgeon inspected the regimental hospital he found that Surgeon Supple had 'administered a full purging dose' to one patient who was suffering merely from 'a trifling contusion' – this was a cavalry regiment. There was also a fatal case of beri beri, which Surgeon Supple had mistaken for rheumatism. One Lieutenant Thompson was suffering from ophthalmia, but Surgeon Supple had unaccountably diagnosed his ailment as otitis. Finally, the commanding officer complained to the Assistant Adjutant-General that Surgeon Supple, still worried about constipation, had made himself seriously ill by swallowing borax under the impression that he was giving himself a dose of salts. The commanding officer was understandably anxious : 'this occurring at a time when an Officer had been poisoned in Scinde by a Medical Officer administering the wrong medicine, the circumstance caused alarm in the Regiment'. The Madras Government thereupon took action. Surgeon Supple was removed to Bangalore, where he would serve under the constant supervision of the surgeon of artillery.[20]

The appointment of keen and highly-qualified young Eurasians must have troubled many of the old-established medical officers, discontented with the slowness of promotion and aware of suspicions of incompetence. Josiah Dashwood Gillies was an outstanding member of the new generation of Eurasian Assistant Surgeons. He began as an Assistant Apothecary, worked his way through Madras Medical College, and in 1855 at the age of 29 went to Britain to be examined. He was admitted MRCS and was also awarded an MD degree by the University of St Andrews. His examiners at the Royal College of Surgeons were so impressed by his performance that they made a special recommendation that he be appointed an Assistant Surgeon by the East India Company even though he had exceeded the age limit.[21] He was duly appointed, and at first he seems to have had considerable success. But he decided to specialize in women's diseases – sociologically an unwise choice.

He was attached to the 5th Regiment, Madras Native Infantry, and also attended various civilians in the neighbourhood. W.L Heeley, Assistant Magistrate and Collector, Cuttack, later recalled how Gillies had cured Mrs Heeley of 'a more or less exhausting ailment'. He did not say what it was, but merely that she had been suffering 'daily and nightly attacks of acute pain'. Before the Heeleys consulted Gillies, two other doctors 'entirely mistook her case : one of them, indeed, to an extent that would have been ludicrous, had it not been so highly dangerous'.[22] Then Mrs Stonehouse, the wife of a Lieutenant in his regiment, died of puerperal peritonitis while under Gillies' care. Dr Duncan Macpherson, the Inspector-General of Hospitals, who happened to be in the neighbourhood, heard 'rumours of an unfavourable nature', and hastened to Berhampur to investigate.

Macpherson suspended Gillies from duty, and wrote a long and rambling report which he sent to the Director-General of the Medical Department, Madras, in March 1859. His conclusion was that Gillies' professional conduct had been 'disgraceful' and that he was 'a discreditable member of our profession'. In particular, Macpherson instanced 'his worse than empiricism in his treatment of the late Mrs Stonehouse; his insulting and low-lifed behaviour to his female patients, who, be it remembered, have no option, and no escape from him; his abominably filthy habits; his want of veracity and the extreme contempt and dislike evinced towards him by all those with whom he has been associated'.[23]

In due course, Macpherson's report was forwarded to Gillies for his comments. Gillies dealt briskly and at times sarcastically with Macpherson's criticisms. For example 'the view taken by the Inspector-General of the pathology of puerperal peritonitis has been laid aside for many years, and is not now taught in any school of medicine'.[24] Macpherson criticized him for not using chloroform. But although the patient had asked for it Gillies explained that he refused because he had no qualified assistant available and because many authorities had come to deprecate its use in labour.

Gillies seemed indeed to have had some justification for his impatience with Macpherson's criticisms. Macpherson, for example, stated at length how Gillies had reported that 'the foetus descended into the pelvis with its hand resting on the crown of the head. On pointing to him the impossibility of delivery under such circumstances he attempted to show, that by the introduction of his hand he caused that of the infant to withdraw, thus permitting the head to descend alone.' Macpherson concluded triumphantly: 'Now I need not tell you that in all hand presentations the operation of turning becomes necessary. But as this does not appear to have been done, we may conclude that Dr Gillies misstates the case in this particular.'[25] Gillies had no difficulty in showing that this was an ignorant comment and he had in fact delivered the baby successfully. He added: 'I cannot but feel that it is hard to be accused of malpraxis in a point where every obstetrician knows that I am right. . . .' And the Director-General had to agree with Gillies. He merely remarked, with reference to Macpherson's criticism: 'This is an unaccountable error, which I am at a loss to comprehend, and Assistant Surgeon Gillies has readily taken advantage of it.'[26] But Gillies had, after all, been accused by Macpherson of professional incompetence and worse.

On the other hand, the Director-General accepted Macpherson's criticism that the afterbirth should have been removed at once instead of waiting three hours. Gillies answered that the delay had only been

half as long as that. But there had been a delay, in view of the anxiety
felt by his patient, 'an extremely excitable and nervous lady, narrowly
watching every act of mine, and ignorant of anything having to come
away after the birth of the child'.[27] He had assumed, from the size of
the uterus, that the placenta had passed into the vagina, from which he
later removed it. But the Director-General agreed with Macpherson
that the placenta should have been removed immediately.
Macpherson's implication was that Gillies had been too concerned
about his own comfort. He had taken evidence from the dead
woman's ayah, or personal maid, to the effect that Gillies went off to
have dinner and returned three hours later to remove the afterbirth.
But Gillies protested that that he had merely waited in an adjoining
room while his patient recovered from her ordeal.

Macpherson made other criticism of a technical nature, but when
the papers were referred to a committee of senior medical officers they
concluded that in important matters Gillies had acted with 'skill and
judgement', although in certain other respects his treatment was open
to grave objections; however, they were not prepared to say that he
had treated the case so unskilfully as to hasten its fatal termination.[28]

Both Macpherson and the committee were troubled by the nurses'
reports that Mrs Stonehouse had been embarrassed because Gillies
removed the sheet to examine her. On one occasion, Gillies noted that
when she complained of pain, 'I again examined the abdomen she
bore pressure tolerably well over every part save the uterus where there
was some pain on firm pressure'.[29] On this Macpherson commented
that it 'corroborates the assertions of the attendants that this constant
meddlesome and coarse interference occasioned the greatest distress
to the poor sufferer, for each time it was resorted to, the sheet was
withdrawn and her whole person exposed'.[30] Gillies denied that he
had ever exposed her whole body, but pointed out that it was now
expected of a physician that he should examine his patients and not
rely merely on their descriptions of their symptoms.

Macpherson and the committee were also troubled by the fact that
Gillies had excluded the nurses from the confinement and had washed
the patient and applied dressings himself. The committee expressed
surprise at 'his having performed many menial offices on her
person'.[31] But Gillies belonged to a new generation of doctors. He had
been in England when publicity was being given to Florence
Nightingale's early attempts to improve nursing standards. He
considered the available nurses incompetent, and offended two of

them – Mrs Carter and Mrs Cloete – who both testified against him. He had refused to give Mrs Carter a testimonial to her skill in midwifery because, he wrote, she 'knows little or nothing about it'. He remembered, too, that he had annoyed Mrs Cloete by refusing to give her husband a sick certificate to enable him to go home to South Africa for two years : Cloete merely had a slight digestive disorder which he had cured.

Macpherson also accused Gillies of 'abominably filthy habits'. He seems to have been referring to an allegation that Gillies failed to use a pocket handkerchief when sitting at tea with a Major Wyndham and other officers. Gillies replied : 'I never had the pleasure of taking tea with the Major at his table, but often at my own when we were marching to Sumbulpore in the depth of the monsoon.' Gillies had served there during the Mutiny. 'On one of these occasions when we were taking tea under a tree, the Major said to me, "Gillies, you are a jolly fellow, but I observed a while ago that you blew your nose through your fingers."' Gillies had answered that he did not remember having done so, and would be careful not to do so. Gillies added that the incident had not deterred the Major from coming to tea again, or from inviting Gillies to dine, or from dining with Gillies at Berhampur.[32]

Macpherson's final indictment against Gillies was of 'his want of veracity and the extreme contempt and dislike evinced towards him by all those with whom he has been associated'. The idea that he was untruthful seems to have arisen from a statement from Dr Cooper, Superintending Surgeon, to the effect that he advised Gillies to be careful in answering queries about patients, in that he often gave 'an evasive or general answer ; sometimes that the patient was better when he was the same, etc.'. Gillies, on the other hand, recalled that he had asked Cooper for advice about how to answer queries concerning the illnesses of women patients : 'as the patients were females, this difficulty was the more embarrassing, and it was to avoid it that I had to give evasive or general answers'. However, Cooper nevertheless had a good opinion of Gillies, both as a doctor and as a man. He reminded Macpherson, 'I expressly told you that the Officer Commanding the Regiment gave me a very good character of the estimation in which Dr. Gillies was then held.'[33]

In fact, the evidence of two commanding officers was in conflict. Colonel Richard Shubrick, who commanded the 5th Native Infantry for almost all the time that Gillies served with them, testified strongly in his favour : 'I gave Dr. Macpherson very clearly to understand that as regards your character, conduct, attention to your duties, care of your hospital and general bearing in society, I had no fault whatever to find with you, that I deemed you deserving of all respect – that in no way and in no one particular during the time that you were in medical charge of the Corps had I cause to complain of you, or even to think of you otherwise than very well.'[34] On the other hand, Lieutenant-Colonel Macleane, who commanded the 43rd Native Infantry with whom Gillies had served for two months, had formed a very different opinion during that short period. By a coincidence he and Gillies had sailed to England on the same ship in 1855. Then he had approved of Gillies : 'his habits were very studious indeed, his conduct most respectful and correct'. But he had never thought that Gillies would be 'more than a Veterinary Surgeon'. When Macleane saw Gillies as a medical officer in his regiment he was shocked to see that he behaved with much 'familiarity' to the other officers ; he was even prepared to argue with his commanding officer about the propriety of going shooting with an officer who had a sore foot, on the ground that he would be able to see the effect of exercise. According to Macleane he later denied that he had said this. Macleane concluded that 'Dr. Gillies was not steady to any thing, and therefore not steady to veracity.' It was only to be expected when people rose above their station : 'I believe that he has been totally upset by his rise in the world.' Of course Macleane thought him unpopular in the regiment : 'every one seemed sorry when he was appointed, and glad when he left'. Macleane hastened to add that 'the prejudice was not so much against his extraction, as against his manners and general ignorance'. Unfortunately, Macleane then went on to assert a similar prejudice : 'I should say that no man of Dr. Gillies' class and antecedents can make himself fit for the delicate and responsible position of a Medical Officer.'[35]

But Gillies was able to produce an impressive number of letters in his favour. Major Kempt, Station Commander, Berhampur :' I am of opinion that your general character and conduct was correct, and that you were very attentive to your duties.'[36] Ward, Civil and Sessions Judge, Cuttack : 'Having often met Dr. Gillies in private parties, I have always seen him behave in a quiet and gentlemanly manner and I have never observed the slightest intemperance.'[37] The Rev. W.B. Ottley, Station Chaplain, Berhampur, claimed that he had come to know Gillies well : his behaviour in society was 'satisfactory, marked indeed by much propriety and good sense and feeling'. Anyone who doubted his veracity must have been prejudiced against him 'as one of a class'.[38] There were a number of letters from grateful patients or their husbands. Captain Dixon, Executive Engineer, enclosed a snuffbox and three photographs he had taken of Gillies, as a slight memorial for your able and kind professional services to my dear wife'.[39] Mrs Heeley told Gillies that 'Mamma' had written that everyone at home had drunk his health on Christmas day, and her mother, no less a person than the sister-in-law of a baronet, also wrote to thank him for his 'fatherly kindness' to her daughter.[40]

In short, Gillies had little difficulty in showing that Macpherson was incorrect in asserting that he was unpopular among officers, or that ladies were unwilling to be his patients. But he did not conceal his contempt for Macpherson's failure to keep abreast of developments in medicine, or for his other lapses. For example, when Macpherson referred to statements in 'Gentoo and Malabar', Gillies commented drily, 'Teloogoo and Tamil, I presume.'[41] However, Macpherson's hostility was apparent throughout these proceedings. That Gillies should feel a certain resentment was understandable. But the Director-General of the Medical Department was shocked by such presumption. He pointed out that Gillies had used improper language in referring to the Inspector-General of Hospitals. Gillies was given the opportunity of withdrawing his impolite criticisms, and did so. Then the Director-General submitted his final report, in which he took note of 'the harsh and uncalled-for language' used by Macpherson about Gillies. Macpherson in turn was invited to withdraw such expressions, and did so.[42]

When he first saw Macpherson's report, the Commander-in-Chief had noted that 'neither Assistant Surgeon Gillies nor any other East Indian brought up and educated in India should ever be placed in a position to afford medical aid to European ladies and families'.[43] In his final report on the case the Director-General returned to this point. It was a mistake, he asserted, to give such men commissions. They should have been made warrant officers : 'this course would not have withdrawn them from their own class, or placed them in a false position, one in which though equals in virtue of holding Her Majesty's Commission, they are, nevertheless, not looked upon by the other Officers of the service as on an equality in a social sense'. Making a perceptible effort to be fair, he added that those who by 'superior merit' had raised themselves from the subordinate to the commissioned ranks of the army deserved 'every encouragement and support'. But he concluded 'that objections (prejudices, they may be called) do exist in many instances, against employing them as the medical attendants of European families, and as accoucheurs, is I believe a fact, that does not admit of the least doubt'.[44]

When he saw this, the Commander-in-Chief returned to the attack. Ignoring the evidence, he asserted it to be a fact that no English gentleman would agree to his wife and family being treated by a Eurasian if he could choose.[45] Then the papers came to be considered by the Madras Government. Such an illiberal view could not be officially countenanced. On the other hand, it would have been impracticable to suggest that Gillies had been unfairly treated when the Commander-in-Chief, the Director-General of the Medical Department and the Inspector-General of Hospitals all felt so strongly that Eurasians should never have been given commissioned rank as medical officers. Instead, Members of Council penned a series of mellifluous minutes to demonstrate that they were themselves above prejudice and determined to face the issue squarely, if only in the abstract.

Trevelyan, as Governor, declared that Eurasians as a class ought not to be excluded from the opportunity of responsible medical employment. As with Europeans, their selection must depend on character and education.[46] This was hardly a realistic statement of the case with regard to European appointments, but Walter Elliott, an experienced civil servant, characteristically took his cue from the Governor. In a convoluted minute he first drew attention to his own tolerance by stating that he had met 'East Indians who were gentlemen in every sense of the word'. This was no question of race, he continued. He would object just as much to being treated by a doctor who was 'a low born or vulgar Englishman'. Class prejudice, it appeared, was acceptable, even if race prejudice were not. One must have gentlemen. It was not a matter of medical skill, or even of moral integrity: 'professional tests of ability even supported by testimonials of unimpeachable moral conduct are not sufficient guarantees for the fitness of a practitioner to prescribe for patients of the higher classes of society'. In short, 'the medical attendant of an English lady must be a Gentleman as well as a skilful practitioner'.[47]

This was the root of the matter. The treatment of English ladies might reasonably have been regarded as marginal to the duties of the medical officer of an Indian regiment. Instead, it was regarded as of overriding importance. What was at issue was the insistence of the English elite that their women should be protected from physical contact with Eurasian males. This explains the indignation with which Macpherson viewed the possibility that Gillies had actually removed the bedsheet and seen his patient's body. Similarly, when the committee of enquiry remarked with disapproval that Gillies had 'performed many menial offices on her person' – washing her and applying dressings – they were shocked not merely that a medical officer was doing the physical tasks normally performed by nurses but also at the fact that he was touching her intimately. This also explains the fact that those who felt this were able to ignore the evidence that English ladies had no objection to being treated by a Eurasian doctor. In their reactions, sexual and occupational jealousies were combined. Similarly, it had long been argued that Eurasians must not be appointed to commissions because Indians despised them and would not obey them, and those who so argued were able to ignore the evidence that many Eurasian officers were in fact obeyed as unquestioningly as English officers.

The Governor and his councillors had no qualms about washing their hands of Dr Gillies. Clearly, he could not be dismissed. They merely resolved that his fitness for employment in any particular duties was a professional question to be decided by the Director-General of the Medical Department. There was, however, a general question which could not be ignored. He had been appointed under the old system of patronage. This had now been replaced by competitive examinations. It was conceivable that persons who succeeded in competitive examinations might not be gentlemen. The Governor-in-Council solemnly resolved that 'gentlemanly habits and delicacy of feeling, whether in East Indians or Europeans, depend upon previous education and conduct; and it is very desirable that this essential point of professional qualification should not be over-looked by the examiners to whom the selection of medical officers is now entrusted'.[48]

Sir Charles Wood, the Secretary of State, had no comment to make upon the Madras Government's policy, or lack of policy, towards Gillies. But he sympathized with their anxiety that means should be devised to ensure that gentlemen were successful in the new system of examinations for the selection of medical officers. Under the existing rules a certificate of character was required from a magistrate or clergyman who had known the candidate for at least two years. He would also consider whether it might be wise to require 'some proficiency in the usual elements of a liberal education'.[49] Soon Wood was also arranging with the Civil Service Commissioners for the ICS examinations to be adjusted to favour 'University men who are gentlemen' rather than 'well crammed youths from Irish Universities or Commercial schools'.[50] Extra marks were therefore assigned to Greek and Latin. In public, on the other hand, he asserted that the aim was 'to get well educated young men wherever they are to be found, no matter where or in what manner their education has been acquired'.[51] In both matters, the instincts of elite preservation seem to have been similar.

But times were changing, however slowly. In October 1859, when the Gillies case was dragging to its close, the services of another Eurasian were warmly praised in General Orders. This was Apothecary George Dewsnap, who had served through the Mutiny with Her Majesty's 84th Regiment, sharing in the relief of Lucknow under Havelock. The Madras *Athenaeum* drew attention to this as evidence of the capabilities of Eurasians.[52] But as an Apothecary he occupied a subordinate position, and was no threat to British claims to a monopoly of commissioned rank. He was duly promoted Senior Apothecary in 1860. Here again he was no threat to the claims of gentlemen. But he had a supporter in a medical colleague who was shrewd enough to look beyond Madras. Assistant Surgeon Montgomery pointed out that in the Bengal army several Apothecaries had been promoted to commissioned rank in recognition of their services during the Mutiny. Should the Madras Government be less generous? Stung into belated action, the Madras Government recommended, in 1862, that Dewsnap should be granted the honorary rank of Assistant Surgeon with the relative rank of Lieutenant. But a Senior Apothecary was paid Rs 250 a month, and a Lieutenant or Assistant Surgeon only Rs 225. The Government therefore recommended that Dewsnap continue to be paid his salary of Rs 250 and also be granted a personal allowance of Rs 150.[53] At the India Office, economy prevailed : Sir Charles Wood authorized Dewsnap's promotion to the honorary rank of Assistant Surgeon with the relative rank of Assistant Surgeon with the relative rank of Lieutenant. But a he added sternly that 'it must be clearly understood that he is entitled to no additional allowance in virtue of his Honorary rank'. Any extra allowance would have to be justified by reference to the work that he was doing.[54]

Dr Gillies, meanwhile, was sent to Tinnevelly, as Civil Surgeon. He was released for a much-needed furlough in 1865, but he died at sea. Dr Macpherson went to England in high fettle, and explained to the Royal Commission on the Sanitary State of the Army in India how the Madras Government had taken the initiative in returning to a lock hospital system. But when he came back he was mortified to find himself passed over for promotion. He submitted a succession of memorials. After he had completed the five years allowed him as an Inspector-General of Hospitals, there seemed to be nothing that he could do. He complained that the Government wanted to 'superannuate' him.[55] He asked to be allowed to live in England while unemployed: 'I have devoted my life to intellectual pursuits which I am unable to follow in India, except in the public service.'[56] Not surprisingly, the Government was unimpressed. Finally, he was made officiating president of the Madras Sanitary Commission. But in this capacity he provided repeated evidence of incompetence. He submitted a sewerage scheme which the Governor criticized as being 'of the most crude and unsatisfactory character'.[57] It transpired that he had bullied the other members of the Commission into accepting it against their better judgement. Soon he was in trouble again. The Governor in Council criticized him severely for presenting information on the working of the commissariat system 'in a manner calculated to mislead the Government'.[58] He died in 1867. To those who had sympathized with Dr Gillies, Macpherson's subsequent misfortunes must have seemed like poetic justice.

Like Eurasians, missionaries also occupied an ambiguous position on the margins of the social distance between the ruling race and the peoples of India. They were clearly members of the ruling race, and as teachers and doctors many of them were involved in tasks which engaged some of the official elite. They usually lived in European style, and some of them enjoyed cordial relations with members of the official elite. Dr Miller is an example of this type of missionary. But missionaries as such were also involved in close relations with Indians, especially with Indian Christians. As we have seen, there were some who held that these roles were incompatible, and that, to enjoy close relations with Indians, missionaries should separate themselves from the elite. The Salvation Army followed an Indian lifestyle in India, and other missionaries echoed anxieties expressed with increasing force in England to the effect that Nonconformity was losing contact with the lower classes. So Lunn would criticize Miller for giving higher education to high-caste Hindus instead of raising the condition of lower-caste converts and mingling with peasants. Dyer had entered agitational politics through the Working Men's League for the Repeal of the Contagious Diseases Acts, and he imported into his Indian campaigns the class hostility associated with the campaign against the CD Acts in England.[59] The Rev. Charles Mead, of the London Missionary Society, was a missionary of Dyer's style. He encouraged lower-caste converts to assert themselves, married a Pariah convert as his third wife, and incidentally had twenty-one children.[60] His more conservative colleagues, however, were shocked by such blatant evidence of his evangelistic and other energies.

The position of the lady missionary was particularly delicate, and the case of Miss Pigot is illuminating. Mary Pigot took charge of the Church of Scotland's orphanage and zenana mission in Calcutta in 1870. She quickly established friendly relations with Scots missionaries, with Indian Christians and with many other Indians. In 1878 the Rev. McAlister Thomson, pastor of St Andrew's Parish Church, commended her work in the highest terms. But in the following year a fresh and loud voice was heard in Presbyterian circles in Calcutta. The Rev. William Hastie arrived to take charge of the General Assembly's Institution – a college under the auspices of the General Assembly of the Church of Scotland. He was able and energetic, but he also seemed to be intolerant and domineering.

Hastie was soon involved in several controversies. Many devout Hindus were offended by a series of letters which he wrote to the editor of the Calcutta·*Statesman* and later published under the title *Hindu Idolatry and English Enlightenment*. He was also involved in controversy with Babu Kali Charan Banerjee, an Indian Christian who did some teaching at Mary Pigot's orphanage. He was irritated by certain criticisms of his theological views which appeared in the *Indian Christian Herald* and of which he suspected Banerjee to be the author. After an inconclusive exchange of letters he declared that he would assume that Banerjee was indeed the author and added : 'You do not, cannot, understand the Free Church controversy, no mere native Christian can.'[61]

He asked some other missionaries to support him. When they replied that they had no control over the *Indian Christian Herald* he retorted in exasperation : 'Apart from you, the men as well as the articles are indeed beneath my notice. Any reply deserved by these insolent Babus would have to be delivered from the tip of my boot.'[62]

He told Banerjee not to interfere with Miss Pigot's orphanage, and he told Miss Pigot not to receive him any more. He also tried to assert a general control over the orphanage and zenana mission. Miss Pigot opposed this, and relations soon reached a crisis.

Professor Wilson, the senior lay teacher at the General Assembly's Institution, organized a picnic in Barrackpore Park for Miss Pigot's orphanage. Hastie came too, and noted that Miss Pigot and Professor Wilson talked and sat together. He began to suspect her of immorality. He also heard that Banerjee had been seen sitting on one end of a reclining chair on Miss Pigot's verandah, with Miss Pigot at the other end, and his arms resting over Miss Pigot's feet. There was even a rumour that Banerjee had been seen at a window of the orphanage, with his arm round Miss Pigot's waist. Another rumour, also shocking to earnest Presbyterians, was that Miss Pigot secretly sympathized with the Roman Catholic Church. In an anonymous leaflet from 'a member of St Andrew's Kirk', supporters of the zenana mission were asked: 'Are you aware that you are at present the auxiliaries of the Jesuits in Calcutta?'[63]

Hastie sent this and other documents home to Dr Scott, Chairman of the Foreign Mission Committee of the Church of Scotland, together with a memorandum in which he stated his suspicions of Miss Pigot's morals, and also asserted that she had 'naturally the strongest affinities' with the 'illegitimate half-castes' who were pupils at her orphanage.[64] Meanwhile, Miss Pigot herself went to Edinburgh to argue her claim to be independent of Hastie's control. Dr Scott showed her the various charges against her, and advised her to go back to Calcutta and defend herself there.

She took Hastie to court, and the case came up in 1883, at a time of racial tension provoked by the Ilbert Bill, before Mr Justice Norris, who was notorious for his impatience with Indian witnesses. At first the proceedings seemed to be in Miss Pigot's favour. Norris was clearly irritated by Hastie's self-importance and especially by his reluctance or inability to make a concise statement. Hastie said that he had thought that Miss Pigot's 'manner before men was indelicate'. He was asked for a specific example, but simply mentioned 'a carelessness of external demeanour before men'. Then Norris intervened to insist on something more precise. But Hastie's examples were hardly impressive. He mentioned a dinner-party: 'After retiring from the dining-room into the drawing-room, Miss Pigot without any invitation or suggestion from her host, flung herself upon a sofa, and threw up her legs in a way that I have never seen a lady in such circumstances do before.'[65] Also : 'I remember being struck during the dinner-party with the levity of her conversation and frivolity of manner.' Then at the picnic in Barrackpore Park he had thought that Miss Pigot paid too much attention to Professor Wilson. But he was the host and she was the principal guest ? Hastie clearly had not seen things in that light. Moreover, during the meal he had seen them touching each other ; indeed, 'their two sides' were in 'a continuous contact', and her head was on Professor Wilson's shoulder.

Professor Wilson was brisk in giving his evidence. At the picnic they were all sitting down under a banyan tree, and someone suggested that they should support each other by sitting back to back : that was how Mary Pigot and he came to be sitting in contact with each other. But the Indian witnesses did not fare so well under skilled cross-examination, and Justice Norris allowed his impatience to rise to the surface. It seemed improbable that Kali Charan Banerjee would have been so imprudent as to stand at an open window in a compromising position with his arm around Miss Pigot's waist. He also denied that there had been any physical contact when he sat in her company on the verandah. But Justice Norris considered that his demeanour as a witness was unsatisfactory. Also, the case was dragging on : Justice Norris even said at one point that he wanted to finish it by the end of the week or he would lose some of his holiday. Miss Pigot produced her parents' marriage certificate to prove her legitimacy ; her mother was still living in Dacca, and was presumably Eurasian. Then Norris rebuked Miss Pigot severely when he heard that she had looked at some of the reporters' notes of the proceedings. This seems to have shaken her composure, and the following morning she broke down during a fierce cross-examination in the course of which, so one newspaper calculated, she was asked 333 questions in two hours.[66] Norris allowed her only one anna damages, with each party paying his own costs.

This was a sad disappointment for Mary Pigot. But William Hastie failed to emerge with any credit from the case. Justice Norris was at pains to emphasize that Hastie had declared his suspicions of her morals in 1879 but his willingness to have her as a teacher in the orphanage in 1880 if only she would accept his superior authority. Apparently, in missionary as well as in imperial circles, threats to power and authority could have decisive effects on attitudes to sexual behaviour. Hastie, a missionary who was unduly conscious of his standing as a member of the ruling race, found himself challenged by an Indian who was on friendly terms with a white, or at least a Eurasian lady missionary. Here was a classic occasion for the sexual jealousy to which men of a dominant group are peculiarly liable. But there was sympathy for Miss Pigot in a variety of newspapers, English as well as Indian. A significant comment appeared in the *Bombay Guardian*, a radical Nonconformist journal: 'We incline to think that the case might have been tried before a native with more satisfactory results.'[67] Several Indian newspapers noted that Miss Pigot was well-known for her friendliness towards Indians. The *Indian Christian Herald* put it more perceptively: 'One great aim of Miss Pigot seemed to be to bridge as much as possible the distance which separated the European from the native.'[68] She had visited the noted Hindu religious leader Keshab Chandra Sen when he was ill, and she had given a party to celebrate his son's marriage.

Such things were regarded with gloomy disfavour by those who opposed all attempts to bridge social distance. An anonymous 'District Judge' wrote to the *Friend of India* to explain that in his view Norris had judged the case correctly. He himself thought that zenana missions were morally dangerous for lady missionaries: 'Among several of the missionary bodies it is the practice for young unmarried ladies to proceed, alone or unprotected, to the houses of middle-class Hindoos to impart elementary instruction to the ladies of the household.' It was time that these missionary societies realized that they were putting their young ladies at the mercy of lascivious Hindu men: '. . . the system of family life among the secluded females of a Hindoo household is quite inconsistent with the idea of any protection from familiarity or insult from the male members of the household being afforded by the ladies of the zenana.'

He added darkly: 'I cannot put matters as clearly as I should otherwise wish, because of the extreme delicacy of the subject, and the repugnance with which the mind dwells on such matters.'[69] He seems, however, to have allowed his own mind to dwell rather too freely on matters of which he can have had no personal knowledge. In such ways ignorance could breed the wildest suspicions of Hindu lasciviousness and at the same time resist any approach to a better knowledge of the subject.

A subscription was raised to enable Mary Pigot to appeal, and in 1884 the Appellate Bench of the High Court found in her favour –

specifically, that Hastie had 'published these libels upon the plaintiff without any justification whatever, and that he was influenced in publishing them by malicious motives'.[70] She was awarded three thousand rupees damages, together with costs. Meanwhile, the Foreign Mission Committee in Edinburgh had already relieved Hastie of his post on the ground that his 'temper and disposition' were unsuited to it.[71] He went home to defend himself, omitting to pay Miss Pigot's damages and costs. In Edinburgh he spoke for eight hours before the General Assembly: not surprisingly, they found against him by a large majority.

Then the Foreign Mission Committee appointed a commission of enquiry to investigate matters in Calcutta. Hastie thereupon decided to go there as well, having taken the precaution of making over a sum of three hundred pounds to his mother and sisters. When he arrived in Calcutta in 1885, he was arrested for failing to pay Miss Pigot's damages and costs, which amounted to twelve thousand rupees. After spending nearly a month in the Presidency jail he obtained a declaration that he was insolvent.[72] In due course, the commission of enquiry appointed by the Foreign Mission Committee reported in Miss Pigot's favour, and she was solemnly awarded a pension of forty pounds a year. Ten years later, the Rev. William Hastie became Professor of Theology at Glasgow University.

Late in the nineteenth century, when Indian princes intruded upon the imperial stage equipped with Western education and Western tastes, they also constituted a threat to social distance: although they were not members of the ruling race, they had been born into a ruling class, unlike many of the officials, and were welcome in exalted social circles in England, unlike many of the officials. Racial, social and sexual jealousy can be seen in operation together.

There was anxious consultation among officials in 1893, when it was learnt that the Maharaja of Patiala intended to marry a Miss Florry Bryan. The idea threatened the racial and social hierarchy in various ways. First, there was the disturbing thought of an Indian marrying a white woman. She was of the ruling race and he was not. Yet he belonged to a ruling class and she was of a lower class. It was deeply worrying. The Maharaja asked Lord William Beresford to tell him what the reaction of the Viceroy, Lord Lansdowne, was likely to be. The reply was very discouraging:

I feel bound to tell you that His Excellency regards your intention with the strongest disapproval, and that he will not in any way countenance this marriage. An alliance of this kind, contracted with a European far below you in rank, is bound to lead to the most unfortunate results. It will render your position both with Europeans and Indians most embarrassing.

Europeans will certainly object to treat this lady as a suitable consort for a ruler in your position. They will also resent the idea of a European lady being married to a Native Chief as one of a number of other wives.[73]

But the Maharaja had not been asking the Viceroy's permission, and he married Florry all the same.

Curzon was greatly troubled by the news that the young Raja of Jind had secretly married 'the daughter of a professional aeronaut of low character and of Dutch or German origin'. It always seemed to Curzon that the ruling classes should behave in a dignified manner : he saw this as 'a horrible scandal'.[74] The local press embroidered the news with colourful detail. According to the *Simla News*, Olive, the young lady in question, was the daughter of a Bombay barber named Monalescu, and she had accompanied her mother, who was acting as parachutist to an American balloonist named Van Tassell.[75] From Curzon's viewpoint, this was even worse.

When the young Raja of Pudukkottai wanted to go to England for the Queen's Jubilee, permission was refused. The Madras Government noted several problems. He was extravagant. His personal character was such that 'he would probably get into mischief'. In particular : 'We specially fear his marrying a European woman.'[76] It was subsequently noted that he was 'more a coloured English gentleman with entirely European tastes than a Native Prince'. He was 'an absentee chief and unduly addicted to amusements'. He was 'not fully alive to the impropriety of spending State funds on private objects'. More seriously, he had 'shown a disposition to ignore the Political Agent, and in other ways to adopt an unfriendly attitude towards the representative of the Paramount Power'.

But he soon learnt the wisdom of conciliating the Political Agent. His finances also improved, and in 1898 he was allowed abroad for eight months. Two years later, the Madras Government recommended that he be granted an honorary commission in the British Army. He was now described in rather different terms – 'fond of sport, has a reputation as a good shot, and is a good tennis player'.[77] But Curzon was unimpressed by the usual qualifications for a commission in the British Army, and the recommendation was turned down. Curzon's passion was for efficiency, and he had been looking into the files. When the Madras Government recommended another spell of leave abroad Curzon would have refused, but the Governor complained that the Raja had already been told that his application had been recommended. Curzon reluctantly agreed in order to save the face of the Madras Government.[78] But when 'our fat friend', as he now termed the Raja, wanted to go to London for King Edward VII's coronation, Curzon firmly refused.[79] However, he was pleased to hear that the Raja intended to marry a sister of the Maharani of Kuch Behar, who was herself the daughter of the Hindu religious reformer, Keshab Chandra Sen : 'although the young lady . . . is about as Europeanized as a native can be, it is far better that the Raja should marry her than a European spouse'.[80]

If Indian princes, who were members of a ruling class, behaved like Europeans, married European women, and were accepted in society in Europe, how could one safeguard the social distance between the ruling race and the races of India ?

It vexed Curzon intensely to realize that such things were seen rather differently in the highest circles in England. He was greatly irritated to learn of the Raja of Kapurthala's successes in Europe. He was only 'a third-class chief', and Curzon suspected his morals. But it seemed that he was to be received by the President of the French Republic. Curzon thought that he had only gone to Paris 'in order to have intercourse with French women'. In fact, this was unlikely to trouble the President of the French Republic. Also, he was received at Buckingham Palace. Curzon was infuriated to remember a previous occasion : 'I saw him dancing at the Jubilee Ball at Buckingham Palace in 1897 with the daughter of the Duchess of Roxburgh.'[81]

In Calcutta or Simla he, Curzon, might not always condescend to receive such princes. Then he heard that the Raja had been given a special reception and luncheon at Buckingham Palace. This was too much. Hamilton explained cautiously that the responsibility really lay with the political aide-de-camp at the India Office.[82] This was Sir William Gerald Seymour Vesey Fitzgerald, who had held that post since 1874. Godley, the accomplished civil servant who had been Permanent Under-Secretary at the India Office since 1883, hastily entered the controversy to point out that it would be very unfair to penalize a civil servant like Fitzgerald who would soon be retiring on his pension; instead, he was given leave of absence until his retirement.[83]

Meanwhile, Curzon published a circular letter to local governments in which the Government of India announced that princes would only be allowed to visit Europe for special reasons : their duty lay in attending to the administration of their states. Hamilton thought it 'too pedagogic' : the princes seemed to be treated like schoolboys.[84] Curzon retorted that they were mostly that – 'a set of unruly and ignorant and rather undisciplined schoolboys'.[85] The Maharaja of Jaipur was the type of prince he favoured – 'conservative', 'intensely loyal'. Above all, he was 'capable, if skilfully and sympathetically handled, of being guided where we will'.[86] Princes who acquired European ideas and tastes were more difficult to handle. In Europe they were apt to think of themselves the equals or superiors of the Viceroy and his colleagues.

When he considered which princes should be invited to London for the coronation of Edward vii, Curzon looked especially to the dignified appearance of those with traditional manners. He chose the Raja of Nabha – 'a very fine and noble-looking man'. Also the Maharaja of Jaipur : 'He is a distinguished-looking man, rather heavy and fat, but of eminently dignified and impressive appearance, and when you get them both in their best dress and jewels, he and Nabha will produce a magnificent effect.'[87]

But handsome men might be a problem. The Viceroy and the Secretary of State conferred anxiously about the tastes of Englishwomen. The traditional stereotype of the white woman at risk from lascivious Indians seemed not to accord with realities. Not only the princes but sepoys were at risk in England. When he heard that the King had suggested that a number of Indian orderlies attend his court in London, Curzon warned Hamilton of the risk to their virtue :

> The 'woman' aspect of the question is rather a difficulty, since strange as it may seem English women of the housemaid class, and even higher, do offer themselves to these Indian soldiers, attracted by their uniform, enamoured of their physique, and with a sort of idea that the warrior is also an oriental prince.[88]

After the festivities were over, Hamilton was able to reassure Curzon : 'Making allowance for all the temptations to which they were subject, I think our Indian visitors behaved on the whole with great self-restraint and propriety.' It had not been easy for them. Hamilton agreed with Curzon in detecting what he described as a 'very unpleasant characteristic' in recent years – 'the craze of white women for running after black men'. He embarked upon some social analysis :

Apparently it pervades all classes of society : the smartest peeresses were only too ready to make a fuss with Bikaner and other Indian chiefs, and as you go lower in the social scale, so does this tendency manifest itself more strongly and in a way characteristic of the habits and lives of the respective classes of the community. At Hampton Court the great difficulty of the officers was in keeping the white women away from our Native soldiers.[89]

By now Curzon was looking forward anxiously to the princes' return. He was all the more concerned lest they acquire exaggerated notions of their importance as a result of aristocratic and still more of royal hospitality in England.[90] But there was no real need to worry : 'Fortunately, when these travellers return to India, they fall very quickly into their proper place.'[91] With unpleasing relish Curzon told Hamilton of the contrast between the situation of a certain prince in England, where he was 'a favoured guest at Windsor and Sandringham', and in India, where 'he regards it as a high honour to be asked to dinner at Government House'.[92] It was satisfying to reflect that in India the social hierarchy could be manipulated into conformity with the structure of power. Indians, of course, had different notions of social status. But Curzon devised for the upbringing of young princes an Imperial Cadet Corps, where discipline and status would be based on European military structures.

Even there he encountered difficulties. When he heard that a young prince had shown homosexual tendencies, he sent him to the Cadet Corps to learn self-discipline. Then he began to fear that the young man might be corrupting other cadets. Hamilton confided that he was not at all surprised that this particular prince had taken to 'the special Oriental vice'. Experience in England, it appeared, had shown Hamilton the dangers of such a situation : 'I have had a good deal of experience of schools, seminaries and colleges for boys, and, as I daresay you know, few of these institutions escape being infected with some immorality or other ; but, once it creeps in, it is most difficult to eradicate.'[93] So it was not such a peculiarly Oriental vice after all. But Curzon had grimly drawn up a list of princes with homosexual tastes. He blamed Indian customs : 'I attribute it largely to early marriage. A boy gets tired of his wife, or of women, at an early age, and wants the stimulus of some more novel or exciting sensation.'[94] That English and Indian society might not differ significantly in the proportion of men

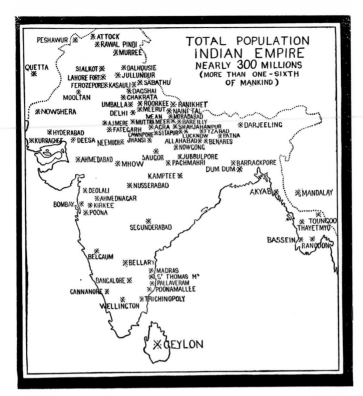

SEVENTY-FIVE OF THE CENTRES IN WHICH STATE-LICENSED-HARLOTRY HAS BEEN ESTABLISHED BY THE BRITISH GOVERNMENT IN THE INDIAN EMPIRE.

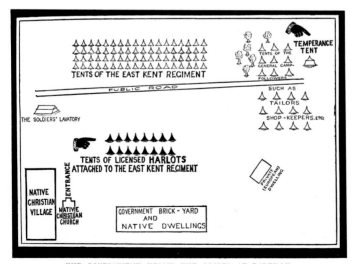

THE GOVERNMENT *VERSUS* THE GOSPEL AT BAREILLY.
(*Sketch taken on the spot by Mr. Alfred S. Dyer, Dec. 30th, 1887.*)

Drawings illustrating Alfred Dyer's research, from *The Sentinel*, 1888

Top : Alfred Dyer, from *The Friend ; Above left :* Mrs Andrew ; *Above right :* Dr Kate Bushnell from *The Sentinel,* 1894

Man Sukh Lal and (*below*) Mrs Man Sukh Lal, from *The Sentinel*, 1894

Top : Milkwomen in the camp, from the *Illustrated London News*, 1864
Left : Lord Roberts

Top : Mahadji Sinde (ruled 1784–94) entertaining two British officers to a nautch in Delhi
Above : Major William Palmer, his Indian wife and their children, with women attendants,
late eighteenth century

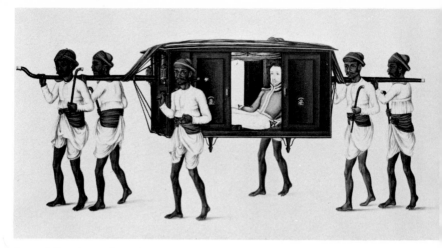

Army Officer in a palanquin at a station, by an Indian artist, *c.* 1828

WHAT IMPUDENCE.

Cartoon from *The Indian Punch*, 1860. Amy: 'Oh, Gussy dear, what do you think that thing of an Ayah says?' Augustus: 'What, dear?' Amy: 'Why, that she has a daughter the very picture of *me*, did you ever hear such impudence?'

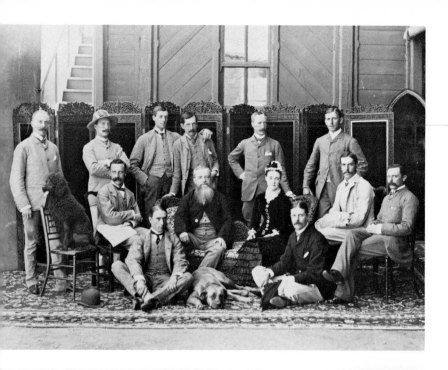

Top : Lord and Lady Ripon and viceregal staff, Simla 1884
Above : Lady Elgin, Bankipur 1896

A British army officer and his household in India (Lieutenant-Colonel C. L. Hervey of the Wiltshire Regiment, *c.* 1880–90)

Missionary picnic, 1902, from the photograph album of the Rev. R. A. Ellis, Wesleyan Methodist missionary, Mysore

with such tastes was a possibility that escaped consideration at this time. This accords with a frequent tendency in the development of stereotypes to attribute to the members of other groups the characteristics most feared in one's own group.

Indeed, it is noticeable that when the dominant group creates stereotypes of those on the margins of social distance it does so by ignoring evidence which contradicts those stereotypes. It was said that Eurasians would never make good army officers because Indian soldiers would despise them. That there were many successful and some famous Eurasian officers was ignored. That Indian rulers had themselves employed Eurasians as army officers was also ignored. It was said that Eurasians would not be effective medical officers because English ladies would not like to consult them. That English ladies had willingly consulted Dr Gillies was ignored. Such stereotypes served to support British claims to a monopoly of responsible office.

Attitudes to sexual behaviour are similarly related to the preservation of vested interests and structures of power. When William Hastie's authority was challenged by Mary Pigot, he suspected her of fornication, but he was prepared to overlook it if she would accept his supervision. Sexual jealousy is recurrent. English hackles were raised at the prospect of an English lady being physically examined by a Eurasian doctor. English women were thought to be in need of protection from lascivious Hindus at the time of the Ilbert Bill agitation. Mary Pigot was accused of fornication with a Hindu who had similarly challenged Hastie's authority. Indian princes were suspected of designs upon white women, and this was seen as a reason for restricting their travels to Europe. Then white women were thought to be attracted to Indian princes, and this was seen as a reason why princes should not linger long in Europe. In both cases, the underlying threat was to the structure of power.

Elaborate techniques from gun salutes to precedence at official receptions were manipulated by the officials to keep the princes at an appropriate distance. If they moved much in high society in England, or if they married Englishwomen, they might lose the habits of deference which they were expected to display before the imperial authority of the Viceroy or of British residents and Political Agents.

English class attitudes are transformed into racial attitudes in an imperial setting. The official elite lived in an aristocratic manner, and the ideal of the gentleman was greatly treasured. The maintenance of a proper distance between them and the populace seemed not only socially appropriate but politically necessary. Those who threatened to bridge that distance aroused great concern. But the ruling race also included many who did not live like gentlemen, and, as we shall see, this was a source of perplexity to the official elite.

5
Low Life and Racial Prestige

The justification of foreign rule was generally assumed to be that it was bringing not only material but moral progress. There were recurrent demands that the official elite should shun the nautch parties given by wealthy Indians at which dancing girls performed. The *Friend of India* in 1835 argued instead for 'conversation parties', where Indians might be edified :

With very small expense, they might in this way be brought under the full power of the courtesy and intelligence of superior minds. A few works of art and portfolios of landscapes, with the ordinary topics of conversation of the day, in the line of foreign politics, Indian measures of administration, Native education and the various schemes of philanthropy continually starting into notice. . .

Such excitement should be reciprocal : '. . . it might easily be intimated to the Baboos that their invitations would be accepted with pleasure, when the entertainments they provided were of the same simple and beneficial character as those to which they were received by their English friends.'[1]

By the second half of the nineteenth century it had become only too clear that many Indians had acquired a more than adequate understanding of Western ideas and were apt not only to discuss but also to criticize British policies. Also, most of them had unaccountably failed to recognize the superiority of Christianity to Hinduism. Were the British setting a sound example of moral progress? Perhaps Indians were aware that some of the entertainments provided in such centres of British rule as the great cities of Calcutta and Bombay were not of that simple and beneficial character envisaged in the reforming era of the 1830s?

The Indian Mutiny of 1857 had shown the importance of British soldiers to the maintenance of imperial rule. But they were notoriously prone to immorality and drunkenness, and when drunk they were difficult to control. Sergeant-Major Walker explained to the Army Sanitary Commission in 1861 that 'the ordinary police of the country, the black police, would not dare to interfere with the men'. Nor was this merely a matter of soldiers. In Chandranagar, under French rule, the officials were much concerned at the arrival of parties of loose women and drunken men by the ten p.m. train from Calcutta. One evening in September 1860 a drunken English officer gave much trouble, and the guard had to be called out to deal with him, since it was well known that the English would not obey Indian policemen. There were anxious consultations between Chandranagar and the French headquarters in Pondicherry. Could the women be expelled? Unfortunately, they were only visitors. They came on outings for pleasure – 'des promenades en parties de plaisir'. The only solution was for the police to redouble their zeal and do the best they could.[2]

At least in British India it was hoped that the 1864 Act would enable the military authorities to exercise a tighter control over the recreations of the unruly soldiery. But there seemed to be a growing number of unruly Europeans among the lower classes in Calcutta and Bombay.

The Mariscano scandal in 1866 prompted sombre reflections. Clementi Mariscano, described alternatively as 'an Italian musician' and a 'loafer', was found guilty by a coroner's jury of culpable homicide and sentenced to eight years' penal servitude. He had killed Isaac Greenman, a German Jew, in a Calcutta street after a quarrel over a Polish Jewess with whom Greenman had been living. Greenman was said to have formerly kept a 'grog shop' in Egypt and had brought her from Odessa 'as a slave', as she described it. The editor of the *Friend of India* declared sadly that such events were typical of the life of poor Europeans in Calcutta : 'the conquering race, the white aristocracy, the civilizing power' had 'reason for shame'.[3]

Similar sentiments were expressed by various officials in the following year in the course of enquiries into the problems raised by European vagrants. The Commissioner of Bhagalpur thought that 'disreputable white men' lowered 'the English character in every bazar and town' where they were seen.[4] The Officiating Commissioner of Patna feared political danger as a consequence of such a reduction in the distance between the ruling race and the Indian people :

The sight of Europeans in the lowest depths of degradation brought on by drinking and profligacy must tend to degrade our race in the eyes of all who see them, and must go far to weaken our prestige amongst a nation avowedly ruled by the respect and fear in which they hold their conquerors.[5]

Many of the European poor seemed respectable enough. Some were seamen discharged by unscrupulous ship's captains who wanted to avoid paying crew while waiting in harbour and counted on engaging fresh men at rock-bottom wages when they were ready to leave. But others were suspected of having dubious occupations, and the Mariscano case encouraged rumours of a white slave traffic between eastern Europe and India.

It was thought that the 1868 legislation would facilitate police control of the red light districts in Calcutta and Bombay. In Calcutta, the police seemed unable to do very much, and brothels flourished in many areas, but in Bombay these were, and still are, confined to Kamathipura, a rectangle bounded by Bellasis Road, Duncan Road, Grant Road and Cursetji Sukhlaji Street. Alfred Dyer visited the area in 1887 and sent back a report which was published in the *Sentinel* under the arresting title, 'Must India Perish through Britain's Sin?' He described houses with 'the ground floor open to the road, like native shops. In these lower as well as in the upper rooms were native women calling to the male passers-by of various nationalities.' These, he explained, were women licensed to sin under the 1868 Contagious Diseases Act. There were also houses 'tenanted by European women, more bold and shameless'. He saw 'groups of native men who were watching the scene'. Indeed, he added, 'this is one of the sights of the city to the natives'. He concluded with relish: 'Conspicuously displayed in one of the shops of this licensed market of sin, I noticed a large framed portrait of "Victoria, Queen of Great Britain and Empress of India".'[6] In this and subsequent articles Dyer was at pains to demonstrate that Europeans were behaving badly in the presence of Indians.

The Bombay Government made a brief response to reformist pressure in 1887 and tried to clean up the area, but desisted in the face of protests from residents in districts to which prostitutes moved. The Government concluded that segregation stirred up less trouble than dispersion.

The 1868 Act was repealed in 1888, and in the same year Alfred Dyer settled down in Bombay as editor of the reformist *Bombay Guardian*, leaving his brother George to manage their religious publishing house at Paternoster Row in London.[7] For a time he was much occupied with his campaign against the military authorities, but like-minded missionaries and others applied pressure to the Bombay Government. Their activities were duly reported with approval in the *Sentinel*, the *Bombay Guardian* and the *Banner of Asia*. The *Banner of Asia* was another reformist journal which acquired an editor with a talent for publicity – Man Sukh Lal, formerly a London journalist named Ward who was converted to the Salvation Army, came out to India and in accordance with Salvation Army practice adopted Indian dress and an Indian lifestyle as well as an Indian name. He continued in this manner after he left the Salvation Army. He also married an Indian wife.

Towards the end of 1891 the case of Fanny Epstein attracted some public attention to these problems in Bombay. Born in Warsaw, she had settled with her parents in London, where her father, Victor Epstein, was a tailor. She worked as 'a fur machine hand' but had been unemployed for a time, and she was restless at home. She was engaged to be married, but impatient at the prospect of a long engagement. Yet she was only eighteen.

Then Alexander Kahn appeared. He was thirty-four, well-dressed, seemingly prosperous. He would have liked to marry her, he said, but his divorce had not yet come through. By what must have seemed a happy coincidence, he had a friend, Isaac Stirling, who knew a friend of Fanny's, Annie Gould. They planned an adventure together. Fanny secretly left her home in Whitechapel and met her friends at Cannon Street Station. There they took the boat train for Paris, where they stayed for a week. Victor Epstein came there in search of Fanny, but they eluded him. They went on to Marseilles, took a cargo boat to Port Said, and thence to Bombay.[8]

Back in London, Victor Epstein continued to enquire after Fanny, and he was helped by the National Vigilance Association. Its members were playing a leading part in the social purity movement in England, and were active in supplying the police with information about the traffic in women, especially the 'white slave trade'. This seemed a typical case. The girl had probably been taken either to Cairo or to South America: Kahn had said that his wife was in Buenos Aires. Enquiries were therefore made at the Foreign Office. In due course, Sir Evelyn Baring, Her Majesty's Agent and Consul-General at Cairo, reported that the police at Port Said had information that Fanny was living in Kamathipura, Bombay.[9] Similar information had already been received at the India Office, where T.F. Myres, of the National Vigilance Association, was soon pressing for action. Miss Epstein should be helped by the police to escape from her abductors. A telegram should be sent at once. This last suggestion prompted an office minute : 'The question is who is to pay for the telegram. Mr Myres does not offer to pay : and it is not easy to see why India should pay.'[10] But Myres was insistent, and he finally offered to pay on Mr Epstein's behalf. This prompted another office minute. The Secretary of State would be asked to authorize the sending of a telegram to the Bombay Government, but an emphatic warning was added : 'It will not be actually sent until Mr Myres produces the money to pay for it.'[11] These civil servants could show that they were practical men. Their caution seemed to be vindicated when Myres declined to pay after all ; so the telegram was never sent. Instead the Secretary of State sent an official despatch to the Bombay Government to put the matter in the hands of the detective police so that Miss Epstein could be found and offered such help as might seem necessary.[12]

But when Fanny was interviewed by the police she declined their help. She maintained that she had come to Bombay of her own accord in company with Annie Gould. Inspector Henry Hiscocks, in charge of Kamathipura Section, reported that he saw Fanny at a brothel in Bazar Road, and Annie at another brothel in Gilder Street, and that Annie corroborated Fanny's statement.[13] Victor Epstein, however, soon received an anonymous letter warning him that his daughter was 'in the hands of a very bad gang', and that the police had been deceived by another woman who had impersonated her.[14] This was firmly denied by H.G. Gell, Police Commissioner, who also interviewed Fanny and claimed that he had positively identified her from a photograph. He had been impressed by her demeanour : 'Her manner of speech and bearing showed me that she belonged to a rank superior to that from which the women in that line of life, who come to Bombay, are recruited.'[15]

He urged her to go back to her father. But she seemed to have no regrets and no embarrassment at her present position : 'Throughout the interview her manner struck me as singularly calm and self-possessed, there being no approach to nervousness, and she gave me the impression of being a somewhat determined young woman and well able to look after herself.'

Inspector Hiscocks also reported that there was no question of Fanny being under any sort of restraint : he had seen her driving about the fort area on two occasions. Moreover, she had been approached by various Protestant missionaries, but to no effect.

Then Mr H. Samuel, President of the Israelite School Committee, asked if a police officer would accompany him to see Fanny, so that he could read her a letter from her father. But they found that she had gone. Inspector Hiscocks made further enquiries. Fanny herself had rented the brothel for three months at sixty rupees a month and had now disposed of the lease. Isaac Stirling said that there had been a disagreement, as a result of which he and Annie had moved to Gilder Street. He added that Alexander Kahn was a dealer in women : indeed, they had first met in Buenos Aires, a city which was notorious for such things.[16]

The police were informed that Fanny, travelling as Mademoiselle Kahn, had embarked with Alexander Kahn for Aden, where they were booked to tranship to the *Océanien*, a Messageries Maritimes steamer bound for Marseilles. This information was promptly transmitted to London, and when the *Océanien* docked at Marseilles Victor Epstein was ready waiting. He took charge of Fanny and brought her home to London.

Meanwhile Alexander Kahn was arrested and prosecuted by the National Vigilance Association for taking Fanny Epstein, an unmarried girl of eighteen years, out of the possession of her father and against his will. But Fanny's evidence did not help the prosecution's case. She said that she first met Alexander Kahn at a club where she had been singing. Soon 'something was said about marriage'. She knew that he already had a wife in Buenos Aires, but expected that he would soon be divorced. She introduced him to her father, and she left home of her own accord. Kahn had given her the money for the establishment in Bombay. He had also given her 'valuable jewellery'. She did not know what the house in Bombay had been used for before she took it over. She ran it as 'a saloon bar'. She was 'mistress of the bar, in which were two young ladies', who were 'either Austrian or German', and who were paid a commission on the champagne which was sold to gentlemen. In addition to the bar there were three rooms with ordinary suites of furniture. She, Kahn and the two young ladies slept on the premises. Then the police came with their enquiries and she disposed of the house at a loss. Her evidence effectively destroyed the case against her lover. The magistrate said, however, that the case had been a proper one to bring before him : 'Kahn had been guilty of shameful behaviour in living with the girl ; but there were legal obstacles in the way. Therefore the defendant would be discharged.'[17]

As the Bombay police had discovered, Fanny Epstein was a competent young lady. The episode revealed the effectiveness of the sources of information available to the police. Fanny's whereabouts were known both in Cairo and in Bombay. But they were reluctant to act, and prosecutions might well collapse because of lack of evidence.

A Vigilance Committee was soon founded in Bombay, public meetings were organized, and petitions were presented to the Bombay Government. 'More effectual measures' were demanded for 'the repression of prostitution' and for the deportation of 'foreign procurers'. Special attention was paid to Cursetji Sukhlaji Street, where annoyance was said to be caused by 'open indecency and immorality'.[18] According to the Police Commissioner, 'most of the European courtezans' lived there, as well as 'other prostitutes, such as Japanese, Jewesses from Arabia and natives of India'.[19]

The Bombay Government resisted much of this pressure. It solemnly resolved that it was 'a lesser evil to segregate brothels as far as possible in one quarter'.[20] But it deported ten procurers.

This was not enough for the reformers. Dyer protested in the *Sentinel* that the Government was ignoring the interests of respectable people in the area. There was a mosque there, and three apartment blocks for sweepers had recently been built in the same street. These sweepers were British subjects and had the right to bring up their families in a moral atmosphere. The ten procurers who had been deported were indeed 'notorious traffickers in European women', but there were a hundred more of such 'foreign ruffians', who constituted an 'organized gang' known as 'the German Jewish club', occupying a house off Grant Road.[21] Many of Dyer's assertions had a factual basis, and it does seem that the majority of European women were Jewish refugees from persecution in eastern Europe. In 1884, when registration was in force, thirty-one of a total of thirty-four registered Europeans were recorded as 'Jewesses from Russia, Roumania, Servia, etc'.[22]

Early in 1894 the Russian ambassador approached Rosebery, Foreign Secretary in Gladstone's last ministry, to ask for the return of Dina Gontcharoff. He asserted that she had been induced to leave Odessa for Bombay in May 1893, and was now exploited in a 'maison de tolérance'. The papers were referred to the India Office, and Kimberley asked the Bombay Government to 'place the matter in the hands of your detective police', so that the girl could be traced and given help and protection.

The Bombay police traced Dina Gontcharoff to a house in Grant Road, and reported that she had come from Odessa to Bombay with 'a woman named C. Sbilanisky, *alias* Jinny Kraft'. Dina was brought before the Police Commissioner and said that she was nineteen years old. The Commissioner noted coldly : 'she looks older.' She also told him that 'she was a prostitute before she left Odessa, and she is still carrying on prostitution in Jinny Kraft's brothel of her own free will'.[23] It was clear that she did not want to go back to Russia, and it was decided that the ambassador should be told that the authorities were 'powerless to render any assistance in the matter'.[24]

The authorities in Calcutta also seemed lethargic, and in 1893 two American missionaries embarked upon a dramatic adventure. No doubt remembering how the journalist W.T. Stead had attracted attention to the abuse of minors in London by procuring a girl for supposedly immoral purposes, they paid fifty rupees to Suki Raur, Dinu Das and Gangaram Das for a girl of eleven years whom they said they wanted to seduce. The police, whom they had informed beforehand, were waiting outside the brothel and promptly arrested the three procurers. But when the case reached the High Court, Justice Pigot discharged the accused on the ground that the law required proof of 'a continuous letting or hiring for an unlawful or immoral purpose', whereas the missionaries had only said that they wanted the girl for one occasion.[25] But their adventure was successful in attracting publicity and support for their cause.

A kidnapping case attracted similar publicity at about the same time. The police received information that Kulsum Raur, a brothel-keeper, together with some of her relatives, had for some time been abducting girls from their homes in the Calcutta suburbs and in Midnapur district. The police raided her house and other brothels and found fourteen Hindu girls between seven and fourteen years old who had passed through her hands in the previous six months. Panchi, a child wife aged about twelve, had been kidnapped while playing in the street near her home in Tollygunge. Most of the girls were restored to their homes, but four, who had been in Muslim brothels, were outcast and their families refused to have them back. They had to be sent to an orphanage. Sentences of seven years' rigorous imprisonment were passed on Kulsum Raur and her associates.[26]

Soon afterwards, sixteen procurers were arrested for kidnapping girls in Midnapur District and taking them to brothels in Calcutta. Of the sixteen, six were Brahmans, eight Hindus of various other castes and the remaining two a Muslim man and woman. Eleven girls had been kidnapped, one of them a Muslim, the rest low-caste Hindus; their ages ranged from six to fifteen, and four of them were widows.[27]

At this propitious time the Calcutta Missionary Conference organized a meeting on social purity in the town hall. There was much enthusiastic oratory, and Protestant missionaries were joined by Hindu, Muslim, Parsi and Roman Catholic speakers. Everyone expressed impeccable sentiments in support of social purity, and Bishop Thoburn of the Methodist Episcopal Church, who took the chair, presented an argument dear to the English, to the effect that self-restraint accorded with self-interest, for sinful behaviour in public places had a depressing effect on property values: 'whole neighbourhoods have become so infested with bad characters that the price of real estate is seriously affected. . .'. South Calcutta was particularly troubled: 'with the exception of a few select quarters in which the more wealthy Europeans live, there is hardly a street or lane through which decent people can take their children with them if they wish to go for an evening stroll. . .'. And Europeans were conspicuous in all this:

> It is a striking fact that the most shameless characters in the city are not Indian but persons imported from Europe, and hence our Indian friends in the northern part of the city are subject to less annoyance in some respects than those who live in the European quarters, but they also have enough of which to complain.

Such things could not be eliminated, but they should be less conspicuous: vice should be 'compelled to shrink back into its own congenial darkness, and not disfigure our streets'. The traffic in young girls should be stopped. There was also a traffic in more mature women from Europe. This aspect of the problem stretched the bishop's oratorical powers to the utmost as he contemplated the spectacle of 'a colony of foreigners of both sexes – a colony which has been established in the interests of public vice'. These people were 'moral lepers'. They were 'devoted to the propagation of vice in all its forms'. Even worse, 'they take possession of houses that ought to be occupied by decent people, depress the value of real estate and dishonour the European name in the eyes of Eastern people'.[28]

The meeting had an impact. The Indian journal *Reis and Rayyet* promptly accused 'the Puritywallahs' of hypocrisy in choosing to attack 'the feeblest interest in the community' – the prostitutes. But the Government paid careful attention. Some of the reformers wanted the law to be amended on the lines of the English Criminal Law Amendment Act of 1885, making it a punishable offence to keep a brothel. Sir John Lambert, the Police Commissioner, strongly opposed this as impracticable. In 1880, when the registration system was in operation in Calcutta, there were 2,458 brothel-keepers on the books and 7,001 prostitutes. Only 8 or 10 of these brothel-keepers were Europeans and of the prostitutes only 46 were Eurasians and 65 Europeans. According to the recent census there were 20,126 prostitutes and brothel-keepers. It would be impossible for him to deal with such numbers. He then produced a familiar argument : it would be 'a change which the people do not ask for, and which they would resent as interference with the conditions of Eastern life'.[29]

Lambert claimed that the existing law was adequate in that brothels could be closed if members of the public complained. From 1892 to 1894, 50 had been closed in this way. The Rev. H. Anderson, of 37 Elliott Road, complained of 7 establishments in that street. Anderson produced evidence that in each case a public nuisance was caused, and Lambert duly issued notices calling on the occupants to discontinue their activities within fifteen days. He subsequently extended this period for some who needed time to sell their effects before leaving India. Of these 7 establishments, 6 were occupied by 'European women (foreigners)'. The occupants of 4 left India ; the occupants of the other 3 moved to different parts of Calcutta.[30]

Similar action followed other complaints. Dr S.P. Sarvadhikari, for example, complained against Rajubali for using 7-1-1 Beadon Street as a brothel. He lived next door. It was closed. Kalinath Nag and others complained against Kamini Raur and Sarojini Raur for using 155 Cornwallis Street as a brothel. It was closed. Miss E. Maxey, superintendent of the Diocesan Home, complained against Marie Rosenthal for using 2 Wellington Street as a brothel. It was closed. There were a number of complaints about establishments in Free School Street. The Rev. W.H. Hart complained on behalf of the congregation of Free School Church against Maggie Reid of 28 Free School Street, Dansi Raur of 29, Manna Raur of 30 and Shama Raur of 31. J. Zemin and the Rev. Fr Naish complained against Natalia Zerska for using 44 Free School Street as a brothel 'under the guise of a cigar shop, to the annoyance of the congregation of St Thomas' Chapel'.[31] The number of closures following complaints enabled Lambert to claim that the law was adequate.

The Social Purity Committee which emerged from the town hall meeting also pressed for the deportation of foreign procurers. They alleged that there were some 145 'foreign dealers in vice', organized in 'clubs'. They specified the addresses of some of these clubs. 'It is possible that some of these club-men, who are mostly German or Roumanian Jews, may pose as tobacconists and the like.'[32] Lambert was at pains to minimize the seriousness of such assertions. He claimed that European procurers and prostitutes were declining in numbers. In 1893 there were about 50 European procurers and about 70 European prostitutes. In 1894 there were only about 36 European procurers and about 50 European prostitutes. Indeed, the Bombay Police Commissioner had recently written to Lambert to ask 'what could possibly have induced so many of these undesirable strangers to quit Calcutta for Bombay?'[33]

Characteristically, all that the Police Commissioner thought necessary was to enlarge the powers of individual police officers. Under the existing law they could not arrest anyone for soliciting without independent evidence, but he proposed that any police officer above the rank of native constable could act on his own authority. When he introduced a Bill to this effect he justified it on the ground that it was hard for 'respectable persons' to have to appear in court to testify in this type of case. But the redoubtable nationalist leader Surendranath Banerjea opposed this as a threat to individual liberty and Lal Mohan Ghose opposed it as opening the way to blackmail. They were not reassured by the wording of the proposed Bill, which would only have excluded Indian and not European constables from possession of these enlarged powers. In Banerjea's words, 'The one department of the State which gives the least satisfaction is the Police.'[34] The Bill was amended in accordance with his suggestions, which were grudgingly accepted by Sir John Lambert. Soliciting would be punishable by a fine of fifty rupees or eight days in prison, provided that it was done to the annoyance of the person solicited or of at least two inhabitants or passers-by. A police officer above the rank of native constable could arrest without warrant at the instance of the person solicited or of two inhabitants or passers-by, provided that he did not know and could not ascertain the name and address of the accused person. This was milder than the original proposal. Imprisonment was only included as an alternative penalty because most soliciting was done by 'male touts'.[35]

In Bombay meanwhile the missionaries were increasing their pressure. An American group again took the initiative. The Rev. A.W.

Prautch and the Rev. T. H. Hudson of the Methodist Episcopal Church were the most prominent in this enterprise. They formed the Bombay Midnight Mission to patrol the red light district of Bombay. The title they chose recalled similar ventures in London – the Moonlight Mission run by Lieutenant John Blackmore, RN, in the 1840s, and the Midnight Meeting Movement which started in 1860.[36] They were joined by some Europeans and Eurasians, and the group numbered some twenty-one when they began work in Cursetji Sukhlaji Street in December 1893.

They made a speedy impact. In March 1894 Sara Kameoski and twenty-seven other residents petitioned the Government for protection from the Bombay Midnight Mission, who patrolled from seven o'clock in the evening until three in the morning, knocking at doors and windows. They described themselves as 'defenceless European women' who had lived there for thirty years. This prompted an attack upon foreign procurers in the *Sentinel* : 'The Russian Jewesses (note the name Sara Kameoski at the foot of the memorial) who are decoyed out to Bombay in large numbers by these demons in human form, so far from living *for thirty years* in the country, do not, on the average, survive for thirty months.'[37]

Dyer tried to make his readers understand the depravity to be seen in Cursetji Sukhlaji Street. He had recently walked through it. He was careful to explain that he was accompanied by his wife, and that they were going from the Bellasis Baptist Chapel to the tramway stop at Grant Road corner. 'The scenes to be seen there in broad daylight are too awful for description.' But he proceeded to describe what he had seen – 'one of the European women in broad daylight in the middle of the roadway whose only clothing was a loose nightdress, unfastened, and a pair of slippers'. He seems to have been easily shocked. He then developed his favourite indictment of Europeans misbehaving themselves in the presence of Indians :

> No educated Native thinks he has properly 'done' Bombay unless he has seen the seething hell of European vice. The Native streets of vice are decorous in the extreme compared with Cursetji Sukhlaji Street. The women are decently clothed and many of them veiled, and the contrast is most humiliating.[38]

The Bombay Government's response to the women's petition was to inform them that the courts were open to them as to everyone else if they wished to take legal action. It soon appeared that the courts were not unfriendly. John Hurst, spinning master at the Dadar cotton mills, assaulted two members of the Bombay Midnight Mission – Alfred G. van Haaften and Malcolm Moss, who had been 'walking up and down the street, and quoting aloud such Scripture texts as "Be sure your sin will find you out"'. He was summoned for assault, and a Parsi magistrate found the case proved but warned the missionaries that they were to blame. 'I cannot allow misguided missionaries', he said, 'to invade the streets at night and interfere with the rights and liberties of the public.' Lance-Corporal Chick, of the Lancashire Regiment, who assaulted Malcolm Moss on another occasion, was similarly let off.[39]

Meanwhile, Prautch, Hudson, Dyer and Man Sukh Lal were involved in trouble with the law. They had been campaigning against the sale of opium to the public. According to Dyer himself, he joined this campaign after he had discovered the 'unspeakably painful fact' that the main reason why men took opium was 'to stimulate sexual lust'. They visited some opium clubs and published descriptions of their adventures in the *Bombay Guardian*, in the course of which they criticized Damaji Lakshmichand, an opium contractor, who promptly sued them for libel. They were sentenced to pay a fine or go to prison, and they chose prison. Dyer, Man Sukh Lal and Prautch each served a month, Hudson a week.[40] They then proceeded to extract the utmost publicity from these events. Dyer recalled how he had been accommodated in the Roman Catholic chapel of the jail – 'a curious place', he commented with gusto, for the editor of 'the leading protestant organ of Western India'.[41] While he was in prison he wrote some hymns. These were now published, of course by Messrs Dyer Brothers, in 'a handsome little volume' entitled *Songs in Prison, and Other Songs of Christian Life and Warfare*, price one shilling, and Man Sukh Lal wrote a pamphlet, *Behind Prison Bars in India*, which was also published by Messrs Dyer Brothers. With the help of contributions from readers of the *Bombay Guardian*, Dyer, Prautch, Man Sukh Lal and his wife Phulbai all went to England, where they gave many lectures attacking British policies in India.[42]

Samuel Smith, an MP who was active in the social purity movement, began to ask questions in Parliament. Was the Secretary of State aware that soon after Sara Kameoski's petition the police had driven the midnight missionaries out of the street in which she and the other signatories lived? There was a hasty flow of telegrams. R.H. Vincent, the Bombay Police Commissioner, explained: 'Police much harassed in preventing conflict between midnight missionaries, prostitutes and visitors to a particular street in Bombay, and impartially prevent open conflicts.'[43] Smith also asked about the prosecution of Dyer and his colleagues, and Fowler assured him that it was a private prosecution.[44]

Vincent submitted a more detailed report on the situation to the Bombay Government. Cursetji Sukhlaji Street was not very peaceful these days : 'Before the missionaries came on the scene, the street was as quiet as such a street can be ; but matters are now much worse. . . .' The missionaries would 'parade' up and down, singly or in couples, or station themselves at each end, accosting all men coming into the street. Most of the men thus accosted were Europeans. Some of the missionaries were young women, and occasionally they had been mistaken for 'unfortunates' : 'This was naturally resented by the male members of the Mission, and on one or two occasions a free fight took place between the missionaries and frequenters of the street, which the police had to put an end to.'

There had also been 'frequent rows between the courtezans and the missionaries', who tried to deprive them of clients : 'On several occasions the prostitutes have thrown water on the missionaries from upper windows, and it has been alleged that one or twice the missionaries have been bespattered with oil and other fluids.'

The Police Commissioner was greatly perturbed to be told by certain gentlemen, 'who of course do not wish their names to be disclosed', that the missionaries had stopped them when they were merely driving through the street, quite innocently of course. Indeed there was 'a great deal of ill feeling' because the missionaries had published the names of some of these gentlemen in one of their journals, which was then sent free of charge to their clubs. He even suggested that 'a system of espionage had been established as regards the private life of gentlemen with the view perhaps of making use of the knowledge gained in the journal of the mission'. In such a situation 'the European officers of the Police' on duty in Cursetji Sukhlaji Street had 'thought it right to warn the missionaries of the risk they run of being maltreated. . .'.[45]

After all, gentlemen were entitled to gentlemanly privacy. This view would not have commended itself to Dyer, whose *Sentinel* had already been banned by W.H. Smith from appearing on his bookstalls after it had revealed the names of aristocratic visitors to Mrs Jeffries' chain of high-class Chelsea brothels.[46] In the *Sentinel* he now repeated the theme of aristocratic vice as the threat to disadvantaged women. Cursetji Sukhlaji Street was the street where 'thousands of young women are annually decoyed from South Eastern Europe, and are from thence sold throughout the Indian Empire'. He was apt to exaggerate the numbers involved. Moreover, 'into this street drift eventually the European mistresses and paramours of the officials who protect it'.[47] The *Sentinel* joined with the *Banner of Asia* in congratulating the *Bombay Guardian* for 'scaring away' some 'aristocratic profligates' from Cursetji Sukhlaji Street by publishing a few names.[48] The *Bombay Guardian* duly published the details of a 'brutal assault' by a certain Major Murchison upon Malcolm Moss, of the Bombay Midnight Mission. Malcolm Moss was hit and kicked : 'His offence was the singing of a hymn outside a house of ill-fame in which this officer but not a gentleman was engaged in sin.'[49] But Moss was indefatigable. In November 1894 the *Sentinel* reported with satisfaction :

Mr Malcolm Moss is still engaged in his Midnight Mission work. He has obtained a tricycle, and follows home the carriages of some of the aristocratic official frequenters of the great European vice market of Bombay, finds their names and addresses, then sends them through the post letters of religious advice, tracts and purity literature.[50]

But it was to no avail. In 1900 the *Bombay Guardian* and the *Sentinel* cast another glance at Cursetji Sukhlaji Street. A traveller taking a short cut through the street had been 'assailed by noisy shouts from upper windows and impudent men in the street'. One of these impudent men climbed onto the step of his carriage, 'mentioning European and Parsee women, as well as other nationalities'. The writer could only deplore 'the boisterous impudence of Bombay's abandoned street'.[51]

By then another issue was threatening morality and the prestige of the ruling race. In March 1900 Miss Robinson, a barmaid at Evershed's Hotel, Rangoon, killed herself by swallowing oxalic acid. This aroused a variety of protests. The Rev. W. F. Armstrong, pastor of Immanuel Baptist Church, Rangoon, urged the Burma Government to prohibit the employment of barmaids, as the unfortunate girl must have committed suicide to escape from her position.[52] Mrs Phinney and Mrs Mawson, President and Secretary of the Rangoon Christian Temperance Union, wrote to the Government in similar terms : the liquor licence should be revoked if barmaids were employed.[53] European residents drew up a petition. Europeans should not be allowed to work as barmaids because it was dangerous to their health and also to their morals. Moreover, the employment of European women in a menial capacity was 'humiliating and derogatory to us as the ruling race'.[54]

The officials conferred among themselves. The Deputy Commissioner of Rangoon showed a proper regard for accuracy. The facts were not those assumed by the 'agitators'. Miss Robinson had not killed herself in order to escape from her employment. She had heard of a friend killing herself with oxalic acid; she had a quarrel with a man, and so she followed her friend's example. But the Deputy Commissioner conceded that barmaids were subject to great temptations. At least, he knew of 'two or more' who had 'sunk to a very low pitch'. One had become so 'degraded' as to solicit coolies in public houses. This thought fired the Deputy Commissioner with indignation: 'It is derogatory to the prestige of the ruling nation that such things should happen when they might be prevented.' He advocated decisive action: 'There is no necessity for barmaids at all, they do not sell the liquor, they merely receive orders and make out the bills. Liquor can be sold just as well by men.' Bar owners liked them because they attracted custom but it was 'not to the interest of Government or of the community that bar-keepers should make large profits'.[55]

An anonymous 'private medical practitioner' contributed a note on the historical background. Ten or twelve years ago, he recalled, Rangoon had no barmaids. One bar-keeper was helped by his wife. Then her sister joined them, but left to be married. So they imported a barmaid to replace her, and others followed. But it was not a respectable occupation: 'though Eurasian women are largely employed in stores, shops and offices in Rangoon, not one Rangoon-born girl has gone behind a bar, though the pay is far higher than in the above-mentioned situations, the reason being that the work is looked on as degrading'. No European acted in such menial capacity in Rangoon, except for the mess sergeant of a British regiment. But soldiers were an exception. He agreed that it was 'a source of humiliation and insult that women of the ruling race should be placed in such a position'.[56]

Barmaids were also employed in Calcutta, and in the following year the Bengal Government decided to prohibit it. There were protests from hotel proprietors, and at a somewhat late stage the Police Commissioner was consulted. But he reported that there had been no complaints of improper or disorderly conduct in connection with the thirty-two barmaids in Calcutta. Then the Advocate-General, John Woodroffe, inconveniently declared the Bengal Government's order to be *ultra vires*. This aroused some official anxiety at the possibility of legal action on the part of aggrieved bar-keepers.

When the papers reached the Governor-General's executive council, there was at first little sympathy with these proposals. Denzil Ibbetson briskly dismissed the example of Miss Matheson with her liking for coolies. Coolies could not afford to drink in bars. It must be a case of nymphomania ; Miss Matheson would have sought them out whether she was a barmaid or not.[57] J.P. Hewett dealt with the moral question by using statistics : 36 barmaids had entered Rangoon between 1890 and 1900 ; of the 34 believed still to be alive, 17 had married and 4 were engaged. This showed that barmaids were not led by their occupation into immorality. It was said that it was degrading in the eyes of 'the natives', but he doubted whether they bothered about the matter.[58] Ibbetson added his agreement. He had 'but small belief in making people moral by statute'. But he sympathized with the racial feelings which had been expressed : 'Personally, I have the very strongest repugnance to the idea of Englishwomen serving liquor to natives – a repugnance which most Englishmen will share, I think. But that is no sufficient reason for prohibition.'[59]

Then Curzon pronounced upon the subject. He had no doubt that the employment of European barmaids had a bad effect on the prestige of the ruling race :

> Whether the barmaids do or do not for the most part serve European customers, yet there is nothing to prevent natives from frequenting the bars ; very often they do so ; the girls cannot refuse to serve them ; the spectacle of the service is open to the eyes of natives equally with Europeans, and occasionally, as in Rangoon, incidents occur which are profoundly degrading to the prestige of the ruling race.

A number of them might marry. But he thought that 'in many cases the young men who marry them have been intimate with them in advance'. These speculations were hardly relevant to the case. He hurried on :

> But what I ask is the need for them in Calcutta at all ? Why bring them out from home, whether it be to ruin, to concubinage, or to marriage ? Why place them behind Calcutta bars to tempt in the young English clerks, and persuade the latter to spend their substance in drinking and frivolity, if not worse ? Why make public the spectacle of English girls engaged in duties which must carry

with them some sense of humiliation to the native eye, and which must suggest
the idea of immorality, even where the reality does not exist ?[60]

After the Viceroy's decisive pronouncement, his executive council
agreed to prohibit the employment of barmaids. Sir Thomas Raleigh,
the law member, bravely ventured to assert his belief in their moral
standards : after all, 'by misconduct they lose their chance of getting
married'. But the general standing of European women was the
decisive consideration :

> It is plainly not desirable that English women should serve drink to the men
> of mixed races who drift into the bars of Calcutta or Rangoon. (I sympathise
> entirely with the Honourable Mr Ibbetson's feeling as to this last point : and I
> am informed that the barmaids particularly dislike the kind of young native
> with whom they are brought into contact.)[61]

It was comforting for the official elite to believe that the lower classes
also had the right racial attitudes.

Soon H.H. Risley reported that the Bengal Government's
prohibition was being evaded in the spirit if not in the letter, at least in
Calcutta, where the barmaids no longer sold liquor but were still in
evidence : 'they sit about and exercise whatever attractions they
possess'.[62]

The Excise and Licensing Acts were therefore amended to prohibit
the employment of women in the public rooms of licensed premises
during opening hours. It was officially explained that they could still
do 'honest work', for example 'cleaning the premises, arranging
bottles and glasses, seeing to the linen and crockery'.[63] It was unlikely,
however, that bar owners would go to the expense of importing
European women for such tasks.

The rank and file of the British Army could also bring discredit on the
ruling race. Dyer blamed the military authorities : by forbidding
soldiers to marry they made them frustrated and aggressive ; by
providing Indian women to be used for their convenience they
encouraged soldiers to treat all Indians roughly. The military
authorities, on the other hand, predicted that there would be
unpleasant 'incidents' if the soldiers' energies had no outlet. Towards
the end of the century assaults on Indians by British soldiers came to
attract growing attention : some of these incidents involved women.

In October 1893 an editorial in the *Hindu* of Madras called on the
Government to take up the case of a 'village rustic' who had been killed

by British soldiers because he had defended two Hindu women whom they had been pursuing. What if some Hindu peasants ran after an Englishwoman, and an Englishman were killed for intervening ?[64] A question was asked in Parliament in November by W.S. Caine, a Nonconformist who had devoted much energy to temperance activities in India.[65] It transpired that the Madras Government had taken action, but only after the news had been reported in the *Hindu*.[66] Hampanna, a railway gatekeeper at Guntakal, had been shot by a soldier whom he had attacked with a stick. The Government offered a reward for information and deputed a police officer to investigate.

As a result of the police officer's enquiries Lance-Corporal Ernest Ashford was accused of murder. The District Magistrate of Anantapur, K.C. Manavathan Rajah, committed him for trial before the Madras High Court. Ashford was one of a draft of 120 soldiers who stayed at Guntakal rest camp en route for Secunderabad. They arrived early in the morning, and late in the afternoon half a dozen soldiers followed two women who went into Hampanna's hut. According to the prosecution they tried to go in after the women, but Hampanna stopped them. There was an altercation. Hampanna tried to drive them away with a stick, and Ashford shot him. Ellamma, the first prosecution witness, stood up well to cross-examination. For example:

'How were the Europeans dressed ?'
'Do we observe all that, Sir ? We just went in and shut the door, we, in fact, passed urine – we were in such a fright.'[67]

But there were discrepancies in the evidence of other witnesses. Private Adam Budd said that he asked Hampanna to let him go into the hut and offered him four annas – significantly, the fee customarily charged to privates in regimental brothels. But Hampanna, according to Private Budd, demanded a rupee, and so he went away. Lance-Corporal Ashford said that one of the women signalled to the soldiers. For the defence it was argued that Hampanna and others were chasing the soldiers, that Hampanna raised his stick to strike Ashford and that Ashford then shot him in self-defence. In his summing up the judge drew attention to Ashford's youth : he was only nineteen. The jury acquitted him.

It was common for juries to acquit in such cases. Significantly, the military authorities do not seem to have tried very hard to find the culprit, and the Madras Government took action only after the *Hindu* had reported the case. A local Police Superintendent was compulsorily retired on the ground that he had lacked promptitude and ability in his handling of the matter, but he was apparently not the only person at fault in this way.

This was one of the defects of imperial rule that Curzon decided to rectify. At an early stage in his viceroyalty he told Hamilton : 'The fact is there is no justice in this country where Europeans and Natives are concerned, and the fault lies not in our institutions but in the racial spirit that is deeper than any institution.'[68] If the normal institution of justice could not function properly, they would have to be supplemented. But this was to tread on dangerous ground, morally as well as politically.

When some men of the 1st Battalion, the West Kent Regiment, were cleared of raping a Burmese woman, Curzon suspected the local authorities of indifference and even of trying to hush things up. He was particularly annoyed with Sir Frederick Fryer, the Lieutenant Governor, for not reporting the matter to him : 'He is perched on his hilltop at Maymyo, and I fancy does not do much more than write a letter or two, per diem, at this time of the year.'[69] It was now the hot season. But Curzon's energies were unaffected, and the result of his tireless persuasions was that a variety of punishments were approved by the War Office. The commanding officer was retired ; another officer was brought in to take his place, and the second-in-command was informed that it would be a matter for future consideration whether he would ever receive further promotion ; the adjutant was deprived of his adjutancy ; the battalion Sergeant-Major was retired ; the eight soldiers who were thought to be the chief offenders were summarily discharged ; finally, the battalion was posted to Aden, reputed to be one of the hottest and most uncomfortable stations in the Empire.[70]

Curzon's suspicions were again aroused when he heard of a murder at Sialkot. The 9th Lancers arrived there one evening from South Africa. A few hours later an Indian cook was beaten up so severely that he died, but there seemed to have been no serious attempt to identify and deal properly with those responsible. Again Curzon was shocked by the unbridled lust of members of the ruling race : '. . . two of the soldiers had set upon a wretched native and beaten him so savagely, for failing to provide them with a woman or women, that he died 9 days later.'[71] Again he was even more shocked by what he considered to be the failure of officers to act in a proper manner. Again an extra-judicial punishment was ordered. Officers and men on leave in India were recalled ; there was to be no more leave for a year ; meanwhile, extra sentry duties were ordered.

Godley hastened to congratulate Curzon on his 'triumph' over the Lancers, which he thought would 'do real good'.[72] But as in the previous case Curzon was punishing the innocent as well as the guilty : perhaps he did not realize how much this would stimulate indignation rather than contrition. The matter was brought up in the Commons in the debate on the Indian budget. Colonel Legge, who had once commanded the 9th Lancers, protested against the injustice of collective punishment. Another military back-bencher said that there were always a number of bad characters hanging around cantonments looking for jobs. If such men had committed this crime they would have done their best to put the blame on the 9th Lancers. Hamilton cleverly turned the tables on Curzon's critics by accepting the high reputation of the Lancers : surely, he went on, such a regiment should have made every attempt to maintain its reputation by finding the culprits and bringing them to justice ! Privately he told Curzon of the concern that he found expressed in high circles about collective punishments. But there were always 'influences' working on behalf of 'smart regiments and particularly of the officers' interests' :

> To stop the leave of some smart young men belonging to a crack Cavalry Corps is a punishment which, it is considered, savours of sacrilege. The trooper may do 'sentry go' till the crack of doom without any public protest, but the officers' ease and leave must not be touched.[73]

However, at the Coronation Durbar, which Curzon planned as an impressive display of the might and majesty of Empire, the Lancers were cheered by the Europeans as they rode by. Curzon pictured himself as one who stood alone for justice. '. . . I sat alone and unmoved on my horse. . . .' He had no doubts. '. . . I felt a certain gloomy pride in having dared to do the right.'[74] He blamed racial feeling. But he may have contributed to it by imposing a collective punishment. Yet he considered it important to deter members of the lower classes from damaging racial prestige by immoral behaviour. The morals of the upper classes also seemed in need of attention at times.

6
Upper-Class Morals and Racial Prestige

Just as officials knew that they must maintain high standards of administrative propriety after the Cornwallis reforms, so they came to feel that they should maintain high standards in sexual behaviour, and the *bibi*, or Indian mistress, soon seemed out of place. Several factors contributed to this important change. There was, first, the consideration that her presence decreased the social distance which seemed so necessary to the authority of the official elite and the prestige of the ruling race. There were also new social pressures. The free entry into British India which was allowed to missionaries from 1813 onwards provided witnesses able and willing to denounce lapses from propriety. Many of these missionaries and some members of the government ecclesiastical establishment were enthused by the evangelical revival. A significant example was Bishop Wilson of Calcutta, who criticized *lal bazars* with such eloquence. The improvement of communication with England encouraged more Englishwomen to live in India. These were important not merely as wives for officials, and so opposed to *bibis* as rivals, but also as the nuclei of inward-looking European social groups in every city and town, as well as in smaller 'stations'.

In places too small for such social groups, as well as in newly-conquered territories where such groups had not had time to develop, a different moral climate was apt to prevail. The case of Captain Walters is of some significance. Captain Walters was stationed at Beawar, Ajmir, where he shared house, or 'chummed', as the expression was, with Dr Nell, the civil surgeon. They were on such good terms that Nell's *bibi* used to mend Walters' clothes, with Nell's approval, and when Nell went on leave he asked Walters to look after her, 'in so far that if she required funds, etc., he should supply her'.[1] That was how Nell himself described the situation.

These harmonious relations were abruptly terminated after Nell returned. One evening in November 1868, as Walters recalled it, a servant told him that 'the bibi sahib' wanted to see him. He went into the garden and saw her there. She told him that she was going to Nell but was afraid. Walters explained that he could understand this : 'I myself on one occasion from my own room heard the sound of blows and of the woman crying, and on taxing Dr Nell with it afterwards he said he would do so again and only wished he had had a cane or a stick at the time.'[2] Walters let her sit in his room, which he also used as his office, 'as it was cold and she was tired', and he gave her a blanket to wrap round herself.

Then Nell came in, assumed the worst, and attacked Walters. An undignified scrimmage seems to have ensued. Walters subsequently demanded an apology, which Nell refused in a sarcastic letter which implied that Walters was lacking in masculinity. Walters had said that he was sorry to have hit Nell, but that he had done so in self-defence. Nell replied :

I am not at all aware that you 'struck me in return' ; if you did I freely forgive you. What did strike me was an idea that the exercise was rather exhilarating at the time. When you closed with me after my whip broke, I threw you on the bed and held you there, and said 'I could strangle you now if I wished, but you are not worth hanging for', or words to that effect, but I did not threaten to take your life as you state in your letter. No doubt the sudden transition from amorous dalliance to whipcord confused your memory.[3]

Walters then appealed to the Commissioner of Ajmir, who referred the matter to a court of enquiry composed of three army officers. They reported that this 'disgraceful brawl over a prostitute' was bound to have an adverse effect on the influence and position of the two officers, as well as detracting from the reputation of the administration of which they were part. They also found that : 'Captain Walters failed to resent the great personal insult which had been inflicted upon him in such manner as to properly uphold his social position in the service.'[4]

In other words, Captain Walters had failed to exhibit the aggressive masculinity expected of an army officer, and both he and Dr Nell had failed to behave with the austere dignity expected of government officials. If they remained in office could the British administration still elicit the same combination of fear and respect that ensured submissive obedience from the people ? Both Nell and Walters were deprived of their posts, and Walters also lost his commission.

In British Burma, where there were relatively few missionaries or

Englishwomen at this time, many officials had Burmese mistresses. The Bishop of Calcutta was shocked to learn of such things when he went to Burma, and told the Governor-General. Colonel Fytche, the Chief Commissioner, issued a confidential circular about it in 1867 :

With a race like the Burmese, accustomed under their former Native Government to bribery and chicane, it is probable that in no case is a Burmese mistress altogether free from evil influences. It is a common belief amongst the natives of the country that such women intrigue to prevent suitors and others obtaining a hearing or approaching officers of Government thus situated, except through a corrupt source.

He sent this to Commissioners and heads of departments, instructing them to issue it to every officer under them and to take note of such things when considering promotions.[5]

This aroused dismay among officials in Calcutta. Circular letters might get into the wrong hands. Fytche was accordingly rebuked for being so 'injudicious' as to issue a circular on 'moral considerations of such delicacy, and so to give notoriety to a great scandal'. He headed it 'confidential' but told his Commissioners and heads of departments to issue it to all officers under him. In fact, the newspapers had got wind of it. All that he could do would be to tell any officer living in 'open concubinage' that the Governor-General in Council disapproved and would not sanction promotion in such a case.[6]

The Bishop of Calcutta continued to criticize official immorality in Burma, and in 1871 Sir Ashley Eden, as Chief Commissioner, tried to answer him with statistics. Of 13 deputy commissioners, 11 were married and one was a widower. Of 34 assistant commissioners, 16 were married. The presence of these ladies should make any public concubinage 'impossible'.[7]

But their influence seems to have been inadequate. In 1881 Colonel W. Munro, Deputy Commissioner of Bassein, appealed to the Chief Commissioner because his superior officer refused to recommend him for promotion, on the ground that he had a Burmese mistress. Charles Bernard, the Chief Commissioner, reported that Fytche had many years ago noted against Munro's name : 'Has got a large family about him by a Native woman.' Munro argued that the relationship had begun two decades ago when 'things of this sort were looked at in a much more venial light', and Bernard himself conceded that the custom had continued 'a full generation' longer in Burma than in India. However, he thought that it was now disappearing : 'I believe that in time, with the spread of European ladies over the country, with the increase in the number of the clergy, and with other antiseptic influences, the evil will abate.'[8]

Munro was not promoted, but others do not seem to have been deterred, and in 1888 Sir Charles Crosthwaite, as Chief Commissioner, issued a circular to Commissioners in Upper Burma, where he found it to be 'notorious' that officials were keeping mistresses. He denounced the practice on the familiar grounds that it was scandalous and likely to encourage corruption, and added a new argument – the danger of a Eurasian class. 'The creation of a large class of Anglo-Burmans who are insufficiently educated and left without means of supporting themselves is likely to become a source of difficulty to the Government and to prejudice our name.'[9]

These arguments were repeated in a confidential circular issued by Sir Alexander Mackenzie, as Chief Commissioner, in 1894. He was more concerned to emphasize the danger to racial prestige. An officer who had a Burmese mistress, he wrote, 'not only degrades himself as an English gentleman, but lowers the prestige of the English name, and largely destroys his own usefulness'. He repeated Crosthwaite's warning about the danger of a growing Anglo-Burman class, who would probably 'bring discredit on the ruling race'. He soon began to make public statements on the matter. He explained uneasily to Lord Elgin, the Viceroy, that he had come to think it unlikely that his confidential circular to heads of departments had 'gone beyond the office boxes of the recipients'. Many of them would be 'slow to move in such cases, being unfortunately hampered by ancient sins of their own of the same description'.[10]

He was reported in a variety of newspapers from the *Rangoon Times* to the *Times of India*. The *Sudhakar*, a Bengali weekly, noted with approval that he proposed to punish 'the heartless debauching of Burmese women by English officials', and asked whether stopping their promotion was really an adequate punishment.[11] In Calcutta Sir Antony MacDonnell read the newspaper reports with foreboding. People might be offended. Little good would follow mere exhortation. What he called 'the Indian atmosphere' had been changed by improved communications with England. Would the same process follow in Burma? An additional factor there was 'the greater attractiveness and perfect freedom of Burmese women, who do not regard such connexions as shameful *liaisons*, and who in this are supported by the opinion of their families'.[12]

Mackenzie had himself urged Elgin's predecessor that the remedy was to import more English ladies into Burma. But there were difficulties. There were 'many places where Englishmen are expected to live in mat hovels, to which no gentleman could take an English wife'.[13] In the pioneering days of war and conquest before the Mutiny, Englishwomen had cheerfully endured hard conditions. But Mackenzie's generation thought in different terms.

He also noted that some officials were marrying Burmese wives. He wrote anxiously to Elgin that this would be fatal to their future happiness and 'dreadful for their home folk'. Since marriages usually began as 'illicit connections', he thought that checking the one would also check the other. Apparently it did not occur to him that officials would marry their mistresses rather than send them away.

In 1895 Sir Frederic Fryer, the new Chief Commissioner of Burma, asked the Government of India to transfer two officials because they had married Burmese women. E.A. Moore and H.E. McColl were stated to be 'good officers, of certainly not less than average ability'. But Fryer thought that legal marriages were 'as harmful from the point of view of the administration' as illicit connections. If these officials were in India their wives would be in no danger of bringing local influence to bear on their husbands' work.[14]

On the Governor-General's executive council serious attention was given to this dilemma. J.P. Hewett noted that there were other officials in Burma who also had Burmese wives. He mentioned Colonel Parrott.[15] The mention of the Parrotts roused Sir Alexander Mackenzie, who was now on the council, to mellow recollections : 'Mrs Parrott is a charming lady. I have lived in their house, and she was extremely popular with the ladies of the station.' So personal experience of the household of a mixed marriage could reveal that the spectre was not so terrible – and that English ladies, those guardians of racial purity, in fact had no objections either. Of course, he added hastily, these young men had been 'extremely foolish'. But wives were not as dangerous as mistresses, especially in Burma. 'A man has his wife for good and all, and knows that he must see that she does not compromise him. If he is wise, he will educate and train her, and Burmese women are far superior to Indians in capacity.'[16] Such rash generalizations were necessarily based on ignorance, since officials in India had been effectively discouraged from marrying Indian women, and there the restrictions of caste and *parda* meant that Englishmen had few opportunities of meeting them socially.

It was decided that there were no justifiable reasons why the Government of India should transfer Moore and McColl, although there would be no objection if some voluntary arrangement could be made.[17] But Fryer still asked for compulsion: 'No officer who is so enamoured of Burma that he makes a Burmese woman his wife is likely to consent to leave it because the Government thinks it advisable to remove his wife from temptation.' He now argued that it was the suspicion of corruption, not merely the reality, that he wanted to avoid.[18] In Calcutta L.M. Thornton impatiently dismissed this final plea: 'It is however not uncommon in this country for Government to have to face a popular misconception and trust that it will ultimately give way to a knowledge of facts.'[19]

This was to uncover one aspect of the growing official concern for prestige – a growing lack of official confidence in the ability of the British administration to convince people that its standards were the right ones. Officials were still convinced that their administration was the best for India, but they were anxious now that people should agree with them. Nevertheless, Moore and McColl were not transferred.

The question was revived in 1900 when Curzon received what he described as 'a frantic letter' from Mrs Ada Castle, the wife of Reginald Castle of the Burma police.[20] He gathered that she had 'embarked on a crusade against impurity in Burma', and in her letter she alleged that an Acting Deputy Commissioner was openly living with two Burmese mistresses, one of whom went with him on tour. Curzon strongly objected to open immorality: 'You cannot prevent young English bachelors from consorting with native women. But you can, and ought to, prevent the open practice of these relations by men in responsible positions.' Minns, the official concerned, tried to argue that his mistress had followed him to Kyaukpyu although he had told her not to come, and that she had gone with him on tour 'not as a mistress but as a nurse', because he was unwell.[21] Curzon thought this explanation 'profoundly unsatisfactory', and Fryer agreed.[22] But Minns was soon Deputy Commissioner of Rangoon, although Curzon thought that he should be relegated to obscurity and refused promotion until he had 'purified himself by a course of wholesome living'.[23] Curzon thereafter followed Minns' activities with a critical eye, although Fryer assured him that Minns was 'an excellent Burmese scholar'. His linguistic skill was hardly surprising, for he had discovered the most enjoyable way of learning a foreign language.

Curzon assured Fryer that he had 'no desire to inaugurate a Steadian crusade'. But he was sensitive to all matters which seemed to him to involve the prestige of the ruling race. As for Mrs Castle, he had gathered that 'the Puritanical lady' was 'apt to render her husband's various stations too hot to hold her'. Perhaps he could be transferred to India ?[24] Fryer had already had to move Castle from Pegu because he had criticized the local Deputy Commissioner who was then a respectable married man, although 'Mrs Castle took it upon herself to attack him for previous breaches of the moral law'.[25] Castle was now serving on famine duty in the Central Provinces, and Fryer asked the Chief Commissioner if he would like to keep him. But the Chief Commissioner politely declined.[26] Mrs Castle meanwhile tried through highly placed personages to have her husband transferred to the North-Western Provinces, where his father had served in the police; her letter reached the Queen, who forwarded it to Lord George Hamilton, the Secretary of State, but nothing could be done.[27] Curzon concluded that the Castles were 'constitutionally unfitted to get on everywhere outside of Paradise, and Mrs Castle would probably find immorality lurking even there'.[28]

Lord George Hamilton thought that Mrs Castle was exaggerating :

The Burmese women, I have always understood, are most admirable housekeepers : they are busy engaging females, with a natural aptitude for the society of men, and I am afraid there always will be sexual relations existing between a certain number of Englishmen and their housekeepers in Burma.[29]

Hamilton was uneasily aware of Curzon's reforming energies, and tried to warn him. Englishmen told not to live with Burmese mistresses might marry them, and they could not be warned against marriage : 'we must be careful in public to say nothing that would prick the conscience of the modern puritan.'

Fryer even preferred mistresses to wives : 'The most troublesome cases are those in which civil officers marry Burmese women. The woman, when married, is under no restraint and I was once obliged to tell an officer that I would not give him charge of a district if he allowed his wife to live in the district with him.'[30]

Hamilton also thought that there was much to be said for mistresses : 'These relations do give the officials a good insight into and knowledge of local customs and ideas, but there is always the danger that the mistress might take advantage of her position and receive bribes or embark in other illicit practices.'[31] But as Secretary of State he might be asked some questions. If so, he would have to adopt an attitude of disapproval, and Curzon would then be obliged to force Fryer to take some action. But what action could he take ?

I assume that, if a man chooses to marry his Burmese mistress, he would occupy a position which would free him from official censure, provided she conducted herself with propriety. But a legal marriage would put the European into a lower position in the estimation of the Native, than if he kept the woman as his concubine. Dismissal or retirement from the service would seem too heavy a penalty, and yet, unless you associate some such punishment with the offence, I do not see how you can stop it.

Hamilton also distrusted Fryer's energies, especially in this matter. He had seen Fryer in England : 'He was lethargic and fat, and, even in this more bracing climate, he seemed to have no "go" or "push" about him.'

Then Mr and Mrs McColl attracted Curzon's adverse attention. There was a defalcation in the public treasury where he was serving, and the treasurer, who was found guilty, happened to be the husband of a relative. On another occasion his wife's brother-in-law was found to have similarly benefited himself in the course of his official duties. Fryer applied for McColl to be transferred to India. He thought that McColl was a good judicial officer but that Mrs McColl was 'a very masterful and ungovernable woman'. Instead, Curzon ruled that McColl should not be allowed independent charge of a district for two years. He wanted McColl to 'suffer'. After all, 'We don't want this sort of man and his intriguing Burmese wife in other provinces. It would be a most unfair thing to make them the dumping ground for the men who have committed domestic escapades in Burma.'[32]

McColl appealed against this decision, and to Curzon's indignation Fryer supported him.[33] The papers went to the Secretary of State, and in the India Office there was some sympathy for McColl. In a departmental minute it was pointed out that in the first case McColl had been made to refund half the money lost from the treasury, while in the second case the treasurer had been appointed before McColl arrived, had himself made good the amount claimed, and argued that it was all a mistake.[34] Finally, Hamilton decided that McColl had been sufficiently penalized : this meant in effect that his disqualification would last little more than a year.[35]

Then H.C. Moore, the brother of E.A. Moore who had married a Burmese woman in 1895, decided to follow this fraternal example, and gave due notice of his intention to do so. Fryer soon learnt that H.S.

Pratt, Assistant Commissioner of Bassein, had married a Burmese woman without giving notice. Even his Commissioner, who lived in the same station, was taken by surprise.[36]

Fryer was meanwhile investigating the case of a certain Major Brown, who was thought to have made insufficient provision for his mistress and illegitimate child. Such things did no credit to the ruling race. But the Major explained that he had given her three hundred rupees to open a shop and trade on her own account, and he offered to place their child in a boarding school, but he refused to continue the allowance he had formerly made her because she had since placed herself under the protection of a Muslim gentleman. It was a sad story. Major Brown had married an English lady, but his wife died and he now had his mother-in-law, 'a lady of somewhat austere appearance', living with him.[37]

Troubled by these worrying events, Fryer proposed to issue an order to the effect that no one with a Burmese mistress or wife would be promoted. This aroused concern in the Viceroy's executive council. H.H. Risley solemnly advised against trying to stop officials from marrying : 'English opinion, or at any rate some sections of it, would condemn such action as a reflection upon marriage.'[38] Denzil Ibbetson added : 'And a provocation to the continuance of concubinage.'[39] Risley continued blandly :

But everyone can see that a particular marriage may be open to objection for various reasons, as for instance that the woman had been the officer's mistress or was otherwise of doubtful character and could not be received in society, that she came from a low class, that she had so many relatives and connections in a particular district that she was bound to be credited with exercising influence for corrupt motives.

In this way the Government could make clear that such policies were no reflection on the character of such ladies as Mrs Parrott, who had met with the approval of Sir Alexander Mackenzie, 'a purist in sexual matters'.

After all, Risley added, the high status of the Eurasian Burghers in Ceylon could be explained as the result of their descent from lawful marriages between Dutch settlers and high-caste Sinhalese women. So the dangers of miscegenation, it appeared, could be counteracted by the safeguards of high social status and lawful wedlock. Risley was regarded as something of an authority in such tricky questions : in the ample leisure available to him as an officer of the British raj he had pondered much on the Aryan origins of high castes and paid great attention to the measurements of people's noses, which he carefully examined as evidence of the social and racial status of their ancestors.

Various members of the Viceroy's executive council were eager to give their opinions on what they obviously considered a very important problem. There was support for the view that anyone who married a Burmese wife would be automatically transferred to India : there were precedents in many diplomatic services. A.T. Arundel objected : 'But the public service in Burma would suffer by losing a man so thoroughly acquainted with the Burmese language and by getting in exchange a man who knew nothing of it.'[40] In the old days of the East India Company, many officials were said to owe their fluent command of the vernacular to intensive instruction in such intimate circumstances.

Denzil Ibbetson had a more sarcastic objection : such a rule might be regarded as an incentive, 'since most officers would consider it a privilege to to be transferred from Burma'.[41]

Curzon provided an imperial perspective : 'A man cannot be suddenly taken from one part of India and dumped down in another. There are no vacant dumping grounds. If the guilty man from Burma is to be transferred to India, then an innocent man in India has to be sent to Burma in his place.'[42] In Curzon's eyes, guilt was necessarily attached to intermarriage.

The Burma Government then produced statistics : in January 1903 there were five civil servants and eight police officers with Burmese wives.[43] Curzon wrote privately to Hamilton that 'the evil' was 'assuming increasing dimensions'. Some rules ought to be issued. Officially the Governor-General in Council sent Hamilton a despatch in which they expressed their wish to discourage such marriages as tending to 'domestic unhappiness' and 'grave administrative evils'. They envisaged a deterioration in 'the whole tone and traditions of the Government service in Burma'. To prohibit such marriages might be seen as encouraging 'irregular connections'. But particular marriages might be objected to 'for various reasons', and they cited as examples the instances devised by Risley : 'that the woman in question has lived openly with an officer as his mistress, that she is otherwise of doubtful reputation or belongs to a a low class, or that the character of her family is such as to render the connection administratively objectionable.'[44]

At the India Office Lyall warned that these rules would arouse 'considerable scandal'. A man with a mistress would be urged by his clergyman to marry her. But now 'the fact that a woman has been a man's mistress is urged as a reason for *not* marrying her'. He concluded : 'The clergy will certainly attack the circular if they get hold of it.'[45]

Sir Charles Crosthwaite, now on the Secretary of State's council, also disapproved of the proposed rules :

> I do not think that the Government has any right to dictate to its officers whom they shall or shall not marry. If a man has a wife of whatever race who misconducts herself so as to interfere with her husband's efficiency as a public servant, then he must take the consequences, loss of promotion or in bad cases removal from the service.[46]

But he also questioned the assumption underlying these various discussions. 'I do not see why it should be assumed that every Burmese woman must be dishonest and intriguing. Major Parrott who was married to a Burmese lady was an excellent officer and I never heard anything against his wife.'

Yet even Crosthwaite took it as axiomatic that intermarriages were 'bad'. Therefore he thought that the Lieutenant-Governor ought to warn 'every young fellow' of the 'dangers'. On the other hand, Burmese women were generally admitted to be 'charming', and very willing to comfort English officials doing their imperial duty in lonely places. Here again is that significant ambivalence of attitude to women – seen both as helpful and comforting and also as dangerous and threatening.

It was accordingly decided that the rules should not be issued. In a formal despatch the Secretary of State explained that any such rules would 'multiply connections of the irregular kind'. But the Lieutenant-Governor and his officials should warn 'every young officer' on his arrival that if he took a Burmese wife or mistress his official prospects would almost certainly be damaged.[47]

Curzon received this with some resentment : 'I suppose you are alarmed at the possible misinterpretation of our orders by Exeter Hall. I should have been quite willing myself to run that risk.'[48] Concubinage might be declining but marriage was growing, and he agreed with Fryer that marriage was worse because it was so permanent. He himself, he asserted, would have been prepared to defend such a proposition in the House of Commons, which was in such matters 'one of the most pharisaical bodies in the world'. But Curzon was not a tactful man.

The importance attached to moral propriety in English political life had been illustrated by the difficulties experienced by the Irish leader Parnell after his involvement in the O'Shea divorce case in 1890. A similar scandal soon disturbed official circles in India. Towards the end of 1893 Lord Wenlock, the Governor of Madras, learnt that the non-official members of his legislative council were about to propose Eardley Norton, a prominent Madras lawyer, for appointment to the Governor-General's legislative council. The procedure authorized under the Indian Councils Act of the previous year left it to the Governor-General to decide whether to accept any such nomination. But this scheme of indirect election had been hailed as the beginning of a new era of representative institutions, and the general assumption was that names put forward would normally be accepted. Wenlock carefully explained the difficulty to the Governor-General. Norton's wife was in England, and he was known to be living with another woman, a planter's wife. If he were appointed, there might well be 'an outcry from the purity folk'. On the other hand, it would be convenient to remove him from Madras to Calcutta :

He is also, as you know, a hot Congress-wallah, and by pen and speech has for many years made himself as disagreeable as he could to the Government, almost, if not quite, amounting, at times, to sedition. He is altogether a pestilent fellow, and, personally, I should be very glad to see him removed to other spheres.[49]

If he were disqualified he was quite capable of delving into 'the discreditable records of every public servant for years'. There was also the consideration that it might be politically unwise to disqualify someone so well-known for his sympathies with Indian nationalism.

When the aggrieved husband learnt that Norton had indeed been chosen by the non-officials he protested to the Governor. Surely the moral character of a member of the supreme legislature should be beyond reproach ? He would certainly be citing Norton as co-respondent.[50] Wenlock forwarded this disquieting news to the Governor-General, Lord Lansdowne, and left it to him to decide.[51] Lansdowne, who was near the end of his term of office, decided to postpone all action on Norton's nomination and leave it to his successor to decide.[52] But Norton soon relieved them all of further perplexity by withdrawing his name.[53]

Then the Indian National Congress faced a similar problem. There was what the *Madras Mail* described as 'an exciting scene' when the members of the Congress assembled in that peaceful city for their annual meeting in 1894. Norton was about to move a resolution to the effect that the Secretary of State's Council should be abolished. Suddenly there was a disturbance. Henrietta Muller, a visitor from England, stood up and moved that the name of Eardley Norton be removed from the list of speakers. There was 'a great uproar and confusion'. But Miss Muller persisted, in spite of the cries of 'Shame' which were directed against her. Her amendment, she said, was 'quite constitutional'. The chairman was also a visitor – Alfred Webb, an Irish Nonconformist MP. He ruled her out of order, and she left, accompanied by 'some of the prominent members of the native community'. Norton then made his speech, and the proceedings continued. Later Webb offered a personal explanation. He said that he had ruled Miss Muller out of order because her amendment had nothing to do with the resolution, and he asked whether members considered that he had followed the 'rules of fair play'. There were 'cries of "You have", "You have", and a frantic outburst of cheering'.[54]

Miss Muller wrote indignantly to the *Madras Mail* to explain that she had always supported the social purity movement, and added that a place at the meeting had even been reserved for Norton's mistress, under the name of 'Mrs Norton'.[55] Among those who left with Miss Muller was G. Subramaniya Aiyer, the Brahman editor of the *Hindu*, and she was strongly supported by R. Venkata Ratnam Naidu, a school headmaster, whose exposition of ideas of purity accorded closely with the arguments of Alfred Dyer himself.

In fact, the Congress had always concentrated on political issues. The campaign against the CD Acts in the House of Commons could not be ignored, at least when it became a political issue, and some appropriate sentiments of moral outrage were expressed in the 1888 session of the Congress, but there were signs of impatience : soon some members were shouting 'Enough !' When the matter came up again in 1893 D.E. Wacha, who introduced the relevant resolution, concentrated on 'official mendacity', for which he found evidence in the Russell Report, and C.C. Mitter, who supported him, merely expressed the hope that they would not again have to deal with 'a subject of such a delicate nature', and added 'the less said on the question the better'.[56]

However, ideas of temperance and social purity were acceptable to many politically-minded Indians. On the one hand, such ideas were advocated by Nonconformists whom they respected for their disposition to criticize British policies in India. On the other hand, such ideas accorded with an ascetic tendency in Hinduism whereby self-denial, vegetarianism and continence were highly esteemed as facilitating spiritual development. Social purity and temperance were among the matters discussed at the National Social Conference, which was founded in 1887 and met after the annual sessions of the Congress. They were also discussed with enthusiasm in a variety of other associations organized on a basis of locality or caste. It was easier to agree on a resolution in favour of social purity than on the desirability of legislation to raise the age of consent to twelve. Sir Romesh Chunder Mitter, a former High Court judge, led the opposition to the Age of Consent Bill in 1891, but he actively supported the social purity campaign inaugurated by Bishop Thoburn in Calcutta in 1893.

In Madras, Venkata Ratnam Naidu was a leading figure in such campaigns. He denounced a variety of pastimes ranging from 'that hideous sin engendered by vice and practised in solitude' to the watching of nautch dancers, and urged men to sign a pledge that they would avoid 'indecent pictures', 'impure thoughts' and nautch dances.[57] Throughout the nineteenth century a prestigious but expensive form of hospitality was still to provide a nautch, or more properly *nach*, a performance of traditional dancing, for one's guests, who often included members of the official elite. Such dances were provided in honour of the visit of the Prince of Wales in 1875 and of his son Prince Albert Victor in 1890. But on the latter occasion there were protests. The Bishop of Calcutta forwarded a memorial to Lord Lansdowne, the Viceroy. He claimed that such performances had an immoral character. Lansdowne, however, replied glumly that the proceedings had been 'perfectly decorous'.[58]

The *Sentinel* noted with disapproval that Dr Miller, that missionary who consorted with the upper classes, was a member of the reception committee which organized such a deplorable entertainment for the young prince: 'A Nautch dance is performed by Hindu prostitutes, who usually sing songs of the most lascivious character, accompanied by gestures and movements of the body having an obscene meaning.'[59] Most of the dancing girls were in fact attached to temples, as *devadasis*, or 'slaves of God', and were often involved in prostitution. But the *Sentinel* emphasized the erotic character of their dancing : contrary to Lansdowne's impression that their movements were decorous, Dyer predicted darkly that 'in the case of the young men present' such performances were 'generally followed by acts of sin within a few hours after the exhibition'.[60]

A public meeting was organized in 1893 at Madras Christian College, at which the unfortunate Dr Miller, as Principal of the College, was obliged to preside. Subramaniya Aiyer, the formidable editor of the *Hindu*, took a leading part in the proceedings, and memorials were drawn up calling upon the Governor and Governor-General to shun receptions at which nautch girls were to dance. Wenlock hastily asked Lansdowne's advice. He had no liking for these 'grotesque contortions'. But dancing girls were 'attached to some temple or other', and one ought not to offend religious susceptibilities. Subramaniya Aiyer was so 'advanced' that he was ostracized by more conservative Hindus. There seemed to be difficulties either way : 'I am rather puzzled as to what the best answer should be to these people, and of course I am not prepared to be a bit more virtuous than you are.'[61] One could hardly follow such puritanical principles in England : '. . . we shall not be able to attend any theatrical performance till we have satisfied ourselves as to the moral character of all the performers.' The *Madras Mail*, however, called on Europeans to support the anti-nautch campaign : 'The Hindu social reformer is the product of our Western education, and he must not be left to struggle on alone.'[62]

Lansdowne privately asserted his distaste for Indian dancing : 'I need not say how gladly I would for myself and my successors abjure nautches and all kindred entertainments, but I am not much inclined to surrender at discretion to these well-meaning but intolerant gentlemen.'[63] He thought it sufficient to reply as he had replied to the Bishop of Calcutta in 1890.

In the end, Wenlock's official reply to the campaigners was one of polite disagreement. He had attended several nautches and had never seen any impropriety. Moreover, he had no wish to pry into the morals of dancing girls :

It has never occurred to him to take into consideration the moral character of the performers at these entertainments any more than when he has been present at performances which have been carried out by professional dancers or athletes either in Europe or in India.[64]

Lansdowne's reply was to the same effect. He had never seen any impropriety during any of these performances. Moreover, the performers came to exercise their professional skill as dancers, in accordance with the customs of the country.[65]

These replies were duly published in the *Hindu*, and the editor commented severely that no one had suggested that any impropriety had been shown on such occasions : 'Thank God the Hindu society has not sunk to that depth of degradation.'[66] The objection was that these dances were 'directly suggestive of ideas of the grossest immorality'. Such arguments were unlikely to appeal to the official elite, who were apt to find Indian dancing boring rather than exciting. But the campaign continued. When the National Social Conference met at Madras in 1894, after the Congress session there, Venkata Ratnam Naidu introduced a resolution condemning nautches, and prophesied hopefully that Indian dancing and music would benefit when they were purged of immorality.[67] Meanwhile, the Lieutenant-Governor of Bengal, Sir Charles Elliott, was assailed in a Bengali journal because he had attended a nautch : 'His Honour has been in this country for a long time, and does he not know to what class these dancing-girls belong ?'[68]

There were times when it seemed a lost cause. The reformers ventured an approach to Lord Curzon, who was well known for his stern views of the moral conduct required of the ruling race. But his reply was cold. Like other high personages he professed his unconcern : 'The Viceroy is not himself interested in these performances ; but he hardly thinks the matter is one upon which he is called upon to make any pronouncement or to take any action.'[69]

But the reformers won a victory in 1905. Another Prince of Wales was to visit Madras with his Princess. The executive committee appointed to administer the fund collected for their reception unanimously decided against a nautch.[70] A 'native entertainment' was indeed provided when they came, early in the following year : it included 'Hindustani music', but the most exciting items seem to have been 'Herculean feats by Ramamurti (the Indian Sandow)', and 'Magic and Conjuring by Professor Swaminatha Sastriar'. As in other times and places, moral censorship proved detrimental to aesthetic standards. Moreover, in such matters Western-educated Indians seemed to be absorbing all too readily the ideas and assumptions that prevailed among the British in India.[71]

7
Epilogue

It was not only among the opponents of the regulation of prostitution that suspicious were aroused when the VD statistics fell so swiftly after the military authorities had won their long campaign for a system of control. Major F.C. Rasch, an MP who wanted more stringent regulation, asked the Secretary of State in 1899 whether the practice of treating men in barracks rather than in hospital for 'constitutional', or secondary, syphilis meant that the statistics were now underestimating the number of soldiers with VD.[1] This prompted some official enquiries. The Government of India claimed that outpatient treatment was preferable if one considered the soldier's welfare and military efficiency, and added : 'this is more important than statistical accuracy'.[2] But the military authorities had professed great concern for the statistics when they were rising.

It was in the context of rising statistics that systems of control were successively established and abolished in the nineteenth century. This pattern can first be detected in Madras. The VD statistics were rising, and lock hospitals were therefore established in 1805. But the statistics continued to rise. The efficacy of the system was questioned, and some lock hospitals were closed. But the statistics continued to rise, and the lock hospitals were therefore reopened. A similar pattern can soon be detected on an all-India basis. The statistics continued to rise, the efficacy of the system was questioned, and lock hospitals were closed from 1830 onwards. But the statistics continued to rise, and lock hospitals were therefore reopened, first locally and from 1864 as a matter of all-India policy. The statistics continued to rise, and the efficacy of lock hospitals was questioned in 1881. Some lock hospitals were therefore closed as a social experiment, but the statistics continued to rise and they were hastily reopened. Moral reformers then began to apply pressure, and the lock hospital system was abolished in principle in 1888 and in practice in 1894. The statistics continued to rise, and it was re-established in 1897.

The figures for British troops in India were indeed high. But so were the figures for Dutch troops in the Dutch East Indies. The mean for the three years 1890–2 was 438·1 per 1,000 for the former and 455·6 for the latter. The figures for British troops at home were lower, at 203·7, but not as low as for the armies of European powers.[3] But the force of such comparisons was weakened by the existence of a conscript element in those armies.[4]

Perhaps scepticism can be carried too far. When every allowance has been made for the crudities of contemporary diagnostic criteria and for the idiosyncrasies of medical officers, it is hardly possible to deny that there was a considerable increase in the incidence of VD among British soldiers in India for the greater part of the nineteenth century and a considerable decrease thereafter. The military authorities congratulated themselves on the results of their policies :

VD admissions per 1,000
British troops in India[5]

1901	276
1902	281·4
1903	249·6
1904	200·3
1905	154·3
1906	117·3
1907	89·9
1908	69·8
1909	67·8

This is an impressive, indeed extraordinary, achievement if the statistics can be taken at face value. A reduction from 522·3 per 1,000 in 1895 to 154·3 per 1,000 in 1905 is difficult to explain by reference to the methods of treatment then prevalent, even if the exclusion of readmissions reduce the earlier figure to 391 per 1,000. There was talk of improved methods – treating syphilis by injections of mercurial cream and gonorrhoea by irrigation.[6] This was before Wassermann had improved the diagnosis of syphilis by blood tests or Ehrlich had improved its treatment by using Salvarsan. Clearly, other explanations must be sought. Venereal, like other diseases, seems to wax and wane, and the early twentieth century was a period of waning.[7] There were also the various policies of the military authorities. The reintroduction of control meant that many infected women were confined in hospital at a time when they were particularly infectious. Improvements in educational and recreational facilities no doubt provided a variety of new interests for soldiers. Finally, War Office opposition was overcome, and financial penalties were inflicted upon soldiers who caught VD.[8]

However unreliable the nineteenth-century statistics may be as evidence of medical realities, they are a necessary background to any analysis of the attitudes and assumptions of the military authorities. British soldiers were regarded as vulnerable. They were often referred to as 'our young soldiers'. On one occasion General White even wrote of the danger to 'our boy soldiers'. They were seen as 'reckless', heedless of danger as soldiers should be, but heedless also of the danger of VD. Endowed with the urges of healthy men, they were seen as lacking, because of their lower-class origins, the moral and intellectual resources required for a life of continence. Not that many regimental officers thought a life of continence possible or even desirable. Indeed, there was much sympathy for the view expressed so forcibly by Dyer and his colleagues that the right solution was to allow more soldiers to marry, and there were instances of commanding officers ignoring official policy and allotting married quarters to soldiers who had married without permission.

Indian prostitutes were therefore seen in a positive role as necessary to the satisfaction of the soldiers' physical needs. If those needs were denied satisfaction, dire consequences were envisaged. The soldiers' masculinity would be at risk: the prospect of homosexuality was revealed in guarded terms by the authorities whenever there was talk of excluding prostitutes from cantonments. On the other hand, the women were seen in a negative role as threatening soldiers with a disease which might destroy their manhood. A distinction was often drawn between respectable prostitutes, who accepted the control of the military authorities, and disorderly vagrants, who infested shadowy haunts at night and tempted unwary soldiers to destruction.

Because prostitutes were seen as necessary, there was no attempt to reform them in the lock hospital regime. This was also justified on the ground that they were hereditary prostitutes. The military authorities often emphasized how respectable these professionals were, unlike the deviants alienated from society in Europe. Here we must enquire into the reality behind such stereotypes.

A flourishing industry was revealed to horrified reforming circles in England in 1893. The main military brothel in Lucknow cantonment was a substantial building. In Indian style there were two courtyards, with fifty-five rooms opening onto them.[9] Mrs Andrew described the matron of the Lancers' brothel as a very prosperous person, wearing 'a great deal of solid gold jewellery'. She was also 'a fine-looking woman, that is,' added Mrs Andrew grudgingly, 'judging by the native type'. She kept her correspondence in order, and as evidence of her professional standing with the authorities produced a letter from the Lancers' Surgeon : 'You have not brought your women from Meerut and Ferozepore. You will have to do it or the Colonel will think you have broken faith.'[10] A matron of this type would supply the labour force, take a percentage of their earnings, supervise them and sometimes lend them money, so strengthening her authority by establishing a creditor relationship.

The Lancers' matron was on intimate terms with a British NCO, Orderly Sergeant Edward Theobald. She kept his letters. As Mrs Andrew put it, 'his letters were very fulsome, and he told her that he had forsaken his family for her'. She referred to him as her husband, and he signed his letters 'Your loving husband'. He had petitioned the Cantonment Magistrate for permission to build a house in the cantonment for them both. There was another petition to the effect that he wanted to settle down with her in India until he died. But the Cantonment Magistrate seems to have been unsympathetic, for the sergeant went back to England, presumably under orders.[11]

The Ibbetson Commission noted that four out of a dozen women turned out of a regimental brothel promptly got married. As in England and France, the picture of the fallen woman ending her life in destitution and disgrace did not always accord with reality. But although some prospered and eventually got married, usually to the sons of prostitutes or to pimps, it did not follow that no disrepute attached to their occupation. It was said that in cantonments the registered women prided themselves on their social superiority to sweepers. But under the caste system sweepers were universally despised. Additional discredit attached to those women who had contact with unclean foreigners. Medical officers would often refuse to admit prostitutes to general hospitals on the ground that their presence would drive respectable women away.

Nor were vacancies adequately filled by heredity. Under Stansfeld's questioning Ibbetson conceded that from ten to twenty per cent of the women in military brothels came as a result of socio-economic hardship : some were young widows, the result of child marriage ; some were destitute.[12] Other observers noted an influx of rural women into prostitution in times of famine. Nor did such incentives always suffice, as was demonstrated by the kidnapping crimes in Calcutta and Midnapur. The case was similar with the European women driven by hardship into urban brothels : many were refugees from anti-semitism in eastern Europe. Dina Gontcharoff refused to go back to Russia. Fanny Epstein came out of boredom and a spirit of adventure, but she did not stay. These two, and others who appear for a moment in the archives, were women of an independent spirit, determined to make the best of things.

There is an obvious contradiction between the care with which the military authorities provided facilities for sexual relations between British soldiers and native women, and the care with which other authorities tried to discourage sexual relations between British officials and native women. In both cases the fundamental concern was to preserve the structure of power. In the one case the soldiers' virile energies had to be maintained. In the other case the social distance between the official elite and the people had to be preserved. Captain Walters suffered not only because he damaged the prestige of the ruling race by brawling over an Indian mistress but also because he lacked pugnacity in defending his honour.

The official elite lived like an aristocracy. They were often so described, and they so regarded themselves. Not merely were they mainly recruited from a middle class which admired the lifestyle of the landed aristocracy in England. They themselves had an analogous function in the imperial structure, dominating the administrative and military systems, deriving their incomes from a predominantly agrarian economy and playing a paternalistic role among respectful peasants. So they saw themselves, and social distance seemed essential to their authority : because they were remote they would be feared as alien and trusted as incorruptible.

The stereotypes which were formulated to defend this social distance and to justify the privileges of the ruling race proceeded by a circular reasoning which ignored inconvenient evidence. Eurasians, it was said, did not show the qualities which were needed in responsible posts, and which were shown by the British who occupied the responsible posts from which Eurasians were excluded. Eurasians, it was said, could not be army officers because they would be despised by Indian soldiers. This was to ignore the fact that Eurasian officers had risen to high rank in the service of Indian rulers as well as in the Company's army before their exclusion. Eurasians, it was said, could not be medical officers because they would not be accepted as equals by British officers and would not be consulted by their wives. In the case of Dr Gillies the evidence that he was on good terms with many officers and was consulted by English ladies was similarly ignored. As an alternative argument it was suggested that he was not a gentleman : attitudes to race and to class could readily be deployed to the same effect.

Fundamentally, the Gillies case reveals the sexual jealousy latent in males of a dominant group with respect to males of subordinate groups. Official hackles were raised at the prospect of an English lady being physically examined by a Eurasian doctor. Later in the century, Western-educated Indians are seen as rivals and similar stereotypes are deployed against their claims. There was opposition, in 1888, to the prospect of Indian medical students examining European women patients at the Eden hospital, although it was known that one Indian doctor in particular was on occasion consulted privately by Englishwomen.[13] There was a significant persistence in such attitudes. In 1919 a British soldier acting as an untrained hospital orderly in Lahore was put into difficulties when a European woman was brought in as a patient and the only medical officer available was an Indian who was not supposed to touch white women patients. He could only tell the British soldier what should be done.[14]

Similarly, Indian princes as members of a ruling class but not of the ruling race are seen as threatening the social hierarchy carefully manipulated by the official elite to accord with the structure of power. This threat was perceived towards the end of the nineteenth century when princes were acquiring a Western education and Western tastes. If they married English women, or if they moved in high society in Europe, it was feared that they would learn to infringe the distance separating them from the ruling race. Their designs upon white women were seen as an important reason for restricting their visits to Europe. When a different perception of reality obtruded, and white women were seen as having designs upon them, this was still seen as a reason for keeping them away from Europe. Whatever the shape of the stereotype, it was made to serve the needs of the structure of power.

The case of Miss Pigot is an extreme example of the way in which a threat to authority could condition a person's attitude to sexual behaviour. When she resisted his control, Hastie suspected her of misbehaviour with an Indian who had also challenged him, but he was prepared to overlook it if she would only accept his authority. Mary Pigot was seen to be consciously trying to bridge the distance between the ruling race and the people, and missionaries in general occupied an ambiguous place in the imperial system, on the margins of social distance. Members of the ruling race, occupied in some of its tasks, following a European lifestyle, they often enjoyed close relations with Indians and were sometimes provoked into criticisms of official policy and morals.

In the campaign against the CD Acts and in other issues affecting sexual behaviour, missionaries were able to influence the Government by manipulating parliamentary pressure. Dyer and his colleagues also imported a theme of class hostility to aristocratic vice that had marked the opposition to the CD Acts in England. The official elite were seen as an aristocracy, and missionaries who cooperated with them were criticized for forgetting their duties to the lower classes in India. Indians were quick to join in criticizing lapses from propriety on the part of the ruling race.

This was a sensitive pressure point, for the official elite were uneasily aware of the unruly and immoral tendencies of the lower classes who also belonged to the ruling race. Soldiers could be kept at a distance within cantonments, but this isolation frustrated understanding and encouraged aggressive behaviour when they did come into contact with Indians. The inherent danger of this situation was realized by many observers, not least by Curzon himself. But the alternatives were rejected.

Time and again the idea that more soldiers should be allowed to marry was dismissed as too expensive. The military authorities regulated prostitution, first locally and later on a general and systematic basis. When this policy was abandoned as a result of the campaign led by Dyer and his colleagues, the authorities reverted to less systematic measures. At first these amounted to the compulsory examination of prostitutes, but not to the provision of regimental brothels. But after the First World War, some regiments again began to organize their own brothels.[15]

Apart from the fear that without such provision the soldiers' masculinity would be endangered by disease or homosexuality, there was a deep fear of disorder if sexual behaviour escaped control. A lock hospital system was established at Bangalore in 1855 as an emergency measure on the ground that VD was spreading. But when the VD figures fell, Dr Cole then argued that coercive measures would always be needed to restrain vagrant women. Similar arguments were put forward at other times and places. The fear of a loss of control is recurrent.

The cantonment provided an ordered environment, within which the British soldier could be protected from unsettling contact with Indian life. Most soldiers seem to have accepted the situation, and to have assumed within their world the privileged role of members of the ruling race. They employed Indian servants, and felt the sexual jealousy characteristic of males of a dominant group. Sergeant George and Private Macnally explained in 1893 how the military police would as a matter of course turn Indian males out of brothels used by British soldiers : it seemed only proper to do so. Some soldiers, however, defied convention to the extent of declaring their intention of marrying Indian or Eurasian women. But to the end of British rule the authorities would discourage such unions. All members of the ruling race were supposed to keep their distance.

Source Citations in Notes

Official archives in the India Office Library and Records :

Despatches from London

Bom MD	Military Despatches to Bombay
IMD	Military Despatches to India
ISCD	Statistics and Commerce Despatches to India
MMD	Military Despatches to Madras
M Pub D	Public Despatches to Madras

Letters (Despatches) to London

Bom MLR	Military Letters received from Bombay
IELR	Ecclesiastical Letters received from India
IMLR	Military Letters received from India
MJLR	Judicial Letters received from Madras
MMLR	Military Letters received from Madras

India Office Files

DR	Departmental Reports
J&P	Judicial and Public
Mil. Coll.	Military Collections
RS&C	Revenue, Statistics and Commerce
S&C	Statistics and Commerce

Government Proceedings/Consultations

Bg GP	Bengal General Proceedings
Bg MP	Bengal Military Proceedings
Bom JP	Bombay Judicial Proceedings
Bom MP	Bombay Military Proceedings
IFPI	India Foreign Proceedings (Internal)
ILP	India Legislative Proceedings
IMP	India Military Proceedings
MJP	Madras Judicial Proceedings
MMP	Madras Military Proceedings
M Pub P	Madras Public Proceedings
NNP	Native Newspaper Reports

Private Papers:

India Office Library and Records : MSS Eur

D 558	Lansdowne
D 592	Wenlock
E 214	Fergusson
E 243	Cross
E 355	Fryer
F 84	Elgin
F 108	White
F 111	Curzon

National Army Museum

7101–23   Roberts

Public Record Office

30/48   Cardwell

British Library

Add. MSS 43574 Ripon

Notes

Introduction

1 Hyam 1976, 135 ff.
2 King 1976, 97 ff.
3 Mason 1974, 263, 318 f.
4 It was provided by statute that a majority must have served or lived in British India for at least ten years, and must not have left British India more than ten years before their appointment.
5 Ballhatchet 1978, 192.
6 British soldiers are included in the number of Europeans.
7 Moore 1966, 103 ; Compton 1967, 100.
8 Gopal 1953, 135.
9 Beveridge 1947, 228.
10 Gopal 1953, 138.
11 Hutchins 1967, 111 f.
12 Spangenberg 1971, 353 f.
13 Compton 1968 (1), 274 f.
14 Miller 1976, 6 ff.

Chapter 1

1 Memorandum, Oct. 1886, PP 1888, LXXVII (158), 235 ff.
2 Walkowitz 1974, 10 ff.
3 Adj.-Gen. to Govt, 22–6–1799, Bg MP 16–7–1799, 12 ; Mil. Bd to Govt, 11–12–1797, Bg MP 15–12–1797, 392 f.
4 Adj.-Gen. to Govt, 5–9–1807, Bg MP 15–9–1807, 28 ; General Orders 21–9–1807, Bg MP 21–9–1807, 145.
5 Med. Bd 25–3–1805, MMP 22–4–1805, 2686 ff.
6 Govt resolution 22–4–1805, MMP 22–4–1804, 2686 ff.
7 MMD 7–9–1808, para. 31.
8 Govt to Med. Bd, 30–11–1808, MMP 30–11–1808, 11203 f.
9 Med. Bd 1–5–1809, MMP 9–5–1809, 3310 ff.
10 Med. Bd to Govt, 12–6–1809, MMP 16–6–1809, 4387 ff.
11 Med. Bd to Govt, 9–6–1809, MMP 4–7–1809, 4808 ff.
12 Lt-Col S. Gibbs to Assist Adj.-Gen., 19–1–1810, MMP 20–3–1810.
13 Maj.-Gen. F. Gowdie to Minto, 14–3–1810, MMP 20–3–1810, 2011 f.
14 Med. Bd 4–5–1810, MMP 11–5–1810, 4340 ff.
15 Govt resolution 11–5–1810, MMP 4340 ff.
16 Weekes to Govt, 27–2–1805, Bom MP 29–6–1825, 29.
17 Govt to C.-in-C., 25–6–1825, Bom MP 29–6–1825, 32.

18 O.C. Rajkot to Assist Adj.-Gen.,
27–6–1825, Bom MP 29–6–1825,
30 ; Bom MP 7–9–1825, 32.

19 Suptdg Surgeon, Poona,
16–7–1825, Bom MP 17–8–1825,
59 ; Suptdg Surgeon,
Suvarndurg, 7–9–1826, Bom MP
18–10–1826, 10.

20 Adj.-Gen. to Govt, 20–1–1827,
Bom MP 7–2–1827, 17.

21 Med. Bd to Adj.-Gen.,
22–4–1830, Bom MP 23–6–1830,
308a.

22 Minute, n.d., Bom MP 2–2–1832,
482.

23 Malcolm to Beckwith,
29–11–1830, ibid. 484.

24 Further minute, n.d., ibid. 485.

25 Suptdg Surgeon, Poona,
16–7–1825, Bom MP 17–8–1825,
59.

26 Med. Bd, 1–8–1825 ; Mil. Secy,
C.-in-C., 6–8–1825 ; ibid.

27 Govt to Mil. Secy, C.-in-C.,
28–2–1827, Bom MP 28–2–1827,
110.

28 Govt to Adj.-Gen., 22–11–1830,
Bom MP 24–11–1830, 64.

29 Bg MLR 10–7–1830, para. 3.

30 Bombay Govt to Supreme Govt,
11–11–1831, Bg MP 23–1–1832,
20.

31 Minute, 27–12–1831, Bg MP
23–1–1832, 23.

32 Burke to Supreme Govt,
21–4–1832, Bg MP 28–5–1832,
19.

33 Burke to Supreme Govt,
21–3–1834, Bom MP 21–5–1834,
2471.

34 Carr to C.-in-C., 20–9–1834,
IMP 19–12–1863, 513 f.

35 Carr to C.-in-C., 22–9–1834,

ibid. 514.

36 Wilson to Bombay Govt,
26–1–1836, ibid.

37 Bom MLR 16–7–1834, para. 2.

38 Bom MD 27–4–1836, para. 4.

39 Med. Bd to Govt, 8–1–1835, GO
16–1–1835, MMP 16–1–1835,
66 f.

40 Smith to QMG, 20–2–1830, Bom
MP 10–3–1830, 30.

41 Burton to Adj.-Gen.,
10–8–1839, ILP 2–8–1841, 11.

42 Adj.-Gen. to Govt, 13–8–1839,
ibid.

43 *Sadr Faujdari Adalat* to Govt,
7–9–1839, MJP Sept. 1839,
7435 f.

44 MMLR 22–4–1840, paras 19–20.

45 MMD 13–4–1841, para. 16.

46 G. of I. to Madras Govt,
2–8–1841, ILP 2–8–1841, 12.

47 MMD 22–3–1842, para. 28.

48 Murray to Deputy Adj.-Gen.,
14–7–1838, MMP 21–8–1838,
10250 ff.

49 Med. Bd, 4–10–1838, MMP
21–8–1838, 10323 ff.

50 MMP 21–8–1838, 10336.

51 Ibid. 10262.

52 Ibid. 10267.

53 Med. Bd to Govt, 7–5–1842,
MMP 7–6–1842, with MMLR
Encls.

54 Madras Govt to G. of I.,
6–11–1838, MMP 6–11–1838,
with MMLR Encls.

55 Med. Bd to Govt, 7–5–1842,
with MMLR Encls.

56 Minute, 1–6–1842, ibid.
Quarterly Review, LXX (1842).

57 Govt minute 2603, MMP
7–6–1842.

58 MMD (5) 25–1–1843, para. 5.

59 Report on VD ward, 16–5–1844, MPubP 9–7–1844, 1443 ff.

60 Report on VD ward, 14–6–1844, ibid. 1452.

61 Ibid. 1449 ff.

62 MPubD 28–4–1847, paras 13–15.

63 Order by Capt. Morgan, 28–11–1844, MMP 10–7–1849, 7637 f.

64 James to Adj.-Gen., 15–1–1849, ibid. 7638 ff.

65 Ibid. 8324 ff.

66 Milner to Brigade Major, Cannanore, 19–11–1848, MMP 10–7–1849, 81.

67 Young to Brigade Major, Malabar and Canara, 10–1–1849, ibid. 81.

68 Young to Med. Bd, 6–6–1849, ibid. 129.

69 GO 2570, ibid. 130.

70 J. Macandrew, Deputy Inspector-General, HM's Hospitals, to QMG, 20–6–1855, MMP 17–7–1855, 4885 f.

71 GO 2020, ibid, 4888.

72 MMD (46) 7–5–1856 para. 5.

73 Suptdg Surgeon, Mysore, to Deputy Assist Adj.-Gen., 6–9–1855, MMP 2–10–1855, 6464 ff.

74 Report on Bangalore Lock Hospital, MMP 26–8–1856, 2132 f.

75 Beresford to Adj.-Gen., 25–10–1858, MMP Sept.–Oct. 1859, 3086 f.

76 Assistant Surgeon in charge, Bangalore Lock Hospital, to Suptdg Surgeon, Mysore, 4–1–1860, 6–1–1860, IMP 19–12–1863, 639.

77 Suptdg Surgeon, Hyderabad Subsidiary Force, Secunderabad, 24–11–1858, MMP Sept.–Oct. 1859, 3088.

78 Principal Inspector-General to Adj.-Gen., 7–5–1860, IMP 19–12–1863, 639.

79 GO 2462, 6–7–1860, ibid.

80 Principal Inspector-General to Adj.-Gen., 6–7–1863, ibid. 664.

81 In fact, the distinction between Regulation and Non-Regulation territories was relative.

82 Adj.-Gen. to Govt, 8–7–1846, Bom MP 7–10–1846, 4551.

83 Med. Bd to Adj.-Gen., 27–8–[1846], Bom MP 20–9–1848, 3601.

84 A. Alexander, Regimental Surgeon, to Lt-Col Twopenny 25–11–1847, Bom MP 5–5–1848, 50.

85 Brigadier Hughes, Commanding, Southern Division, to Deputy Adj.-Gen., 1–12–1847 ; J. Kennis, Deputy Inspector-General, Hospitals, to Lt-Col Havelock, 9–5–1848; Lt-Col Havelock, Deputy Adj.-Gen, to Govt, 16–5–1848 ; Bom MP 5–1–1848, 50 ; 15–7–1848, 2398.

86 Med. Bd to Adj.-Gen., 13–7–1848, Bom MP 20–9–1848, 3601.

87 Govt to Adj.-Gen., 6–9–1848, ibid.

88 Morse to GOC, Poona Division, 16–9–1848, Bom MP 8–11–1848, 4182.

89 Adj.-Gen. to Govt, 2–10–1848, ibid.

90 Minute, 19–10–1848, ibid.

91 G. Lidingham to Lt-Col B. Trydell, 27–12–1849, Bom MP 3–5–1850, 2602.

92 E.W. Edwards to Med. Bd, 14–2–1850, ibid. 2601.

93 Morse to Brigade Major, Poona, 2–1–1850, ibid. 2602.

94 Lidingham to Edwards, 13–2–1850, ibid. 2603.

95 Morse to Brigade Major, 14–3–1850, ibid. 2599.

96 Numerical return, Bom MP 9–10–1850, 6691.

97 Numerical return, ibid. 6693.

98 Numerical return, ibid. 6692.

99 Med. Bd to Adj.-Gen., 24–7–1850, ibid. 6685.

100 Edwards to Med. Bd, 8–7–1850, ibid. 6686.

101 Report, 20–8–1850, ibid. 6695.

102 N. Wilson to Adj.-Gen., 23–8–1850, ibid. 6695.

103 Maj.-Gen. S.B. Auchmuty to Adj.-Gen., 27–8–1850, ibid. 6694.

104 Govt to actg Magistrate, Poona, Bom JP 30–12–1850, 11992.

105 Numerical returns, Bom MP 18–6–1851, 3415 ff.

106 Edwards to Med. Bd, 20–2–1851, ibid. 3413.

107 Med Bd to Adj.-Gen., 7–3–1851, ibid. 3412.

108 Trydell to Assist Adj.-Gen., 29–4–1851, ibid. 3419.

109 Auchmuty to Adj.-Gen., 10–5–1851, ibid. 3418.

110 Numerical return, Bom MP 20–8–1851, 5050.

111 Numerical return, Bom MP 31–3–1852, 1464 ff.

112 Numerical returns, Bom MP 20–8–1851, 5051 ; 31–3–1852,

1464 ff.

113 Numerical returns, ibid.

114 Med. Bd to Adj.-Gen., 27–5–1851, Bom MP 20–8–1851, 5048 ; Edwards to Med. Bd, 13–1–1852, Bom MP 31–3–1852, 1461.

115 Govt to Adj.-Gen., 18–3–1852, ibid. 1467.

116 Minute, 22–4–1863, IMP 19–12–1863, 666.

117 Minute, 26–4–1863, ibid.

118 Govt resolution, 26–5–1863, ibid.

119 Adj.-Gen. to Govt, 2–7–1863, ibid.

120 Principal Inspector-General to Adj.-Gen., 20–8–1862, with MMLR Encls.

121 Major H.K. Burne, Offg Secy, Military Dept, office memorandum, 19–12–1863, IMP 19–12–1863, 667.

122 J.C. Brown (Deputy Inspector-General) to Brigade Major, Lucknow, 9–5–1860, ibid. 634.

123 J.B. Harrison, surgeon, memorandum, 22–7–1862, ibid. 658.

124 Lt-Col E.R. Priestley to Brigade Major, Agra, 17–5–1861, ibid. 643.

125 Maclean to Priestley, 18–5–1861, ibid.

126 Troup to G. Harvey, 20–5–1861, ibid.

127 A.S.M. Philips (magistrate), to Harvey, 27–5–1861, ibid.

128 Surgeon to Adj., 3–1–1863, ibid. 654.

129 J.H. Morris (magistrate), to Brigade Major, Allahabad, 7–1–1863, ibid.

130 Rainier to Adj.-Gen., Lucknow,
15–1–1863, ibid.

131 Lt-Col E.B. Johnson, Offg Adj.-
Gen., Lucknow, to G. of I.,
8–2–1863, ibid.

132 O'Nial to Lt-Col R.O. Bright,
13–1–1863, ibid. 656.

133 G. Hutchinson Ray to O'Nial,
8–1–[1863], ibid.

134 Tucker to Brandreth,
15–1–1863 ; Brandreth to
Tucker, 20–1–1863, ibid.

135 A.C.C. De Renzy to Brigade
Major, Multan, 13–3–1863,
ibid. 662.

136 Errington to Deputy Assist Adj.-
Gen., 16–3–1863, ibid.

137 MMD(15) 30–1–1861.

138 IMD(297) 15–8–1863.

Chapter 2

1 PP 1863, XIX (3184), 67 ff.

2 Act XXII, 1864, xix, 7.

3 Governor-General's legislative
council debates, 30–3–1864.

4 Ibid. Trevelyan had now moved
to Calcutta, as finance member
of the Governor-General's
council.

5 OC, HM'S 58th Regt, to Deputy
Assist QMG, 29–1–1869, IMP
March 1869, 586.

6 OC, HM's 107th Regt, to Deputy
Assist QMG, 29–1–1869, ibid.

7 Col F.D. Atkinson to G. of I.,
16–3–1869, ibid. 587.

8 Draft rules, IMP Nov. 1865, 71.

9 Committee to G. of I.,
14–8–1865, ibid. 70.

10 Duties of MO in charge of lock
hospital, ibid. 72.

11 xxv.

12 J. Jones, report, 28–1–1869, IMP
June 1869, 394.

13 NWP Govt to G. of I.,
12–3–1869, ibid.

14 NWP Govt to G. of I., 4–5–1869,
ibid. 396.

15 G. of I. to NWP Govt, 1–6–1869,
ibid. 395.

16 C. Fabre-Tonnerre to Stuart
Hogg (Chairman of Justices),
16–9–1867, IMP June 1868, 381.

17 Ibid.

18 Bengal Govt to G. of I.,
20–1–1868, ibid.

19 Governor-General's legislative
council debates, 27–3–1868.

20 Governor-General's legislative
council debates, 3–4–1868.

21 Editorial, *Friend of India*
(Calcutta), 17–11–1870.

22 Bench of Justices Meeting,
6–3–1872, *Times of India*,
7–3–1872, 8–3–1872.

23 Govt to Clerk to Justices,
18–3–1872, S & C 823/1881.

24 PP 1871, XIX (408), Q 15129 ff.

25 Baptist Missionary Society, draft
memorial, PRO 30/48/35, 83 f.

26 Cardwell to Argyll, 1–7–1873,
ibid. 91.

27 Argyll to Cardwell, 2–7–1873,
ibid. 85 f ; Cardwell to
Underhill, 15–7–1873, ibid. 81.

28 Maj.-Gen. E.B., Johnson, QMG,
to G. of I., 22–10–1873, with
IMLR Encls.

29 Skelley 1977, 253 ff.

30 Circular memorandum,
20–7–1870, IMP May 1888, 1899.

31 Circular memorandum,
8–5–1876, ibid.

32 Ripon, minute, 21–10–1880,
Add. MSS 43574, 237 f.

33 Govt to Municipal Commissioner, 15–1–1880, S&C 823/1881.

34 Woodruffe to Gore Jones, 8–3–1880 ; Admiral's Secy to Govt, 9–3–1880 ; ibid.

35 Govt resolution, 11–3–1880, S&C 700/1881.

36 Memorial, 30–3–1881, ibid.

37 Bom GLR (16) 7–6–1881, para. 8, PP 1883, L (200), 535 ff.

38 Govt to Municipal Commissioner, 16–10–1880, S&C 823/1881.

39 Mandlik to Ripon, 17–12–1880, ibid.

40 G. of I. to Bombay Govt, 18–3–1881, ibid.

41 G. of I. resolution, 14–1–1881, S&C 1054/1881.

42 J. Lambert, evidence, 31–1–1881, ibid.

43 Memorandum, 28–2–1881, ibid.

44 Committee report, ibid.

45 Bengal Govt to G. of I., 30–8–1881, RS&C 230/1882.

46 IHLR 16–1–1882, PP 1883, L (200), 596 ff.

47 ISCD 26–10–1882, RS&C 1899/1882.

48 Minute, 7–6–1881, S&C 700/1881.

49 Bom GLR 19–1–1883, RS&C 598/1883.

50 IHLR, 20–2–1883, ibid.

51 Office minute, 1883, ibid.

52 K[imberley], minute, 20–3–1883, ibid.

53 Committee minute, 3–4–1883, ibid.

54 ISCD (69) 3–5–1883, ibid.

55 Fergusson to Kimberley,

56 Kimberley to Fergusson, 17–1–1884, Eur MSS E214/1.

57 Cornish to Govt, 8–11–1883, RS&C 2090/1884.

58 Committee report, 19–3–1884, ibid.

59 Minute, 15–5–1884, ibid.

60 G. of I. to Madras Govt, 26–8–1884, ibid.

61 Office minute, 21–10–1884, ibid.

62 K[imberley], minute, 7–11–1884, ibid.

63 Surgeon-General to Director-General, Army Medical Dept, 9–6–1884, PP 1888, LXXVII (158), 192 ff.

64 Surgeon-General's note, ibid. 265 ff.

65 C.-in-C., minute, 23–1–1888, ibid. 219 f.

66 G. of I., resolution, 9–2–1887, ibid. 198.

67 D. Chatterton to Magistrate, Saharanpur, 29–1–1878, DR L1V.

68 NWP & O. lock hospital report for 1878, para 13, ibid.

69 A. Scott Reid, report, 1–1–1878, ibid.

70 Emerson to Offg Magistrate, 11–2–1878, DR, LVII.

71 NWP & O. lock hospital report for 1878, DR, L1V.

72 Circular memorandum, 26–11–1883, IMP May 1888, 1829.

73 Circular memorandum, 12–7–1884, Mil. Coll. 315/14.

74 Circular memorandum, 17–6–1886, PP 1888, LXXVII (197) 289 f.

21–12–1883, Eur MSS E214/3.

75 Collis to Deputy Assist Adj.-
   Gen., 3–1–1887, Mil. Coll.
   315/14.
76 Roberts to Dufferin, 16–3–1887,
   National Army Museum,
   7101–23–98–1.
77 *Pall Mall Gazette*, 19–5–1887.
78 *Pall Mall Gazette*, 21–5–1887;
   Methodist Times, 26–5–1887;
   Christian Commonwealth,
   26–5–1887.
79 Cross to Dufferin, 4–8–1887,
   Eur MSS E243/17.
80 E.F. Chapman, QMG, to G. of I.,
   2–8–1887, PP 1888, LXVII
   (158), 209.
81 Peary Mohan Mookerjee to G.
   of I., 17–11–1887, ibid. 257 f.
82 Bombay Govt to G. of I.,
   28–1–1888, ibid. 233 f.
83 'The Black Hand of Authority in
   India', dated Lucknow
   16–12–1887, *Sentinel*, Feb. 1888.
84 Report, 14–1–1888, *Sentinel*,
   March 1888.
85 'Repentance or Retribution. A
   Serious Crisis in India', *Sentinel*,
   April 1888.
86 Rev. H.O. Moore, Bishop's
   Chaplain, Calcutta, to G. of I.,
   5–3–1888, PP 1888, LXXVII
   (158), 277.
87 Dufferin to Cross, 26–3–1888,
   MSS Eur E243/24. The reference
   was to Sir C.U. Aitchison, best
   known for his massive
   compilation of treaties relating
   to India.
88 IMD (75) 29–3–1888, PP 1888,
   LXXVII (158), 210 f.
89 Chapman to G. of I., 5–5–1888,
   with IMLR Encls.
90 IMLR (81) 18–5–1888, IMP May

1888, 1835.
91 *Sentinel*, May 1888.
92 House of Commons resolution,
   5–6–1888, PP 1888, LXXVII
   (339), 303.
93 IMD 14–6–1888, ibid.
94 Governor-General's legislative
   council debates, 25–7–1888.
95 IMD (123) 17–5–1888.
96 Council minutes, 14–5–1888, PP
   1888, LXXVII (220), 297 ff.
97 Dufferin to Cross, 29–6–1888,
   MSS Eur E243/24.
98 Telegram, 30–7–1889, IMP Aug.
   1890, 1764.
99 G.T. Chesney, Governor-
   General's Legislative Council
   Debates, 14–8–1889.
100 Roberts, ibid.
101 *Indian Spectator*, 18–8–1889.
102 W.S.B. McLaren to Malabari,
   23–10–1889, MSS Eur D558/17.
103 W.S. Caine to Malabari,
   25–10–1889, ibid.
104 Malabari to Roberts,
   9–12–1889, ibid.
105 Lansdowne to Roberts,
   23–12–1889, ibid.
106 A. Rees, Secy, Social Purity
   Committee, Wesleyan
   Conference, to S. of S.,
   3–1–1890, IMP Aug. 1890, 717.
107 Rev. K.S. Macdonald, Secy,
   Calcutta Missionary
   Conference, to G. of I.,
   10–1–1890; IMP Aug. 1890, 716.
108 IMLR 4–8–1890 IMP Aug. 1890,
   732.
109 *Sentinel*, March 1890.
110 Ibid.
111 Memorial, 14–3–1890, IMP Aug.
   1890, 718.
112 Panjab Govt to G. of I.,

8–4–1890, ibid. 725.

113 IMLR 4–8–1890, ibid. 732.

114 *Sanjivani*, 6–4–1889, NNP Bengal, 300.

115 *Suraibi o Pataka*, 20–6–1889, ibid. 553.

116 Stansfeld and Stuart to Cross, 14–2–1890, IMP Aug. 1890, 726.

117 Gorst to Stansfeld and Stuart, 6–3–1890, ibid.

118 Thompson to G. of I., 13–8–1891, IMP Feb. 1891, 1973 ; IMLR 4–2–1891, ibid. 1986.

119 *Sentinel*, January 1890.

120 *Indian Spectator*, 15–9–1889.

121 *Almora Akhbar*, 16–7–1888, NNP NWP.

122 *Hindustani*, 21–6–1893, ibid.

Chapter 3

1 *Times of India Overland Weekly*, 7–1–1893.

2 *Sentinel*, Feb., April 1893.

3 Interview with the Rev. Henry S. Lunn, *Christian Commonwealth*, 15–6–1893.

4 Stansfeld to Russell, 27–2–1893, Mil. Coll. 315/30.

5 A. G[odley] to Kimberley, 1–3–1893, ibid.

6 Statement of Facts, with IMD Encls.

7 Stansfeld to Russell, 17–3–1893, Mil. Coll. 315/30.

8 Kimberley, minute, 7–4–1893, ibid. ; Walkowitz 1974, 355.

9 Ibbetson Commission report, 28–6–1893, para. 32, IMP Aug. 1893, 1411 ; PP 1893–4, LXIV (7148), 269 ff.

10 Lt-Col S. Gildea to Assist Adj.-Gen., 24–6–1893, ibid. 496 f.

11 Capt. P.D. Trotter, comments, 24–6–1893, ibid. 392 f.

12 Pretyman to QMG, 27–6–1893, ibid. 391.

13 Frankfort to QMG, 3–7–1893, ibid. 518.

14 GOC Lahore District to QMG, telegram, 6–7–1893, ibid. 464.

15 O'Connor, statement, 10–6–1893, ibid. 349 f.

16 Campbell, statement, 13–6–1893, ibid. 357f.

17 Hamilton, statement, ibid. 371 f.

18 Macpherson to OC Mian Mir, 24–6–1893, ibid. 519.

19 Frankfort to QMG, 3–7–1893, ibid. 518.

20 Maj.-Gen. C.E. Nairne to QMG, 26–6–1893, ibid. 397.

21 Sir George S. White, minute, 1–7–1893, with IMLR Encls.

22 Mrs E.W. Andrew, evidence, 14–4–1893, Q 534, PP 1893–4, LXIV (7148), 67.

23 Sgt T. George, statement, 8–6–1893, ibid. 335.

24 Maj.-Gen. T. Graham to QMG, 15–6–1893, ibid. 419 f.

25 Macnally, statement, 14–6–1893, ibid. 365 f.

26 George, statement, 8–6–1893, ibid. 335.

27 Para. 53 f, ibid. 297.

28 Carlew, statement, 19–6–1893, ibid. 370 f.

29 Nairne to QMG, 26–6–1893, ibid. 397.

30 White, minute, 1–7–1893, with IMLR Encls.

31 IMLR. 11–7–1893.

32 *Christian Commonwealth*, 11–5–1893.

33 *Christian Commonwealth*, 18–5–1893.

34 *Review of Reviews*, June 1893, 597.

35 Evidence, 4–8–1893, Q 1781, PP 1893–4, LXIV (7148), 107 ff.

36 Q 2292 ff., ibid.

37 Evidence, 11–8–1893, Q 2311 ff., ibid.

38 Note, 11–8–1893, ibid. 189.

39 *Sentinel*, December 1893.

40 Report, 31–8–1893, para. 48 ff., PP 1893–4, LXIV (7148), 23 ff.

41 Dissenting minute, 2–9–1893, ibid. 27 ff.

42 *Christian Commonwealth*, 18–5–1893.

43 IMLR 1–11–1893, para. 11.

44 Report, 19–12–1893, IMP March 1894, 1118 ; IMLR (37) 7–3–1894 ; departmental minute, Mil. Coll. 315/41.

45 Memorandum, 25–1–1894, para. 13, with IMD Encls.

46 IMD (26) 1–3–1894.

47 Minute 27–2–1894, Indian Council Minute Book, 6 ff.

48 Minutes of Council of India, Jan.–June 1894, 96 ff. ; Godley to Elgin, 2–3–1894, MSS Eur F84/29a.

49 IMD (25) 1–3–1894, para. 3 f.

50 Kimberley to Elgin, 9–3–1894, MSS Eur F84/12.

51 Elgin to Brackenbury, 21–3–1894, MSS Eur F84/12.

52 Elgin to Fowler, 22–5–1894, MSS Eur F84/12.

53 Governor-General's legislative council debates, 12–7–1894.

54 Ibid., 24–1–1895.

55 Fowler to Elgin, 20–7–1894, MSS Eur F84/12 ; Miller to Elgin,

56 Chief Commr's Offg Secy to G. of I., 18–8–1894, IMP June 1895, 1542.

57 Chief Commr's Offg Chief Secy to G. of I., 7–9–1894, ibid. 1544.

58 Fendell Currie to NWP. & O Govt, 7–8–1894, ibid. 1546.

59 F. Giles to Commr, Kumaon, 11–8–1894, ibid. 1546.

60 H.E.M. James to Bombay Govt, 27–10–1894, ibid. 1547.

61 Actg District Magistrate, Ahmadabad, to Bombay Govt, 23–8–1894, ibid.

62 Commr to Chief Commr, Burma, 30–8–1894, J&P 346/1895.

63 Commr to Chief Commr, Burma, 27–8–1894, ibid.

64 President, Defence Association, to G. of I., 16–1–1895, IMP June 1895, 1551.

65 Elgin to Fowler, 16–10–1894, MSS Eur F84/12.

66 Elgin to Fowler, 30–10–1894, ibid.

67 Fowler to Elgin, 30–11–1894, ibid.

68 Fowler to Elgin, 21–12–1894, ibid.

69 Fowler to Elgin, 24–8–1894, ibid.

70 Fowler to Elgin, 24–8–1894, ibid.

71 IMD (137) 29–11–1894.

72 Fowler to Elgin, 30–11–1894, MSS Eur F84/12.

73 White to Connaught, 4–9–1894, MSS Eur F108/18.

74 Reay to Elgin, 30–11–1894, MSS Eur F84/29.

75 Harvey to MacDonnell,

9–8–1894, MSS Eur F84/65.

5–1–1895, MSS Eur F84/66.

76 MacDonnell to C.S. Bayley (Viceroy's Private Secy), 5–1–1895, ibid.

77 MacDonnell to Bayley, 6–1–1895, ibid.

78 Viceroy to S. of S., telegram, 7–1–1895, MSS Eur F84/18.

79 S. of S. to Viceroy, telegram, 10–1–1895, ibid.

80 Viceroy to S. of S., telegram, 11–1–1895, ibid.

81 Godley to Elgin, 10–1–1895, MSS F84/30a.

82 S. of S. to Viceroy, telegram, 16–1–1895, MSS Eur F84/18.

83 Viceroy to S. of S., telegram, 21–1–1895, ibid.

84 Governor-General's legislative council debates, 24–1–1895.

85 Minute, 1894, IMP June 1895, 1546.

86 Governor-General's legislative council debates, 24–1–1895.

87 Godley to H. Babington-Smith (Viceroy's Private Secy), 25–1–1895, MSS Eur F84/30a.

88 Elgin to Fowler, 30–1–1895, MSS Eur F84/13.

89 Elgin to Fowler, telegram, 28–1–1895, MSS Eur F84/18.

90 Abdul Razak *et al.* to Governor-General in Council, n.d., IMP Aug. 1895, 1841.

91 Capt. J.C. Sutherland to Deputy Assist Adj.-Gen., 25–5–1895, ibid, 1842.

92 Maj.-Gen. G.E.L.S. Sanford to Deputy Assist Adj.-Gen., 11–6–1895, ibid.

93 Ellis to QMG, 27–6–1895, ibid.

94 G. of I. to NWP Govt, 24–7–1895, ibid. 1844.

95 PMO, minute, 20–7–1894, IMP Sept. 1896, 1482 ; QMG to G. of I., 30–1–1895, ibid. 1782.

96 IMLR(184) 4–11–1896.

97 *Pioneer Mail*, 14–1–1897.

98 *Lancet*, 30–1–1897.

99 Hamilton to Elgin, 19–2–1897, MSS Eur F84/15.

100 Ibid.

101 *The Times*, 20–2–1897.

102 Army Sanitary Commission, memorandum, 9–3–1897, Mil. Coll. 315/50A.

103 Royal College of Surgeons, address, 11–3–1897 ; Royal College of Physicians, address, 29–3–1897 ; PP 1897, LXIII (8402), 613 ff.

104 PP 1897, LXIII (8379), 569 ff.

105 *Daily Telegraph*, 20–3–1897.

106 *Daily Telegraph*, 23–3–1897.

107 *The Times*, 1–4–1897.

108 *The Times*, 5–4–1897.

109 *Lancet*, 3–4–1897.

110 Elgin to Hamilton, 10–3–1897, MSS Eur F84/95.

111 Onslow to Elgin, 12–3–[1897], MSS F84/27.

112 Hamilton to Elgin, 26–3–1897, MSS Eur F84/15.

113 IMD(25) 24–3–1897, paras 11, 12, 14.

114 Hamilton to Elgin, 9–4–1897, MSS Eur F84/15.

115 Princess Christian *et al.* to Salisbury, 24–4–1897, PP 1897, LXIII (8495), 637 f.

116 W.S.B. McLaren, Chairman, memorial, 15–4–1897, ibid. 627 ff.

117 *The Times*, 21–4–1897.

118 Josephine Butler to Frances E. Willard, 29–11–1897, *Sentinel*,

January 1898.

119 Lady Henry Somerset to
Hamilton, 27–1–1898, *Shield*,
March 1898.

120 Hamilton to Elgin, 9–4–1897,
MSS Eur F84/15.

121 O[nslow) to Elgin, 16–6–1897,
Mil. Coll. 315/56.

122 General Order, 14–7–1897, PP
1898, LXI (9017).

123 Hamilton to Elgin, 9–7–1897,
MSS Eur F84–15.

124 Hamilton to Elgin, 18–6–1897,
ibid.

125 War Office to India Office,
26–7–1897, with IMD (94)
1–8–1898.

126 Grass cutters to Garrison
Quartermaster, Fort William,
1–6–1897, IMP October 1897,
1681.

127 Garrison Quartermaster to
Assist Adj.-Gen., 3–6–1897,
ibid.

128 QMG to Lt Gen. Cmdg Forces,
Bengal, 2–8–1897, ibid.

129 *Shield*, March 1900, April 1900.

130 Taylor to G. of I., 9–8–1900, IMP
Feb. 1900, 1333.

131 Taylor to G. of I., 15–8–1901,
IMP Jan. 1902, 2486.

132 *Shield*, Jan. 1901.

Chapter 4

1 House of Commons,
23–4–1793, Parl. Debs, XXX,
675.

2 Eurasians also enjoyed a good
position in Indonesia. Bagley
1973, 43 ff.

3 MD 6–4–1687, para. 8.

4 Court minutes, 19–4–1791, 17 ;
9–11–1791, 576.

5 Ghosh 1970, 84.

6 Bentinck appointed a Eurasian,
Thomas Warden, as Principal
Collector of Malabar. Rosselli
1974, 205 f.

7 Evidence, 30–3–1830, PP 1830,
VI (646), 185 ; cp. Compton (2)
1968, 142 f.

8 Evidence, 23–2–1832, PP
1831–2, XIII (735–V) 17.

9 Evidence, 21–6–1830, PP 1830, V
(655), Q 6049.

10 Evidence, 4–3–1830, PP 1830, VI
(646), 45.

11 IELR 27–5–1835, para. 18.

12 Petition from East Indians of
Bengal Presidency, presented
9–8–1853, PP 1852–3, XXVII
(897), 821 ff.

13 Evidence, 23–6–1853, PP
1852–3, XXXII (627–I), Q 6698
ff.

14 *Athenaeum*, 7–4–1859 ;
9–4–1859.

15 *Annual Report of the Madras
Medical College*, 1858–9, in
*Selections from the Records of the
Madras Government*, LVIII.

16 *Madras Daily Times*, 9–4–1859.

17 *Athenaeum*, 24–5–1859.

18 Reader 1966, 65.

19 *Athenaeum*, 14–4–1859.

20 OC, 7th Light Cavalry, to Assist
Adj.-Gen., n.d., actg suptdg
surgeon to Assist Adj.-Gen.,
27–6–1856, 27–6–1856, MMP
12–8–1856, 1978 ff ; GO 1998,
12–8–1856, ibid. 1984.

21 Board of Examiners, Royal
College of Surgeons,
10–8–1855, MMP Dec. 1859,
3978 Rr.

22 Heeley to Gillies, 12–3–1859, ibid. 3978 Xx.

23 Macpherson to Director-General, 11–3–1859, ibid. 3978 D–N.

24 Gillies, 19–9–1859, ibid. 3978 Rr.

25 Macpherson to Director-General, 17–3–1859, ibid. 3978 Ii9.

26 Director-General to Adj.-Gen., 30–9–1859, ibid. 3972–7.

27 Gillies, notes, ibid. 3972–7.

28 Adj.-Gen., to Govt, 31–10–1859, 3971, 287.

29 Gillies, report, 3978 Q, explanation, 3978 Y.

30 Macpherson, comments, 3978 Q.

31 Committee to Director-General, 30–4–1859, ibid. 3978 D.

32 Gillies, explanation, 19–9–1859, ibid. 3978 Oo.

33 F. Cooper to Macpherson, 28–2–1859, with comments from Gillies, ibid. 3978 Ee5.

34 Shubrick to Gillies, 6–7–1859, ibid. Cc 3.

35 Macleane to Macpherson, 7–3–1859, ibid. 3978 L.

36 Kempt to Gillies, 19–9–1859, ibid. 3978 Hh8.

37 Ward to Dixon, 18–3–1859, ibid. 3978 Zz.

38 Ottley, statement, 29–7–1859, ibid. 2978 Ff6–Gg7.

39 Dixon to Gillies, 16–8–1858, ibid. 3978 Uu.

40 Marianne Heeley to Gillies, 25–2–1859, ibid. 3978 Vv.

41 Gillies, comment, ibid. 3978 Jj.

42 Adj.-Gen. to Govt, 31–10–1859, ibid. 3971, 287.

43 Ibid.

44 Director-General to Adj.-Gen., 30–9–1859, ibid. 3972–7.

45 Adj.-Gen. to Govt, 31–10–1859, ibid. 3971, 287.

46 Minute, 7–11–1859, ibid. 3978 Kk11, 288.

47 Minute, 8–11–1859, ibid. 3978 Ll12, 290.

48 GO 4494, 17–12–1859, ibid. Ll12, 291.

49 MMD (91) 26–5–1860.

50 Wood to Trevelyan, 16–10–1864, cited in Compton 1968 (1).

51 *Hansard* (3rd Ser.), 1865, CLXXIX, 418, ibid.

52 *Athenaeum*, 18–10–1859.

53 MMLR(242) 11–9–1862.

54 MMD(2) 8–1–1863, para. 4.

55 Macpherson to Principal Inspector-General, 25–2–1864, MMP 16–6–1864, 1863 ff.

56 Macpherson to Principal Inspector-General, 3–12–1864, MMP 21–12–1864, 4655.

57 W.T. Denison, minute, n.d., MMP 1–9–1865, 4023 f.

58 GO 3321, 6–9–1865, MMP 6–9–1865.

59 Bristow 1977, 87.

60 Jeffrey 1976, 340.

61 *Friend of India*, 16–10–1883.

62 Ibid.

63 *Indian Daily News*, 10–9–1893.

64 Macmillan 1926, 97 ; *Indian Daily News*, 10–9–1883.

65 *Indian Daily News*, 5–9–1883.

66 *Indian Daily News*, 13–9–1883, 17–9–1883, 18–9–1883, 21–9–1883.

67 *Bombay Guardian*, 24–9–1883,

Opinions of the Indian Press in the Defamation Case, Pigot v. Hastie, 30 f.

68 *Indian Christian Herald,* 5–10–1883, ibid. 49 ff.

69 *Friend of India,* 9–10–1883

70 *Indian Statesman,* 22–4–1884.

71 Macmillan 1926, 106.

72 In re William Hastie (1885), *Indian Law Reports,* 11 Cal 451.

73 Col J.C. Ardagh (Viceroy's Private Secy) to Sir H.M. Durand (Secy, Foreign Dept, G. of I.), 25–4–1893, MSS Eur D558/24.

74 Curzon to Hamilton, 3–10–1900, MSS F111/159.

75 *Simla News,* 11–10–1900.

76 Havelock to Elgin, 10–2–1897, MSS Eur F84/49.

77 Madras Govt to G. of I., 16–6–1900, IFPI, July 1900, 206.

78 Curzon to Hamilton, 12–9–1900, MSS Eur F111/159.

79 Curzon to Hamilton, 21–8–1901, MSS Eur F111/160.

80 Curzon to Hamilton, 10–1–1901, ibid.

81 Curzon to Hamilton, 18–7–1900, MSS Eur F111/159.

82 Hamilton to Curzon, 1–11–1900, ibid.

83 Godley to Curzon, 22–11–1900, ibid.

84 Hamilton to Curzon, 29–8–1900, ibid.

85 Curzon to Hamilton, 29–8–1900, ibid.

86 Curzon to Hamilton, 25–7–1900, ibid.

87 Curzon to Hamilton, 29–8–1901, MSS Eur F111/160.

88 Curzon to Hamilton,

15–11–1901, ibid.

89 Hamilton to Curzon, 17–9–1902, MSS Eur F111/161.

90 Curzon to Hamilton. 20–8–1902, ibid.

91 Curzon to Hamilton, 27–8–1902, ibid.

92 Ibid.

93 Hamilton to Curzon, 19–6–1903, MSS Eur F111/162.

94 Curzon to Hamilton, 3–12–1902, MSS Eur F111/161.

Chapter 5

1 *Friend of India,* 8–10–1835.

2 W. Walker, evidence, 18–10–1861, PP 1863, XIX–I (3184), 491.

3 Commandant, Police, to Chef de Service, 27–9–1860, Archives Nationales, section outre-mer, Inde : Police, Carton 348, Dossier 207.

4 *Friend of India,* 7–6–1866, 17–5–1866, 24–5–1866 ; Compton 1968 (2), 117.

5 Commr, Bhagalpur, to Govt, 18–6–1867 ; Offg Commr, Patna, to Govt, 1–10–1867, Bg GP March 1868, 21 ff.

6 *Sentinel,* January 1888.

7 MS Dictionary of Quaker Biography, Friends House, Euston Road, London.

8 *The Times,* 25–11–1891, 1–12–1891.

9 V. Lister (Foreign Office) to [V. Epstein], 8–10–1891, J & P 1709/1891.

10 Office minute, 29–9–1891, J & P 1607/1891.

11 Office minute, 30–9–1891, ibid.

12 S. of S. to Bombay Govt,
8–10–1891, ibid.

13 Hiscocks, report, 16–11–1891, J
& P 2082/1891 ; Miss Epstein's
statement, J&P 1709/1891.

14 Anonymous letter to 'unknown
friend of Mr Epstein',
8–10–[1891], J&P, 1709/1891.

15 Gell to Bombay Govt,
11–11–1891, J&P 2082/1891.

16 Hiscocks, report, 16–11–1891,
ibid.

17 *The Times*, 14–12–1891.

18 Memorial, n.d., J&P
1083/1894 ; *Sentinel*, March
1892.

19 R.H. Vincent to Govt,
16–5–1894, para. 4, J&P
1083/1894.

20 Resolution, 25–7–1892, ibid.

21 *Sentinel*, Nov. 1892.

22 B. Gordon (Chief Medical
Officer, lock hospital) to
Surgeon-General, 18–6–1884, R
S & C 2090/1884.

23 Staal to Rosebery, 10–1–1894 ;
Kimberley to Governor of
Bombay, 24–1–1894 ; Bombay
Govt to S. of S., 11–4–1894 ;
J&P 90/1894, 760/1894.

24 India Office to Foreign Office,
11–5–1894, J&P 760/1894.

25 Sir John Lambert (Police
Commissioner, Calcutta) to
Govt, 9–3–1894, J&P 950/1895.

26 Ibid.

27 L.P. Shirres, magistrate,
Midnapur, to Commr,
Burdwan, 10–12–1893, ibid.

28 Bishop J.M. Thoburn, speech,
27–11–1893, with Rev. J.P.
Ashton (Secy, Calcutta
Missionary Conference) to Lt

Governor, Bengal, 1–12–1893,
ibid.

29 *Reis and Rayyet*, 2 Dec. 1893 ;
Lambert to Govt, 22–5–1894
(5054), J&P 950/1895.

30 Lambert to Govt, 21–5–1894
(4978), ibid.

31 Tabular statement, ibid.

32 Ashton to Lt Governor of
Bengal, 26–4–1894, ibid.

33 Lambert to Govt, 22–5–1894
(5063), ibid.

34 Bengal legislative council
debates, 19–1–1895, 16–2–1895.

35 Ibid. 23–3–1895.

36 Walkowitz 1974, 26 f.

37 *Sentinel*, May 1894.

38 Ibid., March 1894.

39 Ibid., July 1894.

40 Decision by J. Sanders Slater,
Chief Presidency Magistrate, in
Damaji Lakshmichand v. *Rev. A.W.
Prautch and others*, 19–4–1894,
J&P 1083/1894.

41 *Sentinel*, September 1894.

42 Ibid., October, November 1894.

43 Viceroy to S. of S., telegram,
8–5–1894, J&P 813/1894.

44 J&P 1083/1894.

45 Vincent to Govt, 16–5–1894,
ibid.

46 Bristow 1977.

47 *Sentinel*, March 1894.

48 Ibid., May 1894.

49 Ibid., Sept. 1894.

50 Ibid., Nov. 1894.

51 Ibid., June 1900.

52 Rev. W.F. Armstrong, Pastor,
and Deacons of Immanuel
Baptist Church, Rangoon, to
Burma Govt, 29–3–1900, J&P
561/1903.

53 Mrs Phinney and Mrs Mawson

to Burma Govt, 2–4–1900, ibid.

54 Petition to D.M. Smeaton, Financial Commr, n.d. ibid.

55 Deputy commr, Rangoon, to Commr, Pegu, 4–4–1900, ibid.

56 Note by 'a private medical practitioner', 24–7–1900, ibid.

57 Note on A. Williams, minute, 16–8–1902, MSS Eur F111/279. Williams was Deputy Secretary, Home Dept.

58 Minute, 25–8–1902, ibid.

59 Minute, 26–8–1902, ibid.

60 Minute, 27–8–1902, ibid.

61 T. Raleigh, minute, 3–9–1902, ibid.

62 Risley, minute, 8–10–1902, ibid.

63 J.T. Woodroffe, in Bengal legislative council debates, 24–2–1903.

64 *Hindu*, 10–10–1893.

65 *Hansard* (4th ser.), 1893, XVIII, 1526 f.

66 MJLR (5), 10–4–1894.

67 Trial, J&P 747/1894.

68 Curzon to Hamilton, 15–8–1900, MSS Eur F111/159.

69 Curzon to Hamilton, 14–6–1899, MSS Eur F111/158.

70 IMLR (66), 10–5–1900.

71 Curzon to Godley, 18–6–1902, MSS Eur F111/161.

72 Godley to Curzon, 2–10–1902, ibid.

73 Hamilton to Curzon, 27–11–1902, ibid.

74 Curzon to Hamilton, 8–1–1903, Ronaldshay 1928, II, 247.

Chapter 6

1 Nell, statement, 20–11–1868, IMP March 1869, 589.

2 Capt. J.J. Walters to Col R.H. Keatinge (Commr, Ajmir), 19–11–1868, ibid.

3 G.M. Nell to J.S. Walters, 17–11–1868, ibid. 586.

4 Court of enquiry report, 21–11–1868, ibid. 589.

5 Confidential circular, 19–6–1867, MSS Eur F111/281.

6 G. of I. to Chief Commr, 17–7–1867, ibid.

7 Eden to Bishop of Calcutta, 1871, ibid.

8 Note, 20–8–1881, ibid.

9 Circular to Commrs, Upper Burma, 19–12–1888, ibid.

10 Confidential circular, 8–8–1894, ibid. ; Mackenzie to Elgin, 13–4–1894, MSS Eur F84/65.

11 *Sudhakar*, 21–12–1894. Its circulation was officially noted as two thousand, but each copy was doubtless read by many, as was usual with such journals. NNP, Bengal, 1894.

12 MacDonnell to H. Babington Smith (Viceroy's Private Secy), 17–11–1894, MSS Eur F84/65.

13 Mackenzie to Elgin, 16–4–1894, ibid.

14 Chief Commr's Chief Secy to G. of I., 4–10–1895, MSS Eur F111/281. Fryer soon came to regard marriage as more harmful because more permanent than an 'illicit connection'.

15 Minute, 15–10–1895, MSS Eur F111/281.

16 Minute, 16–10–1895, ibid.

17 Elgin, minute, 17–10–1895 ; G. of I. to Chief Commr, Burma, 23–10–1895, ibid.

18 Chief Commr's Chief Secy to G
    of I., 8–11–1895, ibid.
19 Minute, 21–11–1895, ibid.
20 Curzon to Fryer, 7–4–1900, MSS
    Eur F111/201.
21 Fryer to Curzon, 24–10–1900,
    ibid.
22 Curzon to Fryer, 1–6–1900, ibid.
23 Ibid.
24 Curzon to Fryer, 7–4–1900, MSS
    Eur F111/201.
25 Curzon to Hamilton,
    21–8–1901, MSS Eur F111/160.
26 Castle then served for a year in
    the Bombay Presidency, but
    returned to Burma in 1902,
    where he remained until he
    retired in 1914.
27 Hamilton to Curzon, 1–8–1901,
    MSS Eur F111/160.
28 Curzon to Fryer, 23–11–1900,
    MSS Eur F11/201.
29 Hamilton to Curzon, 4–7–1901,
    MSS Eur F111/160.
30 Fryer to Curzon, 24–4–1900,
    MSS Eur F111/201.
31 Hamilton to Curzon,
    15–8–1901, MSS Eur F111/160.
32 Curzon to Fryer, 22–7–1901,
    MSS Eur E355.
33 Fryer to Curzon, 11–10–1902.
    ibid.
34 J&P 2327/1902.
35 I Pub D (156) 12–12–1902, ibid.
36 Fryer to Curzon, 28–11–1902,
    MSS Eur E355.
37 Fryer to Curzon, 26–9–1902,
    ibid.
38 Minute, 12–12–1902, MSS Eur
    F111/281.
39 Marginal comment, ibid.
40 Minute, 26–1–1903, ibid.
41 Minute, 27–1–1903, ibid.
42 Minute 29–1–1903, ibid.
43 Burma Govt to G. of I.,
    24–1–1903, J&P 517/1903.
44 I Home Pub LR (7), 26–2–1903,
    ibid.
45 C.J. Lyall, minute, 19–3–1903,
    ibid.
46 Minute, n.d., ibid.
47 I Pub D (40), 10–4–1903.
48 Curzon to Hamilton,
    30–4–1903, MSS Eur F111/162.
49 Wenlock to Lansdowne,
    31–12–1893, MSS Eur D558/25.
50 W.S Sullivan to Wenlock,
    8–1–1894, ibid.
51 Governor's Private Secy to
    Viceroy's Private Secy,
    12–1–1894, ibid.
52 Lansdowne to Wenlock,
    27–1–1894, MSS Eur D592–3.
53 Norton to Viceroy, telegram,
    31–1–1894, MSS Eur F84/64.
54 *Madras Mail*, 28–12–1894.
55 *Madras Mail*, 29–12–1894.
56 Indian National Congress
    Annual Reports, 1888, 1893.
57 Chintamani 1901, 249 ff.
58 Lansdowne to Bishop of
    Calcutta, 11–10–1890, MSS Eur
    D558/19.
59 *Sentinel*, Feb. 1893.
60 *Sentinel*, April 1893.
61 Wenlock to Lansdowne,
    9–5–1893, MSS Eur D558/24.
62 *Madras Mail*, 10–5–1893.
63 Lansdowne to Wenlock,
    16–5–1893, 20–5–1893, MSS Eur
    D558/24.
64 Governor's Private Secy to Secy,
    Hindu Reform Association,
    Madras, 4–10–1893, *Hindu*,
    9–10–1893.
65 Viceroy's Private Secy to Secy,

Hindu Reform Association, Madras, 23–9–1893, ibid.

66 Editorial, ibid.

67 Report of Eighth National Social Conference, 19 ff.

68 *Sanjivani*, 8–12–1894, NNP Bengal 1894.

69 Viceroy's Private Secy, 22–12–1900, Report of the Fourteenth National Social Conference, 126ff.

70 Singer 1972, 172.

71 During the anti-nautch period there was a danger that the tradition might be interrupted. Balasaraswati herself saw little of traditional dance during her childhood ; ibid. 181.

Chapter 7

1 House of Commons, 20–3–1899, *Hansard* (4th ser.), LXVII, 1316.

2 Departmental minute M2640, 12–3–1900, Mil. Coll. 315/66.

3 Para. 16. PP 1897, LXIII (8379), 569 ff.

4 Flexner 1914, 371.

5 Mil. Coll. 315–66 ; 315/72.

6 Surgeon-General F.W. Trevor, PMO, HM Forces in India, to G. of I., 14–8–1908, Mil. Coll. 315/66.

7 Flexner 1914, 192 ; Smith 1971, 132.

8 Skelley 1977, 57.

9 PP 1893–4, LXIV (7148).

10 Ibid. 63ff.

11 Ibid.

12 Ibid. 161 ff.

13 *Indian Spectator*, 23–9–1888.

14 Joseph Laidlaw Thomas : oral history interview 924/02 ; Imperial War Museum, London.

15 Patrick Chilton : oral history interview 888/03 ; Dugald Campbell McIver : oral history interview 897/06 ; Edwin Francis Philbrick : oral history interview 871/05 ; Imperial War Museum, London.

Bibliography

ACTON, WILLIAM, *Prostitution Considered in its Moral, Social, and Sanitary Aspects in London and Other Large Cities; with Proposals for Mitigation and Prevention of its Attendant Evil* (London, 1857)

ALLEN, CHARLES, *Plain Tales from the Raj* (London, 1975)

BAGLEY, CHRISTOPHER, *The Dutch Plural Society. A Comparative Study in Race Relations* (London, 1973)

BALLHATCHET, KENNETH A., 'British rights and Indian duties : the case of Sir William Lee-Warner', in O'Flaherty, Wendy Doniger, and Derrett, J. Duncan M. (eds), *The Concept of Duty in South Asia* (London, 1978)

BAXTER, CHRISTINE, 'The genesis of the Babu : Bhabanicharan Bannerji and *Kalikātā Kamalālāy*', in Robb, Peter, and Taylor, David (eds), *Rule, Protest and Identity* (London, 1978)

BEVERIDGE, LORD, *India Called Them* (London, 1947)

BOLT, CHRISTINE, *Victorian Attitudes to Race* (London, 1971)

BOXER, C. R., *The Colour Question in the Portuguese Empire, 1415–1825* (London, 1961)

BRISTOW, EDWARD J., *Vice and Vigilance. Purity Movements in Britain since 1700* (Dublin, 1977)

BUTT, I. A., 'Lord Curzon and the Indian States, 1899–1905', Ph.D. thesis (London University, 1964)

CARROLL, LUCY, 'The Temperance Movement in India : Politics and Social Reform', *Modern Asian Studies*, **X**, 3 (1976)

CHEVALIER, LOUIS (tr. JELLINEK, F.), *Labouring Classes and Dangerous Classes in Paris during the First Half of the Nineteenth Century* (London, 1973)

CHINTAMANI, C. YAJNESVARA (ed.), *Indian Social Reform* (Madras, 1901)

COHN, BERNARD S., 'Recruitment and training of British civil servants in India', in Braibanti, Ralph (ed.), *Asian Bureaucratic Systems Emergent from the British Imperial Tradition* (Durham, N.C., 1966)

COMPTON, JOHN MICHAEL (1) : 'Open competition and the Indian Civil Service, 1854–1876', *English Historical Review*, LXXXIII (1968)

COMPTON, JOHN MICHAEL (2) : 'British Government and Society in the Presidency of Bengal. c. 1858–c. 1880 : an Examination of Certain Aspects of

British Attitudes, Behaviour and Policy', D. Phil. thesis (Oxford University, 1968)

COMPTON, JOHN MICHAEL, 'Indians and the Indian Civil service, 1853–1879', *Journal of the Royal Asiatic Society*, 1967

EDWARDES, MICHAEL, *High Noon of Empire. India under Curzon* (London, 1965)

FLEXNER, ABRAHAM, *Prostitution in Europe* (New York, 1914)

FOWLER, W. S., *A Study in Radicalism and Dissent : the Life and Times of Henry Joseph Wilson, 1833–1914* (London, 1961)

GAIKWAD, V. R., *The Anglo-Indians. A Study in the Problems and Processes Involved in Emotional and Cultural Integration* (London, 1967)

GHOSH, SURESH CHANDRA, *The Social Condition of the British Community in Bengal, 1757–1800* (Leiden, 1970)

GOPAL, S., *British Policy in India, 1858–1905* (Cambridge, 1965)

GOPAL, S., *The Viceroyalty of Lord Ripon, 1880–1884* (Oxford, 1953)

HARRIES–JENKYNS, GWYN, *The Army in Victorian Society* (London, 1977)

HARRISON, BRIAN, 'Underneath the Victorians', *Victorian Studies*, X (1966–7)

HARRISON, FRASER, *The Dark Angel. Aspects of Victorian Sexuality* (London, 1977)

HUTCHINS, FRANCIS G., *The Illusion of Permanence. British Imperialism in India* (Princeton, 1967)

HYAM, RONALD, *Britain's Imperial Century, 1885–1914. A Study of Empire and Expansion* (London, 1976)

JEFFREY, ROBIN, *The Decline of Nayyar Dominance. Society and Politics in Travancore* (New York, 1976)

KAMINSKY, A. P., 'Policy and Paperwork : the Formation of Policy in the India Office, 1883–1909, with Special Reference to the Permanent Undersecretaryship of Sir Arthur Godley', Ph. D. thesis (University of California, 1976)

KING, ANTHONY D., *Colonial Urban Development. Culture, Social Power and Environment* (London, 1976)

MACMILLAN, DONALD, *Life of Professor Hastie* (Paisley, 1926)

MASON, PHILIP, *A Matter of Honour. An Account of the Indian Army, Its Officers and Men* (London, 1974)

MEHROTRA, S. R., *The Emergence of the Indian National Congress* (Delhi, 1971)

MILLER, JEAN BAKER, *Toward a New Psychology of Women* (New York, 1976)

MOORE, R. J., *Sir Charles Wood's Indian Policy, 1853–66* (Manchester, 1966)

MORROW, MARGOT DULEY, 'Origins and Early Years of the British Committee of the Indian National Congress, 1885–1907', Ph. D. thesis (London University, 1977)

MOSLEY, LEONARD, *Curzon. The End of an Epoch* (London, 1960)

NAIDIS, MARK, 'British attitudes towards the Anglo-Indians', *South Atlantic Quarterly*, LXII (1963)

Opinions of the Indian Press in the Defamation Case, Pigot v. Hastie (Calcutta, 1883)

PARENT-DUCHÂTELET, A.J.B., *De la Prostitution dans la ville de Paris, considérée sous le rapport de l'hygiène publique, de la morale et de l'administration*, 2 vols (Paris, 1836)

PARENT-DUCHÂTELET, A.J.B., 'Paris, its dangerous classes', *Quarterly Review*, LXX (1842)

PEARSALL, RONALD, *The Worm in the Bud. The World of Victorian Sexuality* (London, 1969)

PEARSON, MICHAEL, *The Age of Consent. Victorian Prostitution and its Enemies* (Newton Abbot, 1972)

PUNEKAR, S. D. AND RAO, KAMALA, *A Study of Prostitutes in Bombay (with Reference to Family Background)* (Bombay, 1967)

RANGA RAO, M., AND RAGHAVENDRA RAO, J. V., *The Prostitutes of Hyderabad* (Hyderabad n.d.)

READER, W. J., *Professional Men. The Rise of the Professional Classes in Nineteenth-Century England* (London, 1966)

RONALDSHAY, EARL OF, *The Life of Lord Curzon*. Vol. II: *Viceroy of India* (London, 1928)

ROSEBURY, THEODOR, *Microbes and Morals* (London, 1972)

ROSSELLI, JOHN, *Lord William Bentinck. The Making of a Liberal Imperialist, 1774–1839* (London, 1974)

SEAL, ANIL, *The Emergence of Indian Nationalism. Competition and Collaboration in the Later Nineteenth Century* (Cambridge, 1968)

SINGER, MILTON, *When a Great Tradition Modernizes. An Anthropological Approach to Indian Civilization* (London, 1972)

SINGH, S. N., *The Secretary of State for India and His Council* (Delhi, 1962)

SKELLY, ALAN RAMSAY, *The Victorian Army at Home. The Recruitment and Terms and Conditions of the British Regular, 1859–1899* (London, 1977)

SMITH, F. B., 'Ethics and disease in the late nineteenth century: the Contagious Diseases Acts', *Historical Studies* (Melbourne), XV (1971–3)

SPANGENBERG, BRADFORD, 'The problem of recruitment for the Indian Civil Service during the late nineteenth century', *Journal of Asian Studies*, XXX (1971)

SPANGENBERG, BRADFORD, *British Bureaucracy in India. Status, Policy and the I.C.S., in the Late 19th Century* (New Delhi, 1976)

STARK, H.A., *Hostages to India* (Calcutta, 1936)

VICINUS, MARTHA (ed.), *Suffer and Be Still. Women in the Victorian Age* (Bloomington, 1972)

WALKOWITZ, JUDITH R., '"We Are Not Beasts of the Field": Prostitution and the Campaign against the Contagious Diseases Acts, 1869–1886', Ph.D. thesis (University of Rochester, 1974)

WARE, HELEN R.E., 'The Recruitment, Regulation and Role of Prostitution in Britain from the Middle of the Nineteenth Century to the Present Day', 2 vols, Ph.D. thesis (London University, 1969)

WILKINSON, RUPERT H., *Gentlemanly Power. British Leadership and the Public School Tradition* (London, 1964)

Glossary

Anna : Indian coin. There were sixteen annas in a rupee.

Ayah : Nurse.

Babu (baboo) : At the beginning of our period, an educated Hindu gentleman ; also used as a title prefixed to the name of such a person. In the course of the nineteenth century it came to be used increasingly by the British for the Western-educated Bengalis whom they employed as clerks, whom they distrusted as critics of British rule and as rivals for office and whom they derided as incompetent and unmanly. Sensitive to British sneers, educated Bengalis tended, by the end of the nineteenth century, to avoid the term. As a prefix 'Mr' was often used instead. In the twentieth century, with the growth of nationalism, 'Mr' has been supplanted by 'Sri'.

Bibi : Woman ; originally lady ; in British parlance, mistress.

Choultry : Hall or shed.

Devadasi : Slave-girl of God ; a dancing-girl attached to a temple.

Kotwal : Police officer ; bazar official.

Lakh (lack) : 100,000 rupees.

Lal bazar : Regimental brothel. Associated with *lal kurti*, red coat, or British soldier, or by extension the British cantonment.

Nach (nautch) : Indian ballet.

Peon : Constable ; orderly ; messenger.

Sadr : Principal, chief ; headquarters, government.

Sadr Faujdari Adalat : Chief criminal court.

Zamindar : Landholder.

Index